Architecture as Cultural and Political Discourse

This book is concerned with cultural and political discourses that affect the production of architecture. It examines how these discursive mechanisms and technologies combine to normalise and aestheticise everyday practices. It queries the means by which buildings are appropriated to give shape and form to political aspirations and values. Architecture is not overtly political. It does not coerce people to behave in certain ways. However, architecture is constructed within the same rules and practices whereby people and communities *self*-govern and regulate themselves to think and act in certain ways. This book seeks to examine these rules through various case studies, including the reconstructed Notre Dame Cathedral, the Nazi era Munich Königsplatz, the Auschwitz concentration camp and the Prora resort, Sydney's suburban race riots, and the Australian Immigration Detention Centre on Christmas Island.

Daniel Grinceri is a practising architect in Perth, Western Australia; he recently received his PhD on this topic from the University of Western Australia.

Routledge Research in Architecture

The *Routledge Research in Architecture* series provides the reader with the latest scholarship in the field of architecture. The series publishes research from across the globe and covers areas as diverse as architectural history and theory, technology, digital architecture, structures, materials, details, design, monographs of architects, interior design and much more. By making these studies available to the worldwide academic community, the series aims to promote quality architectural research.

An Architecture of Parts
Architects, Building Workers
and Industrialisation in Britain
1940–1970
Christine Wall

**Towards an Articulated
Phenomenological Interpretation
of Architecture**
Phenomenal Phenomenology
M. Reza Shirazi

Architectural System Structures
Integrating Design Complexity in
Industrialised Construction
Kasper Sánchez Vibæk

Space Unveiled
Invisible Cultures in the Design
Studio
Edited by Carla Jackson Bell

Architectural Temperance
Spain and Rome, 1700–1759
Victor Deupi

**Assembling the Centre:
Architecture for Indigenous
Cultures**
Australia and Beyond
*Janet McGaw and
Anoma Pieris*

**The Films of Charles and
Ray Eames**
A Universal Sense of Expectation
Eric Schuldenfrei

**Intersections of Space
and Ethos**
Searching for the Unmeasurable
*Nikolaos-Ion Terzoglou,
Kyriaki Tsoukala and Charikleia
Pantelidou*

Ars et Ingenium
The Embodiment of Imagination
in Francesco di Giorgio Martini's
Drawings
Pari Riahi

Kahn at Penn
Transformative Teacher of
Architecture
James Williamson

**Designing the British
Post-War Home**
Kenneth Wood, 1948–1968
Fiona Fisher

Drawing the Unbuildable
Seriality and Reproduction in
Architecture
Nerma Cridge

**The Idea of the Cottage in
English Architecture,
1760–1860**
Daniel Maudlin

**Cut and Paste Urban
Landscape**
The Work of Gordon Cullen
Mira Engler

**Wooden Church Architecture of
the Russian North**
Regional Schools and Traditions
(14th–19th centuries)
Evgeny Khodakovsky

**Mid-Century Modernism in
Turkey**
Architecture Across Cultures in the
1950s and 1960s
Meltem Ö. Gürel

**Bruno Taut's Design Inspiration
for the Glashaus**
David Nielsen

Conflicted Identities
Housing and the Politics of
Cultural Representation
Alexandra Staub

Through the Healing Glass
Shaping the Modern Body through
Glass Architecture, 1925–35
John Stanislav Sadar

**Architecture as Cultural and
Political Discourse**
Case Studies of Conceptual Norms
and Aesthetic Practices
Daniel Grinceri

**Sacred Architecture in a Secular
Age**
Anamnesis of Durham Cathedral
Marie Clausén

Architecture as Cultural and Political Discourse

Case studies of conceptual norms and aesthetic practices

Daniel Grinceri

LONDON AND NEW YORK

First published 2016
by Routledge
2 Park Square, Milton Park, Abingdon, Oxon OX14 4RN

and by Routledge
711 Third Avenue, New York, NY 10017

Routledge is an imprint of the Taylor & Francis Group, an informa business

© 2016 Daniel Grinceri

The right of Daniel Grinceri to be identified as author of this work has been
asserted by him in accordance with sections 77 and 78 of the Copyright,
Designs and Patents Act 1988.

All rights reserved. No part of this book may be reprinted or reproduced or
utilised in any form or by any electronic, mechanical, or other means, now
known or hereafter invented, including photocopying and recording, or in
any information storage or retrieval system, without permission in writing
from the publishers.

Trademark notice: Product or corporate names may be trademarks or
registered trademarks, and are used only for identification and explanation
without intent to infringe.

British Library Cataloguing-in-Publication Data
A catalogue record for this book is available from the British Library

Library of Congress Cataloging-in-Publication Data
Names: Grinceri, Daniel, author.
Title: Architecture as cultural and political discourse: case studies of
    conceptual norms and aesthetic practices/Daniel Grinceri.
Description: New York, NY: Routledge, 2016. | Revision of author's
    thesis (doctoral)—University of Western Australia, 2011. |
    Includes bibliographical references and index.
Identifiers: LCCN 2015036933| ISBN 9781138916807
    (hardback: alk. paper) | ISBN 9781315689371 (ebook)
Subjects: LCSH: Architecture and society—Case studies. |
    Architecture—Political aspects—Case studies. | Identity
    (Psychology) in architecture—Case studies.
Classification: LCC NA2543.S6 G73 2016 | DDC 720.1/03—dc23
LC record available at http://lccn.loc.gov/2015036933

ISBN: 978-1-138-91680-7 (hbk)
ISBN: 978-1-315-68937-1 (ebk)

Typeset in Sabon
by Swales & Willis Ltd, Exeter, Devon, UK

Contents

List of figures	ix
Preface	x
Acknowledgments	xi

1 Architecture as cultural and political discourse 1
Culture 5
Politics 10
Architecture 12
Aestheticisation 15

2 Meaning and the death of architecture 23
'This will kill that' 24
The gargoyle in architecture 26
The 'spirit' of the age 33
Legibility and the architectural (con)text 39
*The book and the building: the libraries of
    Labrouste and Perrault 44*

**3 Statements on architecture: meaning and
determinism in the Athens Charters** 56
The politics of the Athens Charters 57
The hermeneutics of continuity 67
The Declaration of Dresden 72
Architecture and the statement 77

4 Aesthetics and politics: the building of Nazi Germany 88
Nazi 'evil' and the 'ordinary' 89
Neo-classicism and National Socialism 92
Words in stone 95
The Königplatz 99
'Denazification' 102
Culpability 106

viii   *Contents*

5   **The camp and the resort: exclusion and**
     inclusion associated with 'bare life'   114
     The zone of indistinction   115
     Volkloser Raum   121
     The Nuremberg Law   125
     Strength through Joy   131
     'Ethica more Auschwitz demonstrata'   135

6   **Spatial contestation and suburban riots**   142
     Territory and belonging: the Cronulla riots   143
     Australian ugliness and the myth of the bush   147
     Social exclusion: Macquarie Fields   153
     Disaffected locals: Redfern   158
     Making up the nation   162

7   **The architecture of indefinite and mandatory detention**   167
     The grey zone   168
     The stateless individual   172
     Sovereign power and 'the state of exception'   175
     Managing Australia's borders: inside Woomera   179

8   **Architecture and ethics: competition for the Christmas**
     Island detention centre   188
     Creating 'limbo land'   188
     Island detention   192
     Architecture and ethics   196
     From 'white elephant' to 'breaking point'   200

9   **Apparatus**   206
     Conclusion   206

     Index   211

Figures

2.1	Bird with open beak and unicorn demon chimera, Notre Dame de Paris	31
2.2	'The Community Bookshelf', Kansas City Library carpark	47
3.1	The front entry to St. Mary's Cathedral following completion of refurbishment works in 2009	70
3.2	The reconstructed Frauenkirche Cathedral in Dresden reopened in 2005	73
4.1	'Ehrentempel' and 'Führerbau' (background) on the Königsplatz in Munich, circa 1937	101
4.2	The Führerbau, view from the intersecting roads of the Königsplatz with the remains of one of the Ehrentempels in the foreground, 2007	103
5.1	Prora, building complex, view from sea side, 2008	133
7.1	November Compound, Woomera Detention Centre, 2002	180
8.1	Christmas Island detention centre	193
8.2	Christmas Island detention centre 'break out' cages to allow detainees fresh air during lock down	195

Preface

This book is concerned with cultural and political discourses that affect the production of architecture. Moreover, it examines how these discursive mechanisms and technologies combined to normalise and aestheticise everyday practices. The notion of culture plays a role in constructing meanings and identities. Understanding this is important to architecture because buildings are often thought to bring about this and other ideals. Yet this book queries the role of architecture in the production of 'culture'. It asks whether buildings are capable of informing the attitudes and values of both individuals and populations, as it is popularly believed they do. It asks whether architecture possesses an inherent ability to achieve this end. Some buildings are thought to promote the values and meanings of a particular community as a representation of 'high' culture and art whereby the lives of people are thought to be improved, or alternatively disadvantaged, because of certain types of architecture in their midst. But can buildings alone, their material substance, aesthetics and symbolism provide for such edification? Impinging on this discussion, politics involves the appropriation of certain representational tools, like architecture, to portray and preserve an imagined ideal of the self and 'culture', and by extension, the nation-state. Through such acts of appropriation, governments do not impose such values or systems of belief, but are able to give them representational form and doing so by presuming to act in the interests of 'the people'. Architecture serves to give shape and form to such political aspirations. However, architecture is neither political – it does not coerce people to behave in certain ways – nor produce certain ways of political thinking by itself. Architecture is a component of a cultural and political discourse, constructed within the rules and practices by which people commonly *self*-govern and regulate themselves to think and act in certain ways. This book seeks to examine these rules, in so much as they effect the production of the built environment along with those values which make for a certain type of 'architecture' and the practices of the architectural profession.

Acknowledgments

Special thanks to my family: Megan, Jordan, Taylor and Cameron Grinceri for their patience and support; and to Winthrop Professors William Taylor and Michael Levine for their advice and commitment.

1 Architecture as cultural and political discourse

In the introduction to one of the many books showcasing the work of Rem Koolhaas, arguably one of architecture's most well known and influential celebrities, Aaron Betsky presents a rather simplified and stereotypical image of architects in general. From his description, perceptions of architects oscillate somewhere between being servile capitalists "willing to place large structures where they don't belong",[1] and "diva-like" artists who pursue their own agenda at the expense of client and budget. Perhaps as a result of this egoism, architects, Betsky claims, see themselves as unappreciated, overworked and underpaid, forever "trying to communicate the importance of good design to an uncomprehending public".[2] From my experience as a practising architect it is difficult to disagree with Betsky's observations. On the whole, architects are motivated by a desire to contribute something worthwhile to the built environment. However, no matter how well intentioned, architects are often frustrated by the inevitable process of negotiation and compromise that might significantly impact on a building's suitability, economic viability and public acceptance. Sometimes it is more a matter of how one finds solutions to these frustrations, such as by-laws, budget, client changes and so forth, that produces appropriate architecture rather than any particular talent for design itself.

Yet star architects like Rem Koolhaas, while still complaining about not being understood or receiving the right commissions, seem to be the exception.[3] They have ostensibly risen above the everyday tedium of architectural practice to become, as Betsky puts it, "the conscious collector, manipulator and projector of images".[4] When these architects produce a new work it generally assumes a status of significance. It becomes reviewed in all the major architectural publications and admired for the way it supposedly challenges common conventions and expands the horizons of architecture and design. Moreover, the building itself becomes revered as an object of 'high' art and 'culture' because it, by most accounts, reveals to its observers something about the building's setting and its inhabitants. In other words, so it is assumed, it makes for a better environment in which to live. This sentiment is perhaps best summarised by Kazuyo Sejima in his speech at

2   Architecture as cultural and political discourse

the 2010 Venice Biennale where Koolhaas was presented the Golden Lion award for a lifetime of achievement in architecture. Sejima declared: "Rem Koolhaas has expanded the possibilities of architecture. He has focused on the exchange between people in space. He creates buildings that bring people together and in this way forms ambitious goals for architecture. His influence on the world has come well beyond architecture, people from very diverse fields feel a great freedom from his work".[5] It is this praise that many architects aspire to, in the hope that their 'art' will also be deemed important and somehow transform the way people live and think for the better. I recall, as an undergraduate student both deriding, yet admiring the egocentricism of Ayn Rand's architect hero Howard Roark in the *Fountainhead*, who never compromised his ideals and aspirations for an architecture that would significantly benefit the world. But one might ask: can buildings alone ever achieve this? Certainly, one can point to the many examples of other star architects that have transformed the economy of a city through the addition of one of their architectural 'masterpieces'. Jorn Utzon's Sydney Opera House and Frank Gehry's Guggenheim Museum in Bilbao readily come to mind. These iconic buildings have not only brought in the much sought-after tourist dollar, but also an increased sense of identity and greater recognition to the city in which the buildings reside.[6] Indeed, the success of such buildings has inspired many other cities and institutions to attempt to change a city's identity through architecture.[7] But having said this, architecture is a product that, given the right context, might symbolise certain objectives, but does it have the power to transform, coerce, guarantee or even determine certain economic, social or personal outcomes, like a change to a city's identity?

In this regard, Koolhaas is unique amongst most other architects because he downplays, even denies, the significance of his architecture. As he once acknowledged in conversation with his students: "There is an unbelievable overestimation of the power of architecture in terms of the good it can do, but even more, in terms of the bad it has done or can do".[8] Interestingly, here, Koolhaas echoes Michel Foucault when the philosopher and historian declared in an interview with Paul Rabinow that the "architect has no power". Foucault continues: "If I want to tear down or change a house he built for me, put up new partitions, add a chimney, the architect has no control . . . I would say that one must take him – his mentality, his attitude – into account as well as his projects, in order to understand a certain number of the techniques of power that are invested in architecture".[9] The question of power as addressed in Foucault's later work is essential to this book. It is not my intention to formulate a theory of power and architecture, nor to consider architecture as an object of power, as such a discursive strategy is likely to be "condemned in advance and to set the analysis of power on a wrong course".[10] Foucault's remarks on power dismissed conventional understandings and conceptions of power, yet he offered them not as a theory of power but as a tool kit for the analysis of power relations.[11] With this in mind, this book intends to adopt this 'tool kit' as a means of analysing the built environment and the power relations through which meanings circulate in the formation of the self and the governance of a population. Foucault proposed that the architect and his work are the subjects of power, suggesting that their values and attitudes are constructed within the same field of legibility and understanding as the rest of society. In other words, they do not possess an exemplary and self-evident authority of the kind a doctor might be thought to hold. Thus, according to Foucault, if an architect's work is to resonate with a particular audience it is more likely to be the result of the architect's ability to draw upon and perhaps symbolise or give form to particular ways of thinking that circulate within that audience rather than exhibiting an inherent capacity to change the way people think.

When architects describe the aesthetic effect of a particular building they generally focus on its physical features. Foucault, however, is more interested in the particular ways of thinking that imparted a distinctiveness to such features and made them meaningful. One example given by Foucault is the addition of the chimney to European middle age houses. Foucault explains that at a certain moment it was possible to build a chimney inside the house, as opposed to open fire inside the house. It was at that "moment all sorts of things changed and relations between individuals became possible".[12] Foucault enquires why the chimney came about at that particular point in time, "or why did they put their techniques to this use?"[13] Thus for Foucault the chimney came into existence at a time when people were tending towards a different kind of relationship inside the home. As a result, the chimney facilitated these changes by making the house a more comfortable place in which to live. Typically, such architectural changes which come to be seen as impacting on the lives of individuals are attributed to a single originating idea. However, of interest to Foucault is not the authorship of such ideas like comfort, but rather the exploration of the 'techniques' that made the chimney possible and meaningful in new ways. He explains: "It is certain, and of capital importance, that this technique was a formative influence on new human relations, but it is impossible to think that it would have been developed and adapted had there not been a strategy of human relations something which tended in that direction".[14] By 'strategy', Foucault does not intend to describe a deliberate plan or system with the ability to determine a particular outcome, but rather a 'technique' that derived from a series of needs and innovations. Here, 'strategy' refers to, as Paul Hirst explains: "A definite pattern of means and objectives that can be discovered operating across a number of sites".[15] The chimney is thus one example of a number of techniques that tended towards the improvement of social relationships, comfort and healthy living.

The work of Michel Foucault is important to this study, particularly his writing in *The Archaeology of Knowledge* (1972), which examines how knowledge is put into practice through discursive formations in specific institutional settings to regulate the conduct of others. In particular,

4 *Architecture as cultural and political discourse*

it examines how the circulation of knowledge and power operates within specific mechanisms and technologies, whereby a variety of diverse elements like regulations, laws, scientific statements, philosophic propositions, and, as it applies to this book, "architectural arrangements", become normalised and aestheticised in everyday practice.[16] Arguably, Foucault is one of the most cited authors in the social sciences and humanities and remains popular among architectural theorists. The attraction of architects to Foucault's work may in part be explained by his repeated references to space and particular spaces (like the prison, clinic and asylum) in his writing.[17] However, certain aspects of Foucault's work are often underdeveloped in architecture. For instance, the panopticon is often used as an example of how architecture determines the conduct of individuals and contributes to the meaning of 'penality' and 'the penitentiary' at a given time by assigning various roles to the actors caught within the building's spatial confines.[18] Yet it is not Foucault's intention to assert that the panopticon fully determined the behaviour of its occupants to the exclusion of their subjective responses to the building form and interior arrangement. He uses the example of the panopticon to demonstrate that the architecture has no 'power' over individuals, regardless of the building's form, which could have just as easily been a "large shed".[19] According to Foucault, what makes the inmate regulate his own behaviour is not the architecture of the panopticon, but rather the gaze of the warden, which involves the inmate in a form of disciplinary power and establishes their capacity for self-reflection and moral reform. Contrasting this partial application of Foucault's reasoning, theorists like Paul Hirst and Robin Evans have opened the way for architects to more fully question 'conventional' understandings about architecture, particularly architecture and power.[20] In addition, authors such as Paul Rabinow, and more recently Giorgio Agamben, have employed Foucault's methods for analysing the associations between built form and history, sovereignty and biopower.[21] These will be examined later in this book.

Foucault provides a framework for analysing knowledge and ways of thinking, particular to a time and place. This book follows and develops his arguments that knowledge is caught up in technologies of power that produce individuals as subjects which in effect normalise discursive practices. With this in mind, architecture and its associated components, both parts of buildings and the text written about buildings, can be regarded as forming a 'statement', having specific conditions of emergence and enunciative functions that produce a common interpretation within a particular cultural field.[22] This is an important aspect of Foucault's thinking because it denies that buildings contain any inherent capacity to produce a common meaning for those within a given 'culture'. Instead, his point places the production of such meanings within discursive formations that largely determine what a 'culture' is or can be.

This book examines the built environment, and how architecture participates in the formation of certain values, in particular, those which are commonly held to form part of our cultural identity. Moreover, three key themes are addressed: One, how certain ways of thinking take part in the governance of groups of people, and how this makes use of and brings about certain types of buildings. For instance, amongst other case studies, this book will discuss the Australian immigration detention centre at Christmas Island, in order to demonstrate how buildings are brought about in response to specific discursive constructs (in this case a fear of immigration). Two, this book considers the manner in which space becomes utilised as a resource for power, whereby buildings are co-opted for the production of national identity by including certain people at the expense of the excluded 'other'. Such a case demonstrating the 'resourcefulness of buildings', their availability to define and extend forms of power and knowledge – including attitudes arising from a making of self-knowledge and social recognition – is entailed in the concentration camps and other architectural programmes of the Third Reich. And three, this book raises ethical questions about the involvement of architects in the procurement of such projects, in that architects, like anyone else, are not exempt from ordinary moral requirements regardless of their expertise and professional capacities.

Buildings are produced within discursive frameworks that have a direct impact on one's expectations for meaningful architecture and how one, consequently, conducts oneself within certain spaces. Architecture is best understood not only by examining its form and materiality, but also, and more importantly, by examining the features of discourse that delimit knowledge in a particular field making for certain types of 'architecture'. According to Betsky, the architect is one of a group of "identity providers" who help establish a sense of place or community.[23] Yet such an effect is less the result of the architect's ability to shape the world than to provide form to certain modes of thought, speech and conduct. Understanding how discourse shapes the production, design and usefulness of buildings is significant to architecture; it does not diminish the role of the architect, but perhaps better positions their expectations and capabilities.

Culture

It is worth considering the main terms presented in this book in order to explain their relevance to the various case studies presented in the subsequent chapters. Comprehending how 'culture' participates in the production of meaning – and particular meanings at a given time – is important to architecture because buildings are thought to be consequential and expressive objects representative of core values and identities. It is a basic fundamental of social science that the same thing or object might acquire different meanings dependant on the 'culture' in which it is found. Yet 'culture' is very difficult to define. Terry Eagleton for instance claims that 'culture' is one of the most complex words in the English language.[24] The term itself is highly problematic as it can lend its authority to a variety of concepts

6 *Architecture as cultural and political discourse*

and phenomena: American culture, high culture, modern culture, urban culture, counter-culture, sub-culture and so forth. Given that 'culture' is an imprecise or variable entity, to what extent does 'culture' participate in the production of meanings? Etymologically speaking, culture has its origins in agriculture, crops and their cultivation. However, with modernity it has come to acquire additional and alternative significances. The term has come to denote, for instance: "the arts and other manifestations of human intellectual activity . . . the customs, civilisations and achievements of a particular time and people".[25] Noticing this variability, Eagleton suggests that the word charts a "semantic shift" in the unfolding of human history. It measures changes: "From rural to urban existence, pig-farming to Picasso, tilling the soil to splitting the atom . . . But the semantic shift is also paradoxical: it is the urban dwellers who are 'cultivated' and those who actually live by tilling the soil who are not".[26] Thus, 'culture' is an activity, but it is also used to single out different types and qualities of people, perhaps for the purpose of denigrating them, so that individuals lacking a certain form of 'refinement' might be described as being 'un-cultured'.

While the changing meaning of the word 'culture' is perhaps evidence of humanity's increasing urbanisation, 'culture' also raises numerous, sometimes contradictory, philosophical issues too. For example, it raises questions of freedom and determinism, identity and difference, subjectivity and normalisation – all of which will be explored in greater detail in later chapters. Briefly, however, cultural freedom is encompassed by one's sense of equality and liberty to act in accordance with one's own free will, whereas cultural determinism suggests that one's will is entirely determined by that which surrounds one. From a determinist's perspective, it is believed that one's actions are wholly or partly prefigured and governed by the physical environment, providing very little to no freedom to determine one's own actions. In this regard it is difficult, on the one hand, to accept that the physical environment does not play some sort of role in influencing certain modes of conduct.[27] Yet, on the other hand, buildings cannot guarantee specific outcomes as there are too many other factors at play, such as social, economic, political and personal influences. Similarly, buildings cannot guarantee freedom. Foucault posits that architecture can be neither entirely liberating nor oppressive. He comments: "If one were to find a place, and perhaps there are some, where liberty is effectively exercised, one would find that this is not owing to the order of objects, but, owing to the practice of liberty".[28] Foucault claims that architecture, or the spatial order of a place, cannot solve social problems. Rather, it can produce positive effects when the "liberating intentions of the architect coincide with the real practices of the people in the exercise of their freedom".[29] Similarly, 'culture' as a category of material artefacts cannot guarantee freedom; neither can it determine particular forms of behaviour, for such practices can never be inherent in the structure of things nor in the order of objects.

Architecture as cultural and political discourse   7

'Culture' is typically construed as having a dialectical dimension which suggests that it is involved in the process of human development and progress. However, of main concern here is its 'constructivist' dimension: the notion that the self is shaped and reshaped by a series of discursive practices that cut across multiple disciplines.[30] In this way, knowledge is essentially produced through discourse, whereby certain forms of conduct and speech become normalised and accepted by a group of people as a 'true' reflection of the 'way things are'. This view, according to Foucault, describes the body as "totally imprinted"[31] – not only by the surrounding environment, but by the way it is described and talked about. Constructivism denies the dialectical approach to cultural studies, where history is seen as part of a progression toward a particular end, in preference to a methodology that focuses on the processes through which individuals govern and regulate themselves.[32]

Architects and theorists alike tend to speak of architecture as a cultural object as though it were a register of the past that can teach us something about ourselves.[33] Giving voice to this position is Richard Hooker, who, typically for a historian, declares in his summation of the cultural significance of architecture: "All architecture communicates to the members of a community the 'meaning' of their actions. That is, how their actions relate to the rest of the human, material, and spiritual worlds . . . Architecture can be 'read', that is, you can discover how a culture 'writes' for other members of that culture; it is a culture talking about the meaning and organisation of the life of that culture. This also means that whenever a member of a culture looks at a work of architecture, they understand that it has meaning and that this meaning governs their actions and understanding of the world".[34] According to this position, 'culture' is seen as the origin and substance of built form that not only reveals something of the society to which it belongs, but also ennobles the community that produced it. For instance, significant works of art and architecture are said to be denotive of particular cultures, thus expressive of their way of life, beliefs and attitudes. The prominent architectural theorist K. Michael Hays in his treatise on 'critical architecture', which is concerned with the reciprocal influence between culture and architectural form, asserts that the interpretation of meaning from architecture is simply a matter of uncovering the cultural situation relevant to the time and place it originated. Hays proposes that "each architectural object places itself in a specific situation in the world, which constrains what can be done with it in interpretation".[35] To this end, Hays reveals that a 'critical architecture' is defined by its inherent differences from other cultural manifestations, whereby these differences "produce knowledge both about culture and about architecture".[36] Notwithstanding this common endeavour, this book queries whether architecture possesses any inherent meaning, or imparts any specific knowledge, that reveals something of the cultural situation in which it is found. It asks whether architecture has the capacity to generate

8   *Architecture as cultural and political discourse*

meanings which "govern one's actions and understanding of the world". Moreover, it queries the role of architecture in the production of 'culture', and whether buildings are capable of forming the attitudes and values of a population, and if so, how?

The view that promotes architecture as essentially a cultural activity from which one can derive some knowledge hardly seems a contentious issue. Yet it seems clear that architecture is not akin to a text. If people share a mutual understanding of a building's meaning this is not the result of its ability to be 'read' in any single, clear and mutually comprehensible manner.[37] Rather, as will be argued, a consensus of interpretation depends upon a people's common access to language, whereby an individual's interpretation is as much shaped by social formations as the building under scrutiny is made into an object of significance to be interpreted. In this way, we move away from the view that assumes meaning is an intrinsic characteristic or capacity of an object, to the notion that meanings are socially and personally formative. Stuart Hall's assertion is helpful here, he claims: "Culture is about 'shared meanings' . . . Language is the privileged medium in which we 'make sense' of things, in which meaning is produced and exchanged. Language is central to meaning and culture and has always been regarded as the key repository of cultural values and meanings".[38] Language is capable of constructing meaning, not because there is an inherent link between a word and a thing, but because language operates within a "representational system".[39] This system connects, uneasily at times, words, things and groups of people who are drawn or often obliged to interpret them and so understand themselves in certain ways. Hall continues: "Language is one of the media through which thoughts, ideas and feelings are represented in a culture".[40] Similarly, architecture is capable of representing values, ideas and feelings, not because it is a language, but because it is brought about and utilised as a result of the practices of a group of people. Architecture too is a representational medium.

This book contends that architecture is not endowed with inherent meaning and value, rather, architecture acquires meaning through language, or more particularly, discourse. Discourse, as Foucault proposes, differs from language, although it works within a representational system, it constructs the rules and practices that produce meaning and provides a language for talking about things. Discourse provides the framework to talk about what might be described as 'cultural practices', which refers to those practices that participate in the governance of individuals, not only through forms of sovereign government but also those practices that regulate the conduct, thought and speech of individuals. These practices produce, for example: institutions, regulatory decisions, laws, administrative measures, scientific statements, welfare, medical assistance, philosophical and moral propositions – not to mention architectural forms as well.[41] Foucault calls these practices discursive formations. These consist of a group of 'statements' coincidental to time and place giving rise to meaning. According to Foucault's conception of discourse, as outlined in his work *The Archaeology of Knowledge*, statements are not the free product of the mind, rather they have 'surfaces of emergence' or particular institutional conditions of knowledge under which certain meanings and forms of behaviour appear.[42] An example would be the introduction of laws and policies that regulate minimum requirements for natural ventilation and sunlight into habitable rooms. Although they emerged from growing concerns relating to air quality in nineteenth-century England they still influence building codes today.[43] These regulations not only transformed the way people live (resulting in, for example the abolition of the window tax), but also began to inform a new architectural aesthetic. Typically we refer to this new style of architecture as 'modernism', which is identifiable by an extensive use of glass and clean open spaces, as opposed to the dark cluttered spaces of the Victorian era. Historians tend to acknowledge specific architects like Joseph Paxton designer of the Crystal Palace as the originator of this movement.[44] Yet what is missing in this association is an analysis of the various conditions or 'surfaces of emergence', whether derived from economic, technological or social conditions that gave rise to new modes of social interaction as well as new forms of production and architecture.

In addition, the emergence of a 'statement' is also dependent on what Foucault calls 'enunciative modalities', whereby certain individuals or institutions are qualified to speak with authority on a particular subject, such as a doctor's diagnosis of an ill patient. Michel Foucault's work will be explored in greater depth in later chapters; here it suffices to suggest the relevance of discourse for the study of architecture. As such, architecture is considered a component of discursive formations. Thus, by examining how discourse enters into various fields we can understand how buildings are planned and utilised, becoming representative of certain attitudes and values – typically described as 'culture'.

Further to this specific application of Foucault's work, this book seeks to draw upon aspects of Foucault's work, and others like Stuart Hall and Nikolas Rose, to develop additional tools for understanding the circumstances from which meanings are derived from architecture. Discourse not only constructs meanings but also regulates bodies within space, affecting the way buildings are made to function. In this manner, the following chapters are concerned with how architecture, being a representational construct, is enmeshed within relationships of knowledge, power and space. With reference to Foucault's earlier work, in particular *Discipline and Punish* and *The Birth of the Clinic*, this book investigates the operation of "institutional apparatuses"[45] and their technologies that affect the operation of power and its governance over a population. To this end, power may intercede in discourse in order to modify it and introduce new practices, bringing about changes to not only laws, administrative measures, scientific statements, etc, but also architectural forms and styles. All of these, are generally considered

10 *Architecture as cultural and political discourse*

to be the product of 'culture', yet none are predetermined or fixed, as it is so often assumed, but subject to the way knowledge is proscribed in a particular time and place.

Politics

In making use of the term 'culture' it is important to recognise that the concept also has a spatial dimension, whereby the terms 'culture' or 'cultures' conjure a world of human differences, specifically, differences between people that are physically and geographically – i.e. 'spatially' – specific. As such, different human characteristics or traits are thought to be possessed by people of specific locations. As the anthropologists Gupta and Ferguson explain: "Culture is conceptualised as a diversity of separate societies, each with its own culture . . . a separate, individual cultural entity, typically associated with 'a people', 'a tribe', 'a nation', and so forth".[46] It is taken for granted that each nation embodies a distinct culture relative to their place on a map. Yet cultures do not naturally divide themselves according to a border, a nation or a state. Such a proposition poses many problems in a world of increased communication and mobility (not to mention the global hysteria relating to refugees, displaced and stateless peoples), whereby the presence of 'others' appears to threaten the social stability of an imagined cultural community. While such issues are not new, this book seeks to explore the relationship between culture, space and power, whereby the worldwide phenomenon of increased border protection seeks to protect an imagined idea of 'culture' against those who threaten to destabilise it.

The notion that people become bound to a particular place is important because it explains how people come to identify themselves as adhering to certain customs and traditions. Space, in this sense, becomes a "resource of power",[47] whereby politicised notions of 'culture' and space become a means for identifying the whole and excluding others. As such, buildings become useful not only to carry out state sanctioned activities, but also because they define space. Even at their most basic level, buildings construct physical barriers, they can be used to detain, to keep out, and to represent the strength and fortitude of a nation. Consider, for example (discussed in later chapters), the Nazi concentration camps, or the Australian immigration detention centres. While they do not compare in terms of the harm inflicted upon individual subjects, both can be described as 'apparatuses' for the proliferation of certain imagined ideals through the exclusion of others. In this way, 'politics' as referred to here is concerned with the production of identities and notions of belonging, and in particular the manner in which space and buildings are utilised in this process.

In addition to this, it must be recognised that culture does not establish a site of commonality, uniquely acquired by geographic propinquity, but rather 'culture' is politicised in order to create subjects of individuals by shaping their perceptions of the world around. As Hall points out: "Moreover, they [cultures] emerge within the play of specific modalities of power, and thus they are more the product of the marking of difference and exclusion, than they are the sign of an identical naturally-constituted unity".[48] Identities are neither naturally unified, nor are they possessed or owned by individuals, they are, as Gupta and Ferguson reiterate: "A mobile and often unstable relation of difference".[49] As such, politics involves the "social management" of a population, whereby certain practices like; health, law and education, are passed to government who presume to act in the "interests of the people".[50] At this point 'culture' becomes political, which explains how power, supported by forms of knowledge, intercedes in discourse to modify and transform certain beliefs and practices. Such an explanation, however, suggests that power does not necessarily radiate from a single position, from those in authority, but circulates amongst all forms of social interaction. This implies, as Hall points out: "that we are all, to some degree, caught up in its circulation".[51] What's more, power is not negative, but productive, as Foucault remarks: "It induces pleasure, forms of knowledge and produces discourses. It needs to be thought of as a productive network which runs through the whole social body".[52]

In his writings concerning sovereign power, the Italian philosopher Giorgio Agamben asserts that Foucault seems to have orientated his analysis of power according to two distinct directives of research. Firstly, the study of "political techniques", whereby the State assumes the role of caring for and protecting natural life, and secondly, the examination of "technologies of the self" by which the processes of subjectification bind the individual both to his identity and an external power.[53] Yet according to Agamben the point at which these two directives converge remains unclear in Foucault's work.[54] Hence Agamben proposes to extend Foucault's thesis by declaring that the point at which these modes of power intersect produces the "exception". In this way, the "exception" is a kind of exclusion. Agamben explains: "But what is excluded in the exception maintains itself in relation to the rule in the form of the rule's suspension".[55] In other words, the rule is applied to the exception by being withdrawn from it. In this book, Agamben's theory is exemplified through the spatial dimensions of the 'camp'. Here the 'camp' becomes a place where the law is literally suspended by the law. Examples include the Nazi controlled concentration camps, or the US military base in Guantanamo Bay, and also, as explored in later chapters, the Australian Immigration Detention Centres. In these locations individuals are withheld access to law by the law that allows their incarceration. In effect, this 'exception' has the double effect of excluding unwanted 'others', like Jews, Muslims and 'boat people' respectively, but at the same time solidifies the values of the populous by making distinct their values from the excluded 'other'.

Politics involves the appropriation of certain representative tools, such as laws, institutions and architecture, in order to portray, represent and preserve an imagined sense of identity. Governments do not necessarily impose

12 *Architecture as cultural and political discourse*

such values or systems of belief, but are able to give them representative form by acting in the 'interests of the people'. Having said this, the politicisation of the self, which in relation to this book refers to notions of identity formation, belongingness, sameness and otherness, enables 'socially legitimised authorities', such as politicians, regulators, theologians, academics and other experts to construct the images of a nation. As Nikolas Rose points out, the interference of these authorities takes place in all aspects of daily life and at a diversity of sites, such as schools, clinics, homes, work places and courtrooms.[56] For instance, school curricula might be adjusted, as under the Howard Government in Australia, to reflect certain 'core values' like integration, as opposed to multiculturalism under the previous administration, or through the implementation of laws to ban certain forms of religious apparel, like the burqa or head scarf. In effect, knowledge serves to perpetuate and legitimise specific discursive formations which inform an individual's understanding of certain processes and/or endorse certain modes of conduct, thought and speech. Architecture not only serves to provide shape and form to certain discursive practices but also facilitates certain activities, sometimes to the exclusion of others.

Architecture

In recognising that there is no fixed architectural language for representing political ambitions, policies and other practices, it does not follow that architecture lacks the potential to promote a political agenda – rather it does so as an ingredient in the discursive process. Whether intended or not, architecture may become appropriated to represent a multitude of ambitions. Therefore, it is pertinent to ask: can a building espouse specific principles? Put simply, can a building incorporating certain aesthetic elements, like a neo-classical stone façade or a modern glass curtain wall, be described with all seriousness, as some have claimed, as socialist or democratic architecture? Consider, Norman Foster's restoration work on the German Reichstag in Berlin, in which the cupola (which was partly destroyed by fire during the uprise of the Nazi's and further demolished by the bombing of Berlin during WWII), was replaced by a glass dome. Foster uses the transparency of the glass to make connections between democracy and the Germany government following its reunification.[57] In comparison, Giuseppe Terragni's Casa del Fascio in Como also uses glass as a metaphor for the transparency of Mussolini's fascist government. Given the dubiousness and contradiction of the pair of claims, it is highly unlikely that any building product, style or design – in particular glass – can represent certain beliefs in a straightforward manner. Mindful of this caveat, this book is concerned with the manner buildings are produced in response to certain discursive practices. It asks not only how they might mean something, but how can they respond to particular practices that define the values and morals of a nation?

Architecture as cultural and political discourse   13

In answering this latter question, consider briefly Nicolae Ceausescu's Imperial Palace in Bucharest, or as it is now called the House of the Republic or People's Palace. This example shows that a building, no matter how uncomfortably, may be used to represent the values of a government despite the changed politics of those who occupy it. Built during the 1980s, Ceausescu's Palace required the reconstruction of the centre of Bucharest in an effort to reflect the 'greatness' of his regime through the architecture of the city. To do so, Ceausescu had demolished numerous centuries' old churches, monasteries, hospitals, schools and homes, resulting in the displacement of more than 40,000 residents and hundreds of businesses and other essential amenities in the area. In total, one fifth of the city was razed.[58] In its place, Ceausescu carved through a wide central boulevard lined with water fountains and ornate neo-classical facades to act as the backdrop to a long promenade that focuses on the Imperial Palace at the top of Arsenal hill, the city's highest point. Costing more than $10 billion, the Palace is said to be one of the largest and most expensive buildings in the world. Yet in the aftermath of the collapse of Ceausescu's regime and his subsequent execution in 1989 debate was dominated by concerns about what to do with this grandiose structure that would seemingly be a continual reminder of Ceausescu's violent and hated dictatorship. Some argued that the Palace should be demolished. Others considered that it would be better served as a casino or hotel. Despite these proposals, the new Romanian government decided to make use of the monumental building for its own purposes, whereby the Imperial Palace become transformed into the People's Palace and the house of the new democratic republic.

In the essay *The State as a Work of Art*, Renata Salecl asks how present day Romanians now perceive the Palace. To her surprise, Salecl reveals that Ceausescu's Imperial Palace has become "the most precious symbol of democracy in Romania".[59] Yet this claim is somewhat contradictory, for how can the same building be described as the representation of democracy and freedom, yet have originated in the mind of a tyrant? Could it be that neither democracy, communism, or for that matter any other form of politics, is inherently connected to the built form of the Palace or any other building. Rather, buildings become representative of particular values as a result of how they are described and talked about, to which the physical features of architecture may lend various meanings representative form. Similarly, Barthes described the Eiffel Tower as a symbol of Paris, not because of any inherent capacity to do so, but because it is so easily seen. Such monuments may achieve prominence, becoming representative of a city and a point of attachment for national pride and identity, not because they are examples of 'good', well thought-out architecture, but rather as Barthes points out, because "they are there". He explains: "The Tower attracts meaning the way a lightning rod attracts thunderbolts; for all lovers of signification, it plays a glamorous part, that of a pure signifier, i.e. of a form in which men unceasingly put meaning (which they extract at will

14 *Architecture as cultural and political discourse*

from their knowledge, their dreams, their history), without this meaning thereby ever being finite and fixed: who can say what the Tower will be for humanity tomorrow?".[60] In other words, buildings like the Eiffel Tower in Paris and the People's Palace in Bucharest are capable of forming identities and giving rise to particular meanings because they are so readily identifiable. Such buildings become representative of 'cultural' values and attitudes because they more easily facilitate a connection between the words used to describe the thing and the thing itself. Barthes explains how the Eiffel Tower is perceived by the 'world': "First of all as a universal symbol of Paris, it is everywhere on the globe where Paris is said to be stated as an image; from the Midwest to Australia, there is no journey to France which isn't made, somehow, in the Tower's name, no schoolbook, poster, or film about France which fails to propose it as the major sign of a people and of a place".[61] In this way, it is not the things-in-themselves which produce meanings, but rather buildings become objects of knowledge through discourse. Keeping this in mind, architecture not only derives it meanings through discursive forms but it is also procured in the same manner. As such, particular forms of knowledge may result in the specific utilisation of spaces or the construction of new buildings to carry out particular functions in the interests of certain 'essential' policies or procedures. In effect, the architecture plays a key role in contributing towards the 'aestheticisation' of various political constructs by becoming a 'statement' or a component of discourse giving rise to particular meanings.

The example of Ceausescu's Palace is also noteworthy because it raises another issue addressed by this book, being the ethical responsibility of architects in the procurement of such projects. In other words, one should ask whether architects should be held accountable for facilitating particular building outcomes which adversely affect the wellbeing, freedom and rights of certain individuals. Consider Anca Petrescu and the 700 or more architects who contributed towards the design of the Imperial Palace: one might ask whether they should be held accountable, along with those who ordered and carried out the forced removal of tens of thousands of Bucharest residents so that construction might proceed, for the extraordinary burden placed upon the Romanian citizens to fund the project? Yet questions relating to the effects of certain types of architecture and their political motivations are often ignored in architectural ethics. The ethical debate as it relates to contemporary architecture is dominated by what Karsten Harries describes as the main task facing architects, being the interpretation of "a way of life valid for our time".[62] By this, Harries invokes a complexity in architecture that is more than just aesthetic, but, rather, capable of "speaking to us of how we are to live in the contemporary world".[63] Yet whether architecture is capable of this task, as Harries believes, is open to conjecture as previously discussed. Another popular argument regarding the ethical responsibility of architects focuses on the environmental considerations of building design.[64] However, while such debates are certainly valuable, they do consider the

Architecture as cultural and political discourse 15

full effect of architecture as a component of discourse and its capacity to represent the values of a group of people. Other elements of architectural ethics, like Paul Jaskot's *Architecture of Oppression*, examine the architecture of the Nazi regime and its acquisition of building materials through the use of forced labour. Here Jaskot queries the relationship between art and politics in Nazi Germany, whereby he claims that aesthetic decisions were also political decisions in that both goals "drove the implementation of specific oppressive labour practices or influenced the timing of institutional decisions".[65] With this in mind, this book is concerned with the question of whether architects should lend their expertise to the procurement of building projects that intend to marginalise and exclude certain kinds of people for particular political aims. To this end, architects, like Petrescu, should not escape responsibility for providing the means by which certain regimes attempt to represent themselves through various architectural forms.

Aestheticisation

In view of the preceding illustration of the fluidity of meaning and the implications of 'interpretive regimes' with relation to culture, politics and architecture, this book is further concerned with the question of how certain values and attitudes within society become politically motivated and aestheticised in the built environment. In this investigation, it is necessary to examine how the self – and by extension the population – is produced, and assigned what Ian Hunter calls an "aesthetic existence" – being the means by which the self is identified with its surroundings, thereby bringing about certain expectations for the kind of people we imagine ourselves to be. In exploring how the self is positioned by discourse and whether the constructed object attests to this description of selfhood, it is worth noting Hunter's warning regarding the historical "misconstruction of the ways we relate to the domain of 'aesthetics' in the present".[66] Hunter claims that the conception of 'aesthetics' and its domain of influence has been limited by the narrowly defined field imposed upon it by cultural studies, where the term is seen as part of the study of labour and politics. Thus, aesthetics is relegated to the realm of ethics and taste, and self- and group interests conceived of in an economic sphere without full consideration of the broader social context for aesthetic perception, its production, circulation and consumption by "groups and institutions".[67] Thus, with relation to Ceausescu's Imperial Palace, its meaning is largely (if not entirely) attributable to the interests of the ruling class, not only Ceausescu's communist dictatorship but also, as identified, the new democracy. For this reason, Hunter argues that aesthetics cannot be relegated to the realm of economics and taste, but, rather, the broader social context in which values circulate and ultimately consume the identities of individuals.

In progressing this view, Hunter points to two distinct yet converging theories that overturn this former limited understanding of the aesthetic

16 *Architecture as cultural and political discourse*

domain. The first relates to the reconstruction of the "ethical sphere" itself, as advocated by Foucault, a field that does not consider ideas and values arising in or forming a 'cultural' sphere as naturally existing or 'essential', but instead relates to the way in which the self is constructed. Or as Foucault would say, the ethical sphere is composed of "technologies for problematising conduct and events that permit individuals to compose themselves as 'subjects' of their actions and experiences".[68] In this way, attitudes to do with, for instance: abortion, sexuality, single parents, euthanasia, stem cell research, criminals and asylum seekers, to name a few, are composed within the limits of this ethical sphere (which accounts for some degree of flexibility for a diversity of views while the parameters of the debates remain relatively stable). Thus, for Hunter, following Foucault, aesthetics might belong to ethics, yet it does not simply consist of values, ideas and doctrines. Instead, as Hunter describes it: "Aesthetics should be described as a distinctive way of actually conducting one's life – as a self-supporting ensemble of techniques and practices for problematising conduct and events and bringing oneself into being as the subject of an aesthetic existence".[69] In this manner, aesthetics is not only the consideration of the appearance of things but the art of 'self fashioning'. Similarly, for Foucault, the aesthetics of existence entails "those intentional and voluntary actions by which men not only set themselves rules of conduct, but also seek to transform themselves".[70] Consequently, by considering the self as constructed within a specific social framework one should be better placed to understand how cultural values and meanings are productive and associated with the built environment.

It is within this framework that the issue of Nazi architecture is explored in chapters 5 and 6 of this text. Some conventional histories of this era describe the German people as suppressed and the unwilling participants in the Third Reich. However, in recent years this stance has come under challenge, whereby historians like Daniel Goldhagen have put forward the view that ordinary Germans from all walks of life brutalised and murdered Jews both willingly and zealously.[71] In his account *Hitler's Willing Executioners*, Goldhagen reveals that the 'right to kill' was made possible by the desire to advance one's self above another. Based on this pretence, the 'fashioning' of the self and by extension the German national character was founded on the idealisation of health and improved living standards and required the elimination of defectives, those who were determined to be physically and racially degenerate. In this way, the protection of the national body against those who threatened to destroy it became seen as one's moral duty and thus enabled the systematic extermination of millions of Jews and other so called degenerates.

The second and convergent theory of the 'aesthetic existence', according to Hunter, has grown out of recent criticism of dialectically driven theories of politics and economics formulated by Hegel and Marx and their followers. This criticism includes the scholarship of Nikolas Rose and Peter Miller who argue that the way in which "human beings govern themselves and organise their economic lives" does not derive from the terms of conventional social theory, like class and ideology.[72] Rather, such developments are contingent upon and emerge in a variety of "circumstantial technologies", like those, as Hunter points out, in which Puritanism unexpectedly brought about forms of behaviour conducive to a capitalist economy. Hunter explains: "Such circumstantial technologies lead in no particular direction and realise no general form of 'man' as a 'species being'. From this perspective, then, political, ideological, and cultural interests must be analysed in terms of the available institutions of the formation and deployment; and they must be analysed without recourse to the notion of a privileged set of interests . . .".[73] Rose asks how one might write a history of the contemporary "regime of the self". He reasons that in order to do so one must not attempt to write a history of changing ideas of persons as has been done in philosophy, literature and culture, but rather the approach should involve the "genealogy of subjectification". Rose explains: "My concern, however, is not with 'ideas of persons' but with the practices in which persons are understood and acted upon – in relation to their criminality, their health and sickness, their family relations, their productivity, their military role, and so forth. It is unwise to assume that one can derive, from an account of notions of the human being in cosmology, philosophy, aesthetics, or literature, evidence about presuppositions that shape the conduct of human beings in such mundane sites and practices".[74] For Rose, a "genealogy of subjectification" as it concerns the self not only avoids a history of ideas, but rather, seeks to investigate the practices and techniques from different times and places that produce humans with different emotions, beliefs, psychological and other character traits.

By way of explanation, consider Paul Rabinow's discussion of the 1832 cholera epidemic in Paris. The event set the stage for the abandonment of previously held medical understandings of disease as a result of new social considerations with relation to hygiene, sanitation and health.[75] Rabinow explains how the epidemic had a profound impact upon many aspects of French thought and culture. He writes: "The cholera epidemic not only provided a clear impetus for change, but opened the way for new scientific discourses, new administrative practices, and new conceptions of social order".[76] Newly formed government authorities established and regulated acceptable practices relating to housing standards, sanitation and health. In this manner, the crisis necessitated a fundamental physical and moral change to living standards. As a consequence, city planning schemes implemented public works programmes, rail and canal networks; wider avenues were carved into the densely populated areas of the city; and the water supply was greatly improved. "The cholera epidemic catalysed a new set of relationships, spurring a more precise and powerful analysis of the milieu focusing on 'conditions de vie' that included local biological and social variables . . . The apparatus of finely grained observation of the social body – supervised by

18 *Architecture as cultural and political discourse*

physicians, aided by architects, and backed by the police – in the service of the health of the population and the general good, had a long career ahead".[77] From this event, as Rabinow reveals, health reform significantly modified the way people lived bringing about specific laws, institutions and architectural forms. This transformation of society and the city cannot be attributable to a single idea relating to disease or the 'diseased' person, but rather to changing attitudes towards sanitation and hygiene.

Where this had a direct impact on building design and the city is clearly evidenced by the introduction of underground sewers, flowing water and so forth. But beyond such mechanical changes cities also began the process of what we now call 'modernisation'.[78] For example, popularised notions of miasma resulted in significant changes to the layout of medieval Paris, cramped conditions and interweaving streets were transformed for the purpose of better facilitating air flow and population movement. To this end, Haussmann was responsible for cutting through the densely populated and irregular alleyways of the old city to construct the wide boulevards and open spaces, views and squares typically associated with Paris today.

Changes and transformations in health and sanitisation resulting from the cholera epidemic, for example, became such a part of the daily lives of individuals, not only in Paris but throughout the western world, that they have become normalised and accepted as the standard for living. Yet such reforms were not guided by an evolutionary hand to generate specific cultural outcomes, and do not come ready made. Rather, they have to be, as Rose explains; "invented, refined, and stabilised, to be disseminated and implanted in different ways in different practices – schools, families, streets, workplaces and courtrooms".[79] In effect, the self is subject to processes of 'governance' that regulate acceptable forms of speech, conduct and activity within society. That is not to say that governments per se hold the power to compel certain attitudes and conduct, for it is essential not to 'over-valuate' or too greatly attribute the 'power' of the State and its ability to unify or even functionalise social and economic activity. Indeed, Foucault points out that the power often attributed to the government is a "mythical abstraction" and no more than a "composite reality". He declares: "The State's importance is a lot more limited than many of us think. Maybe what is really important for our modern times . . . is not so much the State-domination of society, but the 'governmentalisation' of the state".[80] Governments, as described by Rose and Miller, are the "historically constituted matrix" that articulates all those normative values held by the people, formalised and expressed through the representational capacity of the governing body source. Thus, by analysing the inter-dependencies between political rationalities and governmental technologies, "we can begin to understand the multiple and delicate networks that connect the lives of individuals, groups and organisations to the aspirations of authorities".[81]

This is evidenced, as described earlier, in the operation and expansion of Australian detention facilities during the Howard era. In this manner, the indefinite incarceration of so-called 'illegal immigrants' was condoned by the majority of Coalition voters who endorsed the government's treatment of asylum seekers at the 2001 federal election, following the Tampa Crisis.[82] This endorsement was not borne out of the government's desire to treat 'others' poorly, but a desire to capitalise on latent and overt prejudices that already existed amongst the general Australian population. This endorsement granted the government a mandate to detain asylum seekers and implement new programs for the prevention of unwanted arrivals. The direct intention was to make known that the government was willing to act upon the majority's concerns and capable of maintaining or restoring the populist perception of what it means to be an 'Australian'.

According to Hunter the convergence of these two theories arising from the 'aesthetic existence' of the self signals the end of a political and cultural theory inaugurated by Hegel. In so doing, we avail ourselves of the tools to better understand the 'aesthetic' domain, by treating 'culture' and society as one of the "contingencies that make us what we are".[83] To this end, this book examines the effect of culture, politics and architecture on the production of the self in order to better understand how meanings and meaningful practices are constructed within the discursive framework of the built environment.

Notes

1 Aaron Betsky, "Rem Koolhaas; The Fire of Manhattanism Inside the Iceberg of Modernism", *Considering Rem Koolhaas and the Office of Metropolitan Architecture* (Rotterdam: NAi Publishers, 2003), 26.
2 *Ibid.*, 27.
3 Refer to Arthur Ludlow, "How Architecture Rediscovered the Future", *The New York Times*, 18 May 2003.
4 Betsky (2003), 27.
5 Quoted in Anna Winston, "Koolhaas Wins Venice Biennale Award", *bdonline*, 20 July 2010. Available at http://www.bdonline.co.uk/news/koolhaas-wins-venice-biennale-award/5002986.article (Accessed January 2010).
6 Refer to Deyan Sudjic, *The Edifice Complex* (New York: Penguin Books, 2005), 318.
7 As Ludlow points out, this development is encapsulated by a remark that the director for the National Center for Contemporary Arts in Rome made to Koolhaas, who had entered the competition (which Hadid eventually won) to design its new museum. "We need a building that does for Rome what the Guggenheim did for Bilbao". In response Koolhaas comments: "That is a staggering statement, because Rome doesn't need to be put on the map". Refer, Ludlow (2003).
8 Rem Koolhaas, *Conversations with Students* ed. Sanford Kwinter (New York: Princeton Press, 1996), 65. Quoted in Rafael Moneo, *Theoretical Anxiety and Design Strategies* (Barcelona: ACTAR, 2004), 311.
9 Michel Foucault, "Space, Knowledge, and Power", *The Foucault Reader* ed. Paul Rabinow (London: Penguin Books, 1991), 247–248.
10 *Ibid.*, 87–88.
11 Refer to Mark Cousins and Athar Hussain, *Michael Foucault* (London: MacMillan, 1984), 225.

20   *Architecture as cultural and political discourse*

12 Foucault (1991), 253.

13 *Ibid.*

14 *Ibid.*, 254.

15 Paul Hirst, *Space & Power; Politics, War and Architecture* (Cambridge: Polity Press, 2005), 170.

16 Refer to Michel Foucault, *The Archaeology of Knowledge* (New York: Pantheon Books, 1972), and Michael Foucault, *Power/Knowledge: Selected Interviews and Other Writings, 1972–1977* ed. Colin Gordon (New York: Pantheon Books, 1980), 196.

17 Refer to Anthony Vidler, *The Architectural Uncanny* (Cambridge: MIT Press, 1992). Beatriz Columina and Jennifer Bloomer, *Sexuality and Space* (New York: Princeton Architectural Press, 1992).

18 Refer to Elliot Felix, "Form and Situated Meaning", *Theory of City Form*, Spring (2004), 8.

19 Hirst (2005), 177.

20 *Ibid.*, 155–178. Robin Evans, *Translations From Drawings to Building and Other Essays* (London: Architectural Associations Publications, 1997), 55–91.

21 Paul Rabinow, *French Modern: Norms and Forms of the Social Environment* (Chicago: The University of Chicago Press, 1989). Giorgio Agamben, *Homo Sacer: Sovereign Power and Bare Life* (Stanford: Stanford University Press, 1995). Giorgio Agamben, *The Remnants of Auschwitz: The Witness and the Archive* (Brooklyn: Zone Books, 1999).

22 Refer to Foucault (1972).

23 Betsky (2003), 26.

24 Terry Eagleton, *The Idea of Culture* (Malden: Blackwell Publishing, 2000), 1.

25 Refer to *The Australian Concise Oxford Dictionary* 4th ed. (Melbourne: Oxford University Press, 2004).

26 Eagleton (2000), 2.

27 Refer to Kevin Lynch, *The Image of the City* (Cambridge: MIT Press, 1960).

28 Foucault (1991), 246.

29 *Ibid.*

30 Stuart Hall, "Introduction: Who Needs Identity", *Question of Cultural Identity* ed. Stuart Hall and Paul du Gay (London: Sage Publications, 1996), 11.

31 Foucault (1991), 83.

32 Nikolas Rose, *Inventing Our Selves* (Cambridge: Cambridge University Press, 1998), 3.

33 Refer to Christian Norberg-Schulz, *Intentions in Architecture* (Cambridge: The MIT Press, 1965), 122.

34 Richard Hooker, *What is Architecture?* Available at http://richard-hooker.com/sites/worldcultures/ARCHI/BASELINE.HTM (Accessed June 2009).

35 K. Michael Hays, "Critical Architecture; Between Culture and From", *Perspecta*, Vol. 21 (1984), 17.

36 *Ibid.*, 27.

37 Refer to Michael Matias, "Is Meaning in Architecture a Myth?" *Philosophy and Architecture* (Amsterdam: Rodopi, 1994), 121–140.

38 Stuart Hall, *Representation: Cultural Representation and Signifying Practices* (London: Sage Publication, 1997), 1.

39 *Ibid.*

40 *Ibid.*

41 Refer to Foucault (1980), 194.

42 Hirst (2005), 157.

43 Refer to Helen Mallinson, 'Metaphors or Experience; The Voice of Air', *Philosophical Forum*, Vol. XXXV, No. 2, Summer (2004), 161–177.

44 Refer Kenneth Frampton, *Modern Architecture: A Critical History* (London: Thames & Hudson, 1980), 32–33.

45 Refer to Michel Foucault, *The Birth of the Clinic* (New York: Vintage Books, 1973), and Michel Foucault, *Discipline and Punish: The Birth of the Prison* (London: Penguin Books, 1977).

46 Akhil Gupta and James Ferguson, *Culture, Power and Place: Explorations in Critical Anthropology* (Durham: Duke University Press, 2001), 3.

47 Hirst (2005), 1.

48 Hall (1996), 4.

49 Gupta and Ferguson (2001), 13.

50 Refer to Tony Bennett, "Putting Policy into Cultural Studies" *Cultural Studies* ed. Lawrence Grossberg et al. (New York: Routledge, 1992), 24–29.

51 Hall (1997), 50.

52 Foucault (1980), 119.

53 Giorgio Agamben, *Homo Sacer; Sovereign Power and Bare Life* (Stanford: Stanford University Press, 1998), 5.

54 For further commentary on Agamben's claims regarding Foucault, refer Jacques Derrida, *The Beast & the Sovereign Vol. 1* (Chicago: The University of Chicago Press, 2008), 92–95, 315–317 and 324–330.

55 Agamben (1998), 16–17.

56 Nikolas Rose and Peter Miller, *Governing the Present* (Cambridge: Polity Press, 2008), 1.

57 Consider Jeremy Till, who states that just because one designs a transparent cupola it does not necessarily mean that the governmental processes within can be deemed equally transparent, rather, this situation "is a fake transparency that demeans the whole notion of democracy". Jeremy Till, *Occupying Architecture: Between Architect and the Community* (London: Routledge, 1998), 61.

58 According to Renata Salecl, Ceausescu intended to represent his ideological ambitions of Romania through the built monuments of his government. To this end, the demolition of the historical district of Bucharest was vital, not only to provide the space for Ceausescu's architectural monuments, but rather the destruction of the city was a deliberate attempt to erase the past. For Ceausescu the architectural remnants of the historical district represented "the previous symbolic order" which he believed no longer applied under his reign. Salecl states: "By razing the historical monuments, Ceausescu aimed to wipe out Romanian national identity, the fantasy structure of the nation that is forged around historical old buildings, churches, and then establish his own version of this identity". Refer to Renata Salecl, "The State as a Work of Art", *Architecture and Revolution* ed. Neil Leach (London: Routledge, 1999), 102.

59 *Ibid.*, 104.

60 Roland Barthes, *The Eiffel Tower and Other Mythologies* (New York: Hill & Wang, 1979), 4.

61 *Ibid.*

62 Karsten Harries, *The Ethical Function of Architecture* (Massachusetts: MIT Press, 1998), 2 and Sigfried Giedion, *Space, Time and Architecture* (Cambridge: Harvard University Press, 1941), xxxii. Refer also to David Watkins, *Morality and Architecture* (Oxford: Oxford University Press, 1977).

63 Harries (1998), 13.

64 Refer to Warwick Fox, *Ethics and the Built Environment* (London: Routledge, 2000).

65 Paul Jaskot, *The Architecture of Oppression* (New York: Routledge, 2000), 3.

66 Ian Hunter, "Aesthetics and Cultural Studies", in *Cultural Studies* ed. Lawrence Grossberg et al. (New York: Routledge, 1992), 347.

22   Architecture as cultural and political discourse

67 Refer to Pierre Bourdieu, *The Field of Cultural Production* (Irvington: Columbia University Press, 1993), 29.
68 Quoted in Hunter (1992), 348. Refer to Michael Foucault, *The History of Sexuality: The Will to Knowledge* Vol. 1 (London: Penguin Books, 1976), *The Use of Pleasure* Vol. 2 (1984) and *The Care of the Self* Vol. 3 (1984b).
69 Hunter (1992), 348.
70 Foucault (1984), 10. Refer to Alan Milchman and Alan Rosenberg, "The Aesthetic and Ascetic Dimension of an Ethic of Self Fashioning: Nietzsche and Foucault", *Parrhesia* No. 2, (2007), 44–65.
71 Daniel Goldhagen, *Hitler's Willing Executioners* (New York: Alfred A. Knopf, 2002).
72 Refer to Eagleton (2000), 1.
73 Hunter (1992), 348–349.
74 Rose (1998), 23.
75 Rabinow (1989), 30–39.
76 *Ibid.*, 15.
77 *Ibid.*, 39.
78 Refer to Francois Delaporte, *Disease and Civilisation* (Cambridge: MIT Press, 1986).
79 Rose (1998). 25.
80 Michel Foucault, "Governmentality", in *The Foucault Effect: Studies in Governmentality* ed. Graham Burchell, Colin Gordon and Peter Miller (Chicago: The University of Chicago Press, 1991), 103. Refer to Alan Hunt and Gary Wickham, *Foucault and Law: Towards a Sociology of Law as Governance* (North Melbourne: Pluto Press, 1994), 25.
81 Nikolas Rose and Peter Miller, "Political Power Beyond the State: Problematics of Government", *The British Journal of Sociology*, Vol. 43, No. 2, June (1992), 175–176.
82 The Tampa crisis gained significant coverage in the news media in August 2001 when it came to light that 450 refugees, mainly Afghanis and Iraqis, had been rescued from their sinking boat by a Norwegian freighter off the cost of Christmas Island. Instead of extending help, the Australian government refused permission for the freighter to dock and ordered the Tampa and its human cargo to leave Australian waters immediately. A standoff ensued in which the freighter's captain refused to turn back and the Australian government refused its entry. After three days the impasse was broken at gun point with SAS troops boarding the ship. The Howard government, still refusing to buckle at mounting international pressure, refused the asylum seekers entry and convinced poorer Pacific nations, such as Nauru, Vanuatu and the Solomon Islands, to accept the refugees for 'processing'. The Tampa crisis is widely acknowledged as having an immediate impact on the result of the Federal election. Arguably, Howard deliberately appealed to people's insecurities with regards to the perceived rising levels of immigrants by implementing laws for the tougher treatment of asylum seekers.
83 Hunter (1992), 349.

2 Meaning and the death of architecture

This chapter presents a historical perspective on how meaning is thought to be related to architecture. Contemplating Victor Hugo's pronouncement two centuries ago that "printing will kill architecture", this chapter examines subsequent attempts to reinstate architecture as culture's primary communicative tool by making built form legible. Hugo insisted that humankind once communicated through architecture as though words somehow inscribed in stone. Accordingly, to make his point he referred to the grand Gothic cathedrals of the middle-ages which he believed once possessed the capacity to reflect and communicate the values of French society. However, it is here forth argued that architecture's capacity to impart such values has not diminished per se, for architecture never possessed an inherent capacity to mean anything in particular, as Hugo's pronouncement presupposes. This is not to say that architecture does not become associated with certain meanings, but rather that the manner in which this occurs is not wholly determined by its designer or through means of some kind of collective intentionality. This chapter allows one to see how expectations that buildings mean something has a history, composed in part by writers like Hugo, but also by the way architects describe their work as meaningful objects.

In analysing the multiple and diverse theories pertaining to meaning in architecture, this chapter highlights the conflated means by which various architectural movements have attempted to align a particular design aesthetic with 'the age'. It also considers the varied theories by which architecture is associated with 'speech' or 'reading' as though the building where a giant book in conversation with humanity. This chapter questions and ultimately rejects the attempts to attribute architecture with the proclivity to narrate and to describe particular meanings relative to a building-as-text. Meaning is subject to the discursive practices arising within and defining a community, ones that associate meanings with form through a complex network of historical, social, psychological and enunciative formations, and not through any capacity inherent in the architectural object to convey complex meaning.

24　*Meaning and the death of architecture*

'This will kill that'

> The Church of Notre-Dame at Paris is doubtless still a majestic and sublime edifice. But, however beautiful it has remained in growing old, it is difficult to suppress a sigh, to restrain a feeling of indignation at the numberless degradations and mutilations which the hand of time and that of man have inflicted upon this venerable monument . . . Upon the face of this ancient queen of French cathedrals, beside each wrinkle we constantly find a scar. *Tempus edax, homo edaciour* (Time is destructive, man is more destructive) – which we would willingly render this – Time is blind, but man is stupid.[1]

The words of Victor Hugo from his nineteenth century romantic novel *Notre-Dame de Paris*,[2] have presented architects with much to ponder since he declared: *"Ceci Tuera cela"* – "This will kill that. The book will kill the building . . . Printing will kill architecture".[3] These words have provided architects with a perennial touchstone from which to construe architecture's semantic capacity and, subsequently, to manipulate building form in the attempt to defy Hugo's prediction and make architecture meaningful in itself. Hugo lamented the decline of architecture's existence as an object of cultural as well as semantic worth. He declared that buildings no longer imparted specific meanings, nor did they any longer provide a sense of community among those available to 'read' them. The novel's setting, the Cathedral of Notre Dame, built during the twelfth and thirteenth centuries, was for Hugo an obvious example of architecture's former capacity to convey meaning. By the nineteenth century, Notre Dame de Paris was in a state of disrepair and on the verge of demolition. However, Hugo's novel led to an increased awareness of the building's heritage as a work of 'culture' and prefigured its eventual restoration a decade later. Hugo's views helped create the idea that buildings could mean something specific, and as such, contributed to an emerging credence in the historical worth of architecture. This view made for the assumption (as evidenced in recent debates regarding *Critical Architecture*)[4] that architectural form participates in the production of 'culture', whereby buildings somehow reveal or impart meanings relating to the values of a particular time and place.

Hugo imbued the cathedral with distinctly 'human' characteristics, whereby its degradation over the centuries became a register for the decline of human values. Simultaneously, in his view, the printed word had superseded architecture as the medium by which humanity represented itself.[5] For Hugo, the writer, was caught up in the irony of his own words, as the cathedral, a representation of the past, was now reliant upon the printed word (including those in Hugo's own writing) in order to maintain its status as a symbol of cultural heritage. Similarly, Stephens recognised: "The book written by the architecture of Notre-Dame de Paris becomes the cathedral written by the book *Notre-Dame de Paris*. This mirroring effect reflects the duality contained within each . . . In this respect, Hugo recognised the cathedral's potential as an emblem of different architectural styles to embody the flux of (human) nature that fascinated him as a poet".[6] The invention of the printing press, as described in 'Notre-Dame de Paris', had elevated the book to the primary medium by which civilisation expressed itself. Compared to the book's emerging ubiquity and obvious 'literariness' architecture, by contrast, was rendered little more than an immobile mass, mute and without values such as timelessness, magnificence and beauty, thus supposedly diminishing the building's affectivity and authority.

With this in mind, many architectural theorists, particularly those interested in semiotics in the past few decades, have attempted to enlist Hugo in their call to arms to "reinstate cultural symbolism in architecture" and ultimately assert "how architecture can recover its ability to express meaning".[7] However, in order to analyse the likelihood of such a recovery, one must ask whether architecture can convey meaning as Hugo once claimed and as theorists today routinely imagine it to? If so, how does it do this? If it cannot, what is at stake behind the claims for the loss of architectural meaning and cultural significance? These questions belong to the broader scope of this book that is concerned with whether architecture possesses any inherent meaning that reveals something of the cultural situation in which it is found. Whether architecture has the capacity to generate meanings which 'govern one's actions and understanding of the world'. Moreover, the role of architecture in the production of 'culture'; asking whether buildings are capable of forming the attitudes and values of a population, and if so how?

From the outset, this chapter argues against the assumptions made by Hugo and taken up by his successors, by asserting that architecture never possessed a spontaneous capacity to express cultural values. Rather, cultural values, it will be argued, are wholly constructed, and one way this occurs is by associating meanings with particular forms. This association occurs in ways that are contingent, arising from and contributing to social norms. Architecture does not inherently possess meanings of any kind, rather, meanings are subject to the manner in which knowledge of the self, of buildings and society is formed and acted upon, visualised and appropriated in any given time and place. This chapter asserts that cultural values and meanings are the production of discursive fields within which the object is immersed and so becomes defined, known and valued. Consequently, meaning cannot be inherent in the forms by which individuals come to represent themselves, but rather are a constituent in these interpretative regimes and a marker of them. In writing about Notre Dame, for example, Hugo's lament for lost meaning alerts us to the assumption that buildings reveal something about the 'culture' to which they belong. However, in order to analyse why architecture assumes a particular appearance or why it has become associated with particular meanings one must first examine the rules and patterns that govern ways of knowing in a cultural setting.

26 *Meaning and the death of architecture*

In addition to this particular assertion about architectural form and meaning, this chapter will examine claims that expound architecture's capacity to speak and articulate social issues. For example, Jennifer Bloomer, who references Hugo in assuming architecture's capacity to tell a story, writes: "If a text can be treated architectonically," she asks, "why cannot architecture be treated as a text? Narratives after all have spatial associations . . .".[8] Yet, one might ask, what sort of text is architecture? For, as Lewis Mumford recognised, architecture the discipline seems to have heightened the association between architecture and literature in assuming a natural link between the two: "The real misdemeanour of the printing press was not that it took literary values away from architecture, but that it caused architecture to derive its value from literature".[9] It is this conflation between architecture as text and its presumed legibility as an aesthetic object that is of concern here. If architecture is thought to vie with literature for cultural ascendency, is this a rivalry that architecture can win? Or, are meanings and their association with architecture constructed in completely different ways than a text, a book or poem?

The gargoyle in architecture

> Great edifices, like great mountains, are the work of ages. Art often undergoes a transformation while they are still pending . . . It is like a budding graft – a sap that circulates – a vegetation that goes forward. Certainly there is matter for very large volumes, and often for the universal history of humanity, in those successive weldings of several species of art at different elevations upon the same monument. The man, the artist, the individual, disappear upon those great masses, leaving no name of an author behind. Human intelligence is there to be traced only in its aggregate. Time is the architect – the nation is the builder.[10]

As outlined so far, Hugo, who bemoaned the loss of historic significance associated with the Notre Dame Cathedral, described architecture as possessing inherent meaning about the 'culture' to which it belongs. As alluded to in the above passage, this image of 'culture' was, for Hugo, an organic and evolving agency that works through means of cultivation (one "budding graft" upon another) yielding a comprehensive image of society and the self. To this end, the architecture of the Notre Dame Cathedral represented the changing values of society, which at the time of Hugo's writing was an image of decline and degradation. Thus the Cathedral, for Hugo, symbolised a nostalgic past, one to which French society should aspire and reconstruct.

The Cathedral (built between 1163 and 1250), initiated by Bishop Maurice de Sully, was a seminal work of architecture in its era, and remains one of the most innovative Gothic structures in Europe. Exemplifying the French Gothic style with its cruciform plan, sexpartite vaulting and flying buttresses, it became a monument to the glory of God and a prototype for future cathedrals.[11] Throughout its history the cathedral underwent many significant alterations. However, the greatest change occurred during the French Revolution, a period of political and social upheaval based on the influence of Enlightenment principles such as equality through citizenship and the inalienable rights of humankind. The Notre Dame Cathedral, which was associated with the monarchy, was ransacked during the Revolution, rededicated to the 'Cult of Reason' and, owing to this new status, was subsequently given a 'rational' purpose as a warehouse for food and livestock. During this time many of the cathedral's invaluable artworks and sculptures, including the gargoyles sitting atop the cathedral, were either pilfered or destroyed.

The politics of the revolution, the changing ideas of an increasingly secularised age – perhaps even a shift in prevailing attitudes of the time – contributed to the view that the Notre Dame Cathedral had become diminished in cultural significance compared to its valorisation in pre-revolutionary times or even today. Hugo, in recognising this and having concluded that architecture had lost its ability to convey meaning, endeavoured to renew the association between French Gothic architecture and the Nation, and hoped to instil '*l'amour de l'architecture nationale*'. As the motivation behind the writing of the novel *Notre-Dame de Paris* (1831), its popularity not only made Hugo one of the most famous writers of the nineteenth century, but also stimulated widespread interest in Gothic revivalism, and managed to highlight and associate the ideals of Gothic architecture with that of the nation. Accordingly, the preservation of such monuments was seen as an essential ingredient to understanding the past, and thus French heritage. As such, it was assumed that such buildings 'spoke' to the nation as though they were an 'open book' of French cultural traditions. It is worth noting that the successful promotion of the association between the Gothic style and that of nationhood led cultural commentators such as Marcel Proust to observe that atheists attached more value to cathedrals than a devout seventeenth-century worshiper. "The cathedral had become *un lieu de memoire*, a treasured part of French heritage".[12]

To oversee the fundraising and restoration of the Notre Dame Cathedral, the *Commission des Monuments Historiques* was established, comprising Parisian artists, aristocrats and members of the emerging bourgeoisie, including Hugo as a member of the board. In 1844 the restoration project was awarded to the then relatively young architect Eugene-Emmanuel Viollet-le-Duc, a family friend of the head of the commission Prosper Merimee, (the author of *Carmen*). Merimee had become familiar with Viollet-le-Duc's previous architectural work and had been highly impressed with his restoration of the Romanesque abbey of Vezelay. This appointment catapulted Viollet-le-Duc into prominence, and from that point on he became a highly influential, but controversial, figure in the aesthetic movement of Gothic revivalism and a well respected architectural theorist whose views, in part, still retain some relevance today.[13]

28 *Meaning and the death of architecture*

Given the cathedral had been much altered over the centuries and was neglected since the revolution, the problem that faced Viollet-le-Duc was in deciding which aspects of the building's fabric required retention, alteration or restoration (or a combination of these interventions). Viollet-le-Duc endeavoured to reveal, through the building's material and structural composition, a meaning that was not only representative of its French cultural heritage but also of the modern age. As the architectural historian Millard Hearn explains: "Viollet-le-Duc's theory of restoration was neither to bring a building back to the end of its living evolution – nor to restore it to a pristine version of its original twelfth century design. Rather it was, in his words, 'to re-establish it in a complete condition that never has existed at any given moment'".[14] By this Viollet-le-Duc endeavoured to discover architecture's relevance for the contemporary age and make the building 'better' in the present and therefore more relevant to the age. The problem though, as indicated by many of the critics of the restoration that followed Viollet-le-Duc was in the necessary 'second guessing' of the building's original form and details, and in the interpretation or abstraction of the original intentions behind the architecture. Thus, Viollet-le-Duc's task was not only a practical one in restoring the building to working order, but also a moral one, in terms of whether the resulting alterations could be described as an 'honest' reconstruction of the past.

Viollet-le-Duc was himself aware of this ethical dilemma and in response theorised that the solution was to be found in adapting the principles of Gothic architecture. He proposed that Gothic architecture represented the superiority of the "white race" and thus was derived from the rationalisation of constructional issues, rather than an overt aesthetic or stylistic manipulation driven by popular 'tastes' or other directives of the time. Here the allusion to the 'organic' nature of 'culture' and its association with Gothic architecture is essential to establishing Viollet-le-Duc's views on race and the origins of architecture and its application to the restoration of the Notre Dame Cathedral. According to Viollet-le-Duc, history demonstrated humanity's progressive transformation of nature, which embodied the process of destruction and renovation. For Viollet-le-Duc, Gothic architecture, as Martin Bressani describes: "delineates the unfolding and emancipation of man's technical powers – in constant battle with nature".[15] To this effect, the origins of architecture were the result of overcoming nature, which was instinctively linked to race and effectively gave man power over nature's laws. Here both "man and nature", as Bressani explains, "follow a linear evolution".[16] From this position, Viollet-le-Duc believed that it was the privilege of the French to succeed in creating a true architecture from the debased utilitarian principles evident in Roman, Greek and other styles of architecture. "Gothic architecture", claimed Viollet-le-Duc: "is the ultimate culmination of that slow evolution".[17]

In applying these principles to the Notre Dame Cathedral, Viollet-le-Duc envisaged a reconstruction based on forms and compositions that he had observed in Gothic architecture. Nonetheless, he did not intend to imitate or make copies of them. Rather, he sought to continue the evolution of the Cathedral by drawing on the past in a way that expressed contemporary materials and technologies. In this sense, Viollet-le-Duc believed that the centuries of the Gothic tradition gave him licence to modify the Cathedral's structure for modern purposes. For example, Viollet-le-Duc modified the form of the flying buttresses along Notre Dame's nave (now considered to have been among the earliest examples of buttressing in thirteenth century Gothic architecture). He also removed original artwork that had survived decades of neglect in order to make modifications to Notre Dame's clerestory. In addition, he added a spire to the roof at the transept on which he incorporated the figures of the apostles and archangels by reasoning that it was a necessary addition in response to the original design intent. However, that for which he is most noted is the restoration of the gargoyles on the tower balustrade that had, by this time, weathered into unrecognisable stubs of stone. Although at the time no one seriously questioned these alterations, twentieth-century archaeologists and restorers have since severely criticised these changes, suggesting that they have destroyed or obscured the original form of the building. For example, the French writer Achille Carlier described Viollet-le-Duc "as one of the greatest criminals in history".[18] Such criticism was seemingly influenced by John Ruskin's proposition, that the 'conservation' of historic monuments should involve a minimal modification to the remnants of the past[19] (as discussed in the third chapter of this book).

For Viollet-le-Duc, architecture was capable of maintaining a dialogue with the community if the restoration work not only enhanced that which was deemed culturally significant by the community (like the gargoyles) but was also representative of the age in which it was restored. Viollet-le-Duc queried: "Shall exterior buttressing which no longer have anything to support be left purposeless? No, certainly. *[sic]* We see, therefore, that in solving problems of this kind, absolute principles may lead to absurdities".[20] These 'absurdities' according to Viollet-le-Duc were revealed in purposeless building components that served no function. If modern materials and engineering eliminated the need for exterior buttressing then, in accordance with Viollet-le-Duc's idea of "rational architecture", they should be removed – regardless of their historical significance. As a consequence, the restored architecture remains purposeful for contemporary needs and functional requirements, continuing to interact with and remain relevant for a new generation of occupants.

The restoration of the grotesques and gargoyles on the Notre Dame Cathedral exemplify this point. Viollet-le-Duc reasons: "In an edifice of the thirteenth century where the water ran off by means of drips – it was thought necessary during the fifteenth century to add gargoyles to the gutters, for the better regulation of the escape. These gargoyles are in a bad state and have to be replaced. Shall we on the pretext of unity substitute gargoyles of the fifteenth century for them?"[21] An alternative course of action might have been to replace them with modern rainwater heads. However,

30 *Meaning and the death of architecture*

Viollet-le-Duc is conflicted, suggesting that imitation might appropriately continue their 'primitive' legacy, while to the contrary, they no longer served any functional nor symbolic requirement and so could have been dispensed with entirely. The gargoyles, as their name – meaning gullet or drain – suggests, once served both a functional and symbolic purpose in fifteenth-century Gothic architecture. However, they were not, as Viollet-le-Duc indicates, part of the original architecture, but fifteenth-century inventions. Functionally, they acted as the heads for drain pipes and facilitated the disbursement of rainwater from the cathedral's roof top by spurting water out through their mouths. Nonetheless, their usefulness was appreciably diminished with the introduction of lead downpipes in the sixteenth century. Symbolically, the gargoyle, a winged demonic figure, representative of creatures from ancient myth, was said to watch over and guard the inhabitants of the building by warning off evil spirits. They were also derivative of the medieval argument, as Dionysius the Areopagite (sixth-century Christian theologian and Philosopher) teaches, that the more "simile becomes dissimilar, the more the truth is revealed to us in the guise of horrible and indecorous figures, the less the imagination is sated in carnal enjoyment".[22] Thus, it could be argued that with the loss of their functional capacity their symbolic value, as demonic figures representative of the Gothic era, has grown. In this way, people in the nineteenth century, as they do today, saw the gargoyles as strange and somewhat disturbing decorative features typical of Gothic aesthetics, and these views, subsequently, furthered the aestheticisation of Gothicism evident in writing by Hugo, Viollet-le-Duc and others of their times.

It is interesting to note that the gargoyles and chimeras did not figure in Viollet-le-Duc's original plan for the restoration, yet they soon became an integral part of the reconstruction project. Loaded with symbolic intent, these gargoyles were the creation of Viollet-le-Duc: they were neither imitations of the original building features nor were they made to function as once intended to. Viollet-le-Duc reintroduced the gargoyles, as Herbert Johnson notes: "to communicate the very idea of medievalism".[23] Michael Camille, in his recent monograph of the gargoyles of Notre Dame, argues that the gargoyles were not just the quintessence of the middle-ages but they also brought the Cathedral into the modern era. He explains: "They symbolised an imagined past whose modernity lay precisely in their nostalgia".[24] In other words, Viollet-le-Duc sought to provide a representation of the past by rupturing the historical continuity of the Cathedral and firmly locating it in the present. As Camille further claims: "These forms were not dark dragons of the medieval past, but critical components of his coherent and functional view of the Gothic. Although the gargoyles had been removed in the age of reason, Viollet-le-Duc saw every good reason to replace them. Nothing for him was more modern, more functional, than the gargoyles".[25] In the middle ages the gargoyles served as a necessary reminder of the dark forces of sin and regression, yet for Viollet-le-Duc the new gargoyles brought the Cathedral notoriety and contributed towards its progression into the future. Recalling their former use Viollet-le-Duc claimed: "They are in this sense

Meaning and the death of architecture 31

Figure 2.1 Bird with open beak and unicorn demon chimera on the balustrade to the north tower of Notre Dame de Paris, designed by Viollet-le-Duc.
Daniel Grinceri.

inbuilt elements of restoration, preserving and protecting the structure",[26] although now they protected the building from destruction rather than perdition. In essence, they provided the necessary intrigue by which Gothic architecture had been constructed in the present.

The gargoyles, therefore, became representations of their present and former purposes, attempting to perpetuate cultural significance in the modern era by the way they construct the past. In this manner, the values that came to be associated with the Cathedral, like French Gothicism and national pride, were more the product of both Viollet-le-Duc's and Hugo's writings and theories about the connection between building elements and history than any intrinsic quality of the architecture itself. The gargoyles, having been destroyed during the age of reason because they represented medieval irrationality, later returned, albeit in different form, as a result of their ability to provide a tangible representation of a fictitious past. Thus, they acquired a different kind of rationality as the amalgam of function and expression.

Today the gargoyles are one of the most intriguing elements of the Notre Dame cathedral for tourists.[27] They serve as a representation of the medieval without necessarily revealing their nineteenth-century origin. Yet they are unequivocally the product the modern era, in that they represent a nineteenth-century view of the past, but also incorporated notions relating to the characterisation of race. Take for example, the nineteenth-century

32 *Meaning and the death of architecture*

English antiquarian Thomas Wright, who, in his *History of the Caricature and Grotesque* (1865), mistook Viollet-le-Duc's modern gargoyles for medieval ones. In decrying the representation of demons during the middle ages, Wright claims that in general medieval figures are "droll but not frightful", they provoke "laughter but create no horror . . . with one great exception". He writes: "There is, however, one well known instance in which the medieval artist has shown himself fully successful in representing the features of the spirit of evil. On the parapet of the external gallery of the cathedral church of Notre Dame de Paris, there is a stone figure, of the ordinary stature of man, representing the demon, apparently looking with satisfaction upon the inhabitants of the city as they were everywhere indulging in sin and wickedness. The unmixed evil – horrible in its expression in the countenance – is marvellously portrayed. It is an absolute Mephistopheles, carrying in his features a strange mixture of hateful qualities – malice, pride, envy – in fact, all the deadly sins combined in one diabolical whole".[28]

Wright not only mistook the modern sculptures for medieval ones, but by referring to their facial features and countenance, also assumed that their physiognomy was somehow part of what made the gargoyles 'evil' and 'horrible'. Although misguided with relation to the history of Notre Dame's gargoyles, Wright's oversight brings to light various contours of discourse governing relations between an architectural object, its representation and distortion of human physiognomy and the values resulting from this.

Viollet-le-Duc had begun to theorise about the connection between race and architecture, proposing that the 'Aryans' – "tall, with long, blond hair, white skin, and blue eyes"[29] – were responsible for the greatest cultural advances and thus its apotheosis in Gothic architecture. He argued, as justification against classical revivalism, that the Romans were "degenerate" and racially inferior to the "white races of the North" for falling into a "hybrid architectural tradition". For Viollet-le-Duc the evolution of humanity and culture coincided with the development of architectural styles, from prehistoric man who built the first hut to the fully evolved and cultured intelligentsia who built in the Gothic tradition. In this sense, architects like Viollet-le-Duc contributed to a discourse that was aligned with a dialectical framework for understanding architectural styles, in which each style became the representation of the progression of civilising humankind. Even in the mind of Hugo, the degradation and subsequent abandonment of the Notre Dame Cathedral signified the decline of humanity. Yet on the contrary, the Cathedral's restoration to working order represented the progression of humanity's civilised ideals.

This approach suggests that architectural style, and by extension its meaning, is brought about through the 'dialectical process' – or the progression in which each cultural era (or civilisation) finds a solution to the contradictions of the previous era. According to Hegel, each age is represented by a common recognition of the 'spirit', or 'zeitgeist', being the dialectical process by which history unfolds throughout time. Hegel states:

"Spirit does not toss itself about in the external play of chance occurrences; on the contrary, it is that which determines history absolutely, and it stands firm against the chance occurrences which it dominates and exploits for its own purpose".[30] Nevertheless, those values which gain prominence at any point in time, such as the superiority of race, superstition or an idealised past, to name a few, are brought about through discursive fields that normalise meaning and associate it with form. In this manner, influential figures like Viollet-le-Duc, brought to prominence through multiple prominent architectural works and publications, have the capacity to influence meaning because of their authority as opposed to naturally representing the values or 'spirit' of a group of people. Architecture which incorporates, for example, grotesque figures (having no functional necessity), are indicative of the manner in which discourse acquires a representative form, (in this case, from the medieval past) – rather than the form, as it is most often assumed, imposing a pre-given meaning upon its viewer. During the sixteenth century, the perceived existence of evil perpetuated the gargoyle's representation and installation atop religious edifices. Whatever 'meaning' or significance gargoyles may have once held in the medieval mind, it is clear that partly through Viollet-le-Duc's writing and works they were co-opted to represent nineteenth-century views of the past and Gothic architecture, the superiority of race and the evolution of 'modern' French society.

The 'spirit' of the age

> Architecture began like all writing. It was first an alphabet. Men planted a stone upright, it was a letter, and each letter was a hieroglyph, and upon each hieroglyph rested a group of ideas, like the capital on the column.[31]

Hugo renders parallel the 'evolution' of human culture with that of the 'evolution' of architecture as though one reflected the development of the other. However, Hugo opposed the popular theories espoused by neoclassicists such as Joseph-Francois Lafitau, Marc-Antoine Laugier and Quatremere de Quincy that architecture derived primarily from the need to find shelter.[32] Rather, he insisted that architecture arose from the same impulse "that gave birth to writing". For Hugo, architecture came about when the "first races" became overburdened by the memory of the past. He wrote: "When the load of recollections which mankind had to bear became so heavy and confused that language, naked and simple, risked its loss by the way, men wrote them on the ground in a manner most visible and most natural. They sealed each tradition beneath a monument".[33] Just as humankind's ability to create more complex prose developed over the course of history so did architecture. "A column was not a tree wrought in stone but was a 'letter'; an arch was not two bent and joined trees but was a 'syllable'; a pyramid was not simply a mountain shape but a 'word' . . . Each

34   *Meaning and the death of architecture*

architectural form evolved from as a linguistic form and, when combined with others, conveyed more complex meanings".[34] For Hugo, the language of architecture assumed its ultimate expression in the forms and ornamentation of the Gothic cathedral. Thus, his pronouncement of the death of architecture can be understood as coincident with the demise of Gothic architecture as a culturally significant style, leading Hugo to declare of his neo-classicist rivals: "architecture had reached an impasse: architects had nothing new to say".[35]

Yet those who continue to envision architecture as a tool for communication, thereby accepting on the one hand Hugo's argument for its capacity to do so, deny on the other hand that it has lost its ability to 'speak'. All such views hinge on the assumption that architecture is not simply a building, nor mute construction composed of functional spaces and tangible materials, but rather, as Neil Levine explains: "architecture is literally a form of expression, giving permanence to human thought in monuments known as buildings".[36] Thus, architecture is at once capable of narrating the collective thoughts of humanity, as an anthem, a constitution or an accumulating body of national literature might when used to convey the collective values of a nation. Nevertheless, the question remains, just how does architecture acquire this capacity? Understanding that words and speech are also open to interpretation, how is architecture rendered wholly comprehensible to a social group or cultural entity?

Architectural theorists, on the whole, suggest that architecture speaks of civilisation and is therefore a record, "written in stone", of cultural values related to 'the age' in which it is produced. Yet, with this in mind, William Whyte, in his exposé on whether buildings contain meaning at all, points out three obvious uncertainties brought about by such assumptions. Firstly, what sort of text is architecture: verbal, linguistic or symbolic? Secondly, to simply present architecture as a text denies the multifaceted nature of interpretation relevant to context and genre. And thirdly, as architecture is both created and/or interpreted, which meaning is correct: that intended by the author or that comprehended by the interpreter?[37] It therefore must be recognised that any likely meaning is the product of the context in which it is interpreted: as such, Hugo's way of speaking about architecture was also a product of his time or that which we now classify as the romantic period. Yet many architects conflate this notion of context as being inherently representative of the 'spirit of the age' and this assumption casts 'meaning' as the consequence of some kind of agency that is viewed, if not partly, but wholly intentional. However, as described in the next chapter, the dominate ideas of the age are not created by a single individual in tune with the needs and demands of society, rather through discursive formations that govern what counts as 'knowledge' – including 'knowledge' of meaning – in a particular period.

There is no doubt that architecture from any age may be able to reveal something of the cultural habits of a particular society. However, this process is not autochthonous; it occurs through, amongst other means, archaeological investigation and academic studies by which historical assumptions are pieced together in order to construct a view of the past. In other words, architecture can only say what we want it to say or expect it to say given such means. Whyte refers to archaeologists who have identified the same problem in their own research. Speaking on their behalf, he writes: "We must ask ourselves whose meanings do such studies retrieve, and how representative are such meanings of . . . society as a whole".[38] Whyte continues: "It is an important problem – and it raises many questions. How should the historian respond to it? Even if architecture does convey meaning, can a historian ever really uncover it?"[39] Despite Whyte's reservations, Hugo's words have resonated with many contemporary architects, and perhaps contributed to structuralist linguistic theory, whereby buildings are thought to be 'readable' as though a component of language. Roland Barthes reinforces this view in his essay *Semiology and the Urban*. He writes: "One of the authors who best expressed this essentially signifying nature of urban space is in my opinion Victor Hugo. In *Notre-Dame de Paris* Hugo has written a very beautiful chapter, very subtle and perceptive . . . Hugo gives proof of a rather modern way of conceiving the monument of the city, as a true text, as an inscription of man in space".[40] Both architects and philosophers have continued to progress this view, further normalising its relevance for understanding and analysing the language of architecture.

Hugo's reflections on Notre Dame were intended to be a call for an architectural 'revolution'. He believed that the 'Romantic' movement, (an aesthetic response based, in part, on opposing the established social and political norms instituted by the Enlightenment) which began in poetry and had already reinvigorated music and painting, would before long, "surely revive sculpture and architecture, which had died long ago".[41] For subsequent architectural movements, Hugo's prophecy of the death of architecture was seen not as a 'prediction of irrevocable doom' but rather as an 'affirmation of resurrection'. His claims provoked many subsequent architects to promote the primary role of architecture as that of expressing the values of the people or the 'spirit of the age'. The endeavour to achieve this illusive goal has, in general, led to an alignment between particular ideologies and design aesthetics, such as that undertaken by the modernists who proposed that social order could be achieved through the use of right angles and glass facades – discussed in the next chapter.

The call to represent the 'spirit of the age' has been echoed in subsequent architectural movements, from Gothic and neo-classical revivalism, to modernism, post-modernism and even the digital age. In effect, each new architectural movement has laid claim to representing the values of a 'new age'. Yet, despite the recycling of architectural styles and their tenuous link with that of the spirit of the age, such exhortations continue to persist. Among the most influential is Sigfried Giedion's assertion that the main task facing architecture is "the interpretation of a way of life valid for our period".[42] He writes: "We are looking for the reflection in architecture of the progress our

36 *Meaning and the death of architecture*

own period has made towards consciousness of itself . . . Architecture can give us an insight into this process just because it is so bound up with the life of a period as a whole. Everything in it reflects the conditions of the age from which it springs. It is the product of all sorts of factors: social, economic, scientific, technical and ethnological".[43]

Yet these factors, as Giedion understood them, change over time. With this in mind, Giedion suggests that the 'spirit' is not simply a repository of unchanging facts, but a living and dynamic thing – like 'culture'. He continues: "However much a period may try to disguise itself, its real nature will still show through in its architecture, whether this uses original forms of expression or attempts to copy bygone epochs. We recognise the character of the age as easily as we identify a friend's handwriting beneath attempted disguises. It is as an unmistakable index to what was really going on in a period that architecture is indispensable when we are seeking to evaluate that period".[44] Hence, for Giedion, architectural style was secondary compared to architecture's innate ability to express itself, so he assumed. Yet how architecture might impart such ideals is not entirely clear. Giedion in writing *Space, Time and Architecture* is obviously attempting to draw parallels with Einstein's *Theory of Relativity*,[45] whereby the perception of time is dependent on the observer's position in space. In this manner, one might be persuaded to accept that one's knowledge is the product of their social context. However, in order to accept such a proposition one must first be clear on the process by which this occurs – whether it occurs through the innate ability of the architecture itself,[46] or by the manner in which discursive forms normalises certain attitudes and values and associates them with form. For instance, how does a monument become representative of the nation or a cathedral of Christianity? Could it be because discourse permits such associations with form? If so, Giedion's tenuous appeal to quasi-scientific certainty does not correlate to the way architecture is likely to acquire meaning as he presupposes the innateness of specific meanings (like nationhood and Christianity) with that of the architecture.

The rest of this section will further examine assumptions relating to architectural 'style' (or as Gideon preferred to call them architectural 'movements') as the inherent representation of 'the age' in order to highlight the mixed and varied arguments that attempt to justify each claim. For Viollet-le-Duc the Gothic style represented the principle of 'process' and was therefore a rational approach to constructional issues. Architecture therefore exhibited meaning because this process represented a particular stage in human development. Accordingly, Gothic architecture did not need to rely on the dictates of past orders and styles, but was new and unencumbered by history. Alan Colquhoun explains this view: "It was precisely the absence of fixed rules which enabled Gothic architecture both to stand for the values of an organic society and to act as the instrument of a society in rapid evolution. It was simultaneously nostalgic and progressive, sentimental and positivistic".[47] According to this view, architecture can be syncretic, in that

Meaning and the death of architecture 37

it can allow for and seemingly accommodate the notions of 'culture' and an 'organic' and evolving entity while at the same time linking the past with the future. Indeed, Gothic architecture was not unique to the nineteenth century – far from it – but had its origins in the twelfth. As such, Viollet-le-Duc proposed that the principles underlying Gothic architecture were most appropriate for the modern era. He declared: "Gothic construction is not, like antique construction, immutable, absolute in its means; it is supple, free, and as inquiring as the modern spirit; its principles permit the use of all the materials given by nature or industry in virtue of their own qualities".[48] Arguably, Viollet-le-Duc's rationalisation for the relevance of Gothic architecture served to justify his own personal tastes. His rationalisation perhaps also served to displace a historical context for understanding buildings, or create an anachronistic history that enabled the recreation of an imagined past as exemplified by the Notre Dame cathedral.

Providing opposition to this view, John Ruskin, who advocated the 'preservation' of Gothic architecture, was one of Viollet-le-Duc's most vociferous critics. Ruskin charged architects to respond to the necessities of the day, by which the 'spirit of the age' or "lamps", as he described them, become the moral imperative of architects in order to express meaning.[49] Yet this call to tangibly link morality with the 'spirit of the age' also seems to have been a pretence to also justify a style of architecture that coincided with Ruskin's sense of aesthetic pleasure, being that of Gothic revivalism.

Equally, Frank Lloyd Wright in his book *The Art and Craft of the Machine*, written at the turn of the twentieth century, described Hugo's comments "as one of the truly great things ever written on architecture".[50] Wright, recognised as one of the early fathers of modernism, declared that throughout history the 'machine' has been used to impede and/or destroy architecture, asserting that it has dealt architecture a "death blow". In order to illustrate his point Wright uses Hugo's example of the printing press, writing: "Down to Gutenberg (inventor of the printing press), architecture is the principle writing – the universal writing of humanity".[51] According to Wright, many ancient cultures used buildings as a form of 'writing', as though buildings were "giant granite books".[52] Wright claimed that the 'machine', like Gutenburg's printing press, superseded architecture as the principle form of cultural expression, and therefore reduced architecture's lasting effect. Wright concludes, reworking Hugo's comments almost literally: "Human thought discovers a mode of perpetuating itself, not only more resisting than architecture, but more simple and easy. Architecture is dethroned. Gutenberg's letters of lead are about to supersede Orpheus's letters of stone. The book is about to kill the edifice".[53] However, Wright does not propose to surrender meekly to the 'machine' but to rediscover its advantages for architecture in a new 'modern' age.

Wright saw himself as leading the charge to once more render architecture meaningful, arguing against the predominant theories expressed by Ruskin and his aesthetic predilections. He declared that the "obedient

38   *Meaning and the death of architecture*

machine" now a tool of the modern age superseded the subservient Gothic tradition.[54] Wright, like so many modernists who followed his lead, argued that modern constructional techniques need not be disguised as Gothic or classical architectural styles, but rather, the 'machine' would generate its own aesthetic. Referring to historicist high-rise buildings of his day, Wright believed it was "better not to build a skyscraper at all than to build one like the Wrigley Building or the Tribune Tower".[55] Like Hugo, who attempted to liberate France from the vestiges of renaissance architecture, the modernist movement attempted to purge architecture of superfluous aesthetisation and thus represent the 'spirit of the age' by making use of new materials and constructional techniques. Wright acted under the assumption that modern architecture was a new form of 'media'. Indeed, Wright attempted to overturn Hugo's assertion by claiming that the 'modern' movement provided 'culture' with a renewed means of preserving and extending itself.

To further highlight the shifting nature of arguments that attempt to imbue architecture with the ability to communicate meaning relative to the 'age', even into the contemporary age, consider Daniel Libeskind, who constructed a full scale model of Agostino Ramelli's sixteenth-century reading machine. The model, exhibited at the Venice Biennale in 1985, was a mechanical device consisting of a large wheel in which books are placed and rotated around at the eye level of the reader. Libeskind claimed to have built the machine in order to rediscover the experience of making architecture by handicraft; it is a metaphor of an architecture that can be read. He continued: "The medieval cathedral was a book where the human body was literally inscribed in the sign of the cross. The architecture served a narrative, the narrative of Christian belief".[56] Libeskind argues that contemporary architecture is no longer expressive of its origins and by extension fails to tell a story amidst the contrivance of modernist ideals. With this in mind, Ersi Ioannidou observes: "According to Libeskind, these particular means of architectural production are at their final stage, 'something' is ending".[57] The "means of architectural production" refers to the 'machine', as advocated by Wright, whereby building components are mass produced and assembled to make a building. The "something" is the inability of modern architecture to narrate the story of western civilisation. The architectural object, as exemplified by the reading machine, should emphasise the materiality and three-dimensionality of built form. Architecture, Libeskind argues, should be a reflection on the process of history, and so "construct a narrative on the actual and metaphysical mechanisation of architecture".[58] Libeskind's model does not pretend to provide answers, but rather it serves to provoke thought on how architecture can recover its ability to narrate the story of humanity. Yet, when applied to architectural form, the communicative ability seems to be reduced to basic elements and 'one liners', as exemplified by his proposal for the World Trade Centre site.[59]

Meaning and the death of architecture 39

Throughout varied architectural movements, from Gothic revivalism to post-modernism, each have repeated the debate on what might be the most appropriate manner in which to express, speak about and narrate the cultural values of humanity. This tendency to find 'appropriate' form suggests that there is not only a lack of intrinsicality with relation to building form and an era, but also a rhetorical and ethical component to a discursive field that constructs such links. Each movement, from Gothicism and modernism to post-modernism, as seen, has seriously questioned the approach of the previous generation and promoted a renewed method for expressing the values of the community. Yet architects and theorists alike continue to pose variable theories with regards to how architecture is capable of expressing meaning. Recently, even those experimenting with the morphed blobs of digital architecture continue to argue that architecture, in a world of mobile phones and the internet, should reflect the age.[60] New architectural movements continue to grapple with the imperative to make buildings relevant to the social setting in which they are located. Determining how well a building might represent the 'spirit of the age' is a matter of whether discursive forms with relation to the appropriateness of certain styles of architecture are linked to the perceived values of the age. In other words, whether the claims of the architect, whether by practice or theory, coincide with the perceptions of those who engage, on whatever level, with the architectural object itself. In this way, the reasonableness of any one claim, whether enunciated by Hugo, Viollet-le-Duc, Ruskin, Wright or Libeskind, depends upon the authority by which their statements are accepted as true and the context in which they are made. They are not a natural response to an all encompassing 'spirit', but rather, components of discourse that delimit knowledge in a particular field.

Legibility and the architectural (con)text

> Architecture will not again be the social art, the collective, the dominant art. The great poem, the great edifice, the great work of humanity will no longer be constructed: it will be printed.[61]

Nearly 170 years after *Notre-Dame de Paris*, Hugo's pronouncement still provokes a challenge to architects in causing them to question how meaning becomes associated with architectural form and how it can be lost. Linguistic theory of the 1960s continued to invoke an architecture with the capacity to speak and literally communicate meaning as though the medium were a language. Theorists such as Charles Jencks, Kevin Lynch and Umberto Eco established parallels between language and architecture by appropriating analytic methods derived from linguistics in order to discover and quantify meaning and describe its relationship to building form. They proposed that the syntactic structure of language could literally be associated with building components, and thus capable of interpretation as if one were

40 *Meaning and the death of architecture*

reading a text. Arising from this is a sense that architectural form can be (or should be) legible, visibly apparent and seen as coherent by the viewer. Nonetheless, the notion that architecture can be read, as though a text, belies the actuality that various 'readings' may differ. Still, let us assume that a group of individuals, with access to a common language, sharing similar cultural values, derive the same interpretation – could this be the result of a legible architecture? Or the way discourse delimits knowledge subjecting individuals to a common interpretation? The following section will seek to examine these claims.

Charles Jencks declared that the "units of a building", such as its doors, windows, columns and walls, were all capable of "motivation",[62] and therefore bear a resemblance to words. In order to discover how architecture communicates, Jencks proposed a new kind of analysis or field of scholarship, which he called "architistics". He wrote in an edited collection of essays called *Meaning and Architecture*: "If the study of how architecture communicates meaning proceeds in accordance with past tradition and linguistics, then we might imagine the following set of abstractions: form, function and technic".[63] The proposed study, involving the combination of architectural and linguistic theory, endeavoured to describe the architectural equivalent of language. Accordingly, the application of a "triple articulation" of architectural language – of form (comprising of the objects shape, configuration, colour and texture), of function (use) and of technic (structure and materials) might become the "formemes, funcemes and techememes" of this proposed architectural language. (They were opposed to the 'double articulation' found in linguistics of 'phonemes and morphemes'.) Not surprisingly, Jencks' proposal was not taken seriously by either linguistic or architectural scholars, even receiving criticism within his own publication by one of his co-editors and contributing author who responds: "I fail to see the parallel between the basic units of linguistics and these proposed architectural ones . . . 'form, function and technique' in architectural theory seem to me hopelessly overworked, and intellectually exhausted. I don't want to see the tedious and gratuitous warfare among them to be fought all over again within architectural semiology".[64] The problem for Jencks is in the very attempt to impose a formula for interpreting architecture. Even if such a formula were composed, one can imagine the limitations it would impose upon architectural design – not to mention the viewer. In this manner, new buildings would become formulaic imitations of pre-existing structures with limited ability to adapt to other constructional variables, like those of the site, environment and economic considerations.

Like Jencks, the architectural theorist Kevin Lynch attempted to formulate a semantic reading of the city. Lynch explored the apparent "legibility" of the cityscape, referring to the ease with which its constituent parts (streets, buildings, paths and districts) can be recognised and organised into a coherent pattern. His theory suggested that just as the text on this paper can be visually recognised and related to symbols that represent words, a legible city is one with distinct and grouped patterns of forms and landmarks. Lynch explains: "Thus an image useful for making an exit requires the recognition of a door as a distinct entity, of its spatial relation to the observer, and its meaning as a hole for getting out. These are not truly separable. The visual recognition of a door is matted together with its meaning as a door. It is possible, however, to analyse the door in terms of its identity of form and clarity of position, considered as if they were prior to its meaning. Such an analytic feat might be pointless in the study of a door but not in the study of the urban environment".[65] Herein lies the dilemma, for while a door is a "hole for getting out" its meaning is associated with its function. If a door acquires other meanings it does so through ways that are independent of the object itself, thus making the object a representation, a symbol, a metaphor or a sign. Likewise, the processes by which meanings become associated with the urban environment are constructed outside the object itself. In other words, cities acquire meanings through a myriad of ways as a result of the customs, practices and attitudes of the people. Barthes in seeking an alliance with architects for his views outlined in *Semiology and the Urban* references Lynch, whom he says seems to be the closest to his view of urban semantics. "But in reality", Barthes comments, his studies "remain rather ambiguous": "On the one hand there is in his work a whole vocabulary of signification . . . These units he calls paths, edges, districts, nodes and landmarks. These are categories of units that would easily become semantic categories. But on the other hand, in spite of his vocabulary, Lynch has a conception of the city that remains more *Gestalt* than structural".[66] By "Gestalt", Barthes is referring to the form-making capabilities of our senses, as opposed to structuralism, to which Barthes stresses that various 'readings' are always provisional and shift with time.[67] Contrary to Lynch, a study of the urban environment and its meaning should analyse the discourses surrounding the object that associates meaning with form, rather than assuming that the tangible qualities of the urban morphology are somehow inherent and permanently fixed to specific meanings.

Umberto Eco also investigates whether architecture's symbolic capacity and that of the spoken word can be quantified and related to one another. Eco analyses the syntactic codification of architecture and queries whether it is possible to transcribe meaning into form – much like the way spoken language transcribes meaning in terms of sounds, syllables and words. He points out: "Catchwords like 'semantics of architecture' have led some to look for the equivalent of the 'word' of verbal language in architectural signs, for units endowed with definite meaning, indeed for symbols referring to referents. But since we know there can be conventions concerning only the syntactic articulation of signs, it would be appropriate to look also for purely syntactic codification in architecture".[68] As such, Eco highlights three varieties of "architectural codes" by which one is able to formulate a reading of architecture: "Technical" codes involve tangible architectural elements like beams, columns, floors, walls and doors. "Syntactic" codes

42 *Meaning and the death of architecture*

are typological forms such as cross plans, labyrinths and high-rises. Finally, "Semantic" codes are the denotative and connotative meanings of the architecture, or that which it refers to other than its self. (In other words, a building which assumes the image of a referent, such as the Crocodile Hotel in the Kakadu National Park, or the 'Big Pineapple' in northern Queensland, Australia.) Eco acknowledges that meaning in architecture becomes apparent not through the memorisation of certain codes and their connectedness with form, but through the 'reference' of certain codes with meaning, and therefore denies that the architectural object itself has the power to determine its own meaning or how it should be interpreted.[69] He concludes by suggesting that the architect should be open to a variety of meanings since architecture is subject to multiple meanings over the course of its history.

Eco incorporates into his discussion an analysis of the Gothic cathedral, in which he states: "The history of the interpretation of the Gothic teaches us that over the centuries the same sign vehicle, in the light of different subcodes, has been able to connote diverse things".[70] Eco, in this regard, differs from Hugo, in that the former suggests that the Gothic cathedral is open to multiple readings and interpretations, rather than one constant and uncompromised meaning. For Hugo, the Gothic cathedral signified the splendour of French national culture, whereby all associated principles – morality, history, geography and science – were literally revealed through the image of the cathedral. Yet Eco questions such a proposition, highlighting the point that while the image of the cathedral may have remained a relative constant throughout time, it has always maintained the capacity to mean different things to different people. With a hint of sarcasm Eco rephrases Hugo's view, stating: "A medieval cathedral was a sort of a permanent and unchangeable TV program that was supposed to tell people everything indispensable for their everyday lives as well as for their eternal salvation. The book would have distracted people from their most important values, encouraging unnecessary information, free interpretation and insane curiosity".[71] According to Eco, the cathedral did not cease to signify, rather, the mass printing and dissemination of books opened the cathedral's image to multiple interpretations and meanings. The development of printing, in the eyes of the clergy – fearing they had lost their privileged role as interpreters of 'the word' – only diminished the cathedral's significance. Eco remarks: "I've written elsewhere about how photography took over one of the main functions of painting: setting down people's images. But it certainly didn't kill painting – far from it. It freed it up, allowed it to take risks. And painters can still do portraits if they want".[72] Eco denies that the mass production of printed books could have reduced architecture's value, instead, that which was more likely diminished were the interests of those who may have controlled the cathedral's image in some way and their ability to prescribe certain meanings.

It is interesting to note that the post-modernist movement also attempted to address similar concerns. Rafael Moneo declared that architecture has

Meaning and the death of architecture 43

lost the status it once had in the past, not as a result of books but of communication technologies. He declared in a lecture at Harvard University: "Victor Hugo said that books had killed cathedral architecture; it wasn't entirely true then, but it seems we could say today that mass communication has reduced architecture's relevance. Architecture is no longer vital, neither as in the most pragmatic point of view that identifies it with cities and housing nor as the reservoir of symbolic communications".[73] Post-modernism promoted the subversion of the 'machine aesthetic' of modernism by "means of a return to ornament, references to the historic past and its symbolism".[74] In other words, the post-modernists opposed modernism's determination to control meaning by attempting to renew the communicative capacity of architecture on the assumption that architecture could mean multiple things.

In offering this view, Moneo features architects of recent decades who wished to return architecture to the formal principles lost during the height of modernism. These architects included James Stirling, Alvaro Siza, Aldo Rossi, Frank Gehry, Robert Venturi and Peter Eisenman. Moneo sees such architects as believing that "Architecture should cleanse itself of all obligation dictated by function, place and technique, or program, and address only those formal principles that helped solve the constructional problem in question".[75] In this manner, the post-modernists endeavoured to create an architecture of multiple meanings, or as Venturi put it, of "complexity and contradiction", of "richness of meaning rather than clarity of meaning",[76] thus circumventing the nigh impossible task of achieving any universally recognised 'clear meaning'. By promoting the multiplicity of meanings, one avoids, so the post-modernists claimed, the didacticism of modernist doctrines.

The adaptation of Eco's views of "communicating more and different values"[77] in post-modern architecture is significant, for it 'freed' architecture of any likely puritanical reductionism of function and form, and permitted experimentation by way of symbology, eclecticism and ornament. Despite this, post-modernism could not free itself from notions relating to legibility. For example, the architect Peter Eisenman, inspired by the structural linguistics of Noam Chomsky, endeavoured to define the norms of the architectural language and restrict people's interpretation whereby meaning would become self-explanatory. Eisenman attempted to imbue architecture with the same semiotic capacities as linguistics in order to make the association between certain meanings and various building forms. His theory attempted to rid architecture of the restrictive aesthetic guidelines imposed by architectural styles, in particular that of modernism, in favour of a composition that aimed to create structures, laws and principles that might guide the "appearance of form".[78] As such, the 'syntax' of architecture, comprising of walls, doors, windows, lines and planes, could be read and interpreted as though a sentence on a page. As Eisenman claims: "any meaning emerging from form must be incorporated within that form".[79] Yet in response to the question as to why others could not read the same meanings into these so described forms, Eisenman argued that their consciousness

44 *Meaning and the death of architecture*

was obscured by "cultural preconception" [80] in which one's knowledge of a thing is constructed. Nevertheless, this is precisely the point: it is because knowledge becomes normalised by discourse that certain buildings are said to have 'cultural' significance. If such meanings are common to a majority it is not because architecture 'motivates' people to think this way. Rather, it occurs because such values are constructed within a network of cultural relationships that have become normalised in everyday speech and activity.

Notwithstanding the attempts of these much acclaimed architects, writers and philosophers to equate building components with syntactic codes, architecture has, to the contrary, proven resistant to a linguistic reading of its structure and likely meaning. William Whyte provokes further thought on the subject by adding: "Architecture is not, in reality, simply a language, and buildings cannot, in actuality, simply be read. Rather, the process of designing, building, and interpreting architecture should be likened, not to reading, but to a series of translations".[81] By "translations" Whyte means that buildings acquire meaning through the association between a particular ideal and the object: "by inhabiting buildings, by looking at them, by experiencing them, we give significance to them and read meanings into them".[82] As such, when people's interaction with the Notre Dame cathedral changed during the enlightenment the building came to acquire alternative meanings, such as the irrationality of the medieval past. This effectively depreciated the value of Christianity and its association with such a magnificent building. Thus, Hugo's lament; in reality the building had not lost its capacity to acquire meanings, only that its meaning no longer coincided with that of the church and others, like Hugo, who appreciated it for its past glory. Architecture does not prescribe meaning, as it is not an inherent quality of architecture itself. Rather, the viewer will associate certain meanings with form based on their knowledge and experience of the building, and so architecture does not therefore speak nor render itself readable.

The book and the building: the libraries of Labrouste and Perrault

> Architecture is the great book of humanity, the principal expression of man in his different stages of development.[83]

In 1840, six years after the publication of *Notre-Dame de Paris,* the young architect Henri Labrouste received his first major commission for the Ste-Genevieve Library. Although a close friend of Hugo's and sympathetic to his views on Gothic revivalism, Labrouste sought to defy Hugo's proclamation that the book would kill the building, by demonstrating architecture's continued capacity to 'speak'. The Bibliothèque Ste-Geneviève Library is unique for the way in which Labrouste incorporated language into the stone façade of the architecture. In effect, elements of the architecture became legible as though it were a book. Decoration was applied to the building through the engraving of 810 names of authors in chronological order and tabular form between the arched windows of the exterior. Labrouste explained: "The names of the principle authors or writers whose works are in the library are written in large letters at just the place on the façade that corresponds to the bookshelves inside containing their books".[84] For Labrouste, the printed books inside, being the building's content, lent the building its aesthetic or visible external appearance. The books themselves, Labrouste explained, "are the most beautiful ornament of the interior";[85] as such, the exterior attempts to reveal that which is therein contained. Thus, Labrouste tried to manipulate the aesthetic surface in order to express the building's function while adopting and extending an accepted neo-classical language most often associated with municipal buildings. According to Levine, Labrouste gave the Bibliothèque Ste-Geneviève a means of signifying that attempted to place the reader in a context by which they became part of its constructed meaning.[86] The words or titles of the catalogued books became stamped onto the architectural object, whereby Labrouste attempted to forestall Hugo's declaration that the book will kill the building, by turning the book *into* a building, so to speak.

The prominent critic, Victor Considerant, a contemporary of Hugo's, warned against assuming that architecture had become a lost art, for he understood that the context in which architecture is located plays a significant part in determining one's association with the object. He recognised that "architecture's vitality depends upon the social programme it is called to fulfil".[87] To the contrary, Labrouste endeavoured to fix the association between the building's function and its significance and therefore relied solely on visual and symbolic cues to express meaning. However, whether a building is expressive of its function or not, the autonomous viewer will only ever make such connections while its "social context", in Considerant's terms, directs them to do so.

'Context', in this sense, refers to the relationship between the human subject and the building itself, rather than merely that which surrounds it. For in this situation, it is clear that the literal engraving of authors' names on the façade of Ste-Geneviève does not offer any visual cues with regards to geographic location. Thus it is possible, as this example demonstrates, to reproduce the same building in alternative locations, as the Bibliothèque Ste-Geneviève has an almost exact duplicate in the Boston Public Library. As such, one might assume that others also found Labrouste's functional aesthetic particularly useful and as a result reproduced it in another location. It therefore can be argued that the Library's aesthetic served a pedagogic purpose in terms of informing the viewer of the building's 'use', much like a sign stating 'Library'. Regardless, this attempt to position the reader in a way that restricts their ability to interpret the object is conditional on the successful use of certain signifying cues, for instance: their ability to read, familiarity with the authors' names, their awareness of library cataloguing systems or their understanding of the neo-classical style. This however does

46 *Meaning and the death of architecture*

not result in a permanent fixity between meaning and the object, rather, it plays on already commonly established signifying practices, like those already mentioned. When such practices lose their value, it is likely that the form will acquire alternative meanings. For instance, neo-classical architecture is today seen as an outmoded revivalism, and so would undermine the view that a given institution occupying the building is progressive. It is therefore pertinent to enquire, what does the same building mean today, now that the Ste-Geneviève library must make provisions for electronic documents and the internet, which have generated an unprecedented change in function, use and operation of modern libraries? Now that the engraved façade no longer relates to the catalogued names displayed inside the library itself, does the building's aesthetic still signify its function?

Consider also the Kansas City library which quite obviously denotes its function as a library by resembling a bookshelf through the display of gigantic book spines. Referred to as the 'community bookshelf', the books represent a collection of the city's most favoured publications. The Kansas City library therefore attempts to manipulate the viewer's interpretation of the architecture by resembling a collection of books. It is precisely this excessiveness of resembling books that causes the architecture to look kitsch. However, it must be recognised, in this case in particular, that although the structure is associated with the library, it is not a library at all, but a carpark. As such, the viewer is fooled into assuming that the visual cues – i.e. giant books – denote the function of a library.

Must it be that for a library to be interpreted as such it must somehow make a literal association with a book? In doing so, the designers invoke a pedagogy that attempts to manipulate the viewer's interpretation of the architecture, perhaps failing to recognise that one associates meaning with form through a complex network of social, psychological and enunciative formations – none of which are the intrinsic property of the object itself. For example, one's experience, expectations and limitations with regards to a particular space all impact on how one perceives architecture, such as the gargoyles which realised the imaginative imperative of medievalism. Meaning is not solely constructed through denotation, for as with the Kansas City library such literal visual cues are likely to be misleading or at least lost over time once the association between the meaning and form changes context.

The overt advertising of a building's function is evidenced in many architectural works, in particular those of libraries. Libraries are often an essential piece of municipal infrastructure which provides a visual representation of the educational and pedagogical standards of the community. The commissioning of such structures requires their importance to be brought to the fore, as though forming a new self-justifying landmark within the cityscape, a beacon of learning and contributor of knowledge to the city's residents. The Bibliothèque Nationale De France, completed in 1996 having been commissioned by the Ministry of Culture under then President Francois Mitterrand and designed by architect Dominique Perrault, also

Meaning and the death of architecture 47

Figure 2.2 'The Community Bookshelf', Kansas City Library carpark.
Richard Cornish.

aspired to such ideals, in being part of, in effect, the same modern pedagogic-governmental formation which gives it purpose.

Anthony Vidler, in his review of the French National Library competition, is highly critical of Perrault's winning proposal for four glass 'L' shaped towers located at the four corners of a vast rectangular concrete podium and garden. He sees the Library as a return to the era of contempt towards the urban environment, proliferated by CIAM, who disregarded historical precedent and proposed to demolish any building not attuned to 'modernist' principles. Aside from the criticism that has since been loaded onto the completed project, as a result of its lack of operational efficiency, Vidler is concerned with how such a proposal could have become attuned to the needs/demands of government and the competition's jury members, in that the competition administrators seem to have overlooked the functional requirements of the library and instead placed priority on the production of a 'new monument' representative of the 'epoch'. Vidler writes: "Indeed the aspirations of Mitterand's cultural advisers and the polemically stated basis of Perrault's design seem quite naturally to support each other, as if the architect had somehow divined the inner aesthetic drives of the jury and the president . . . and given them form".[88] Described by the President of the French Library Association as

48 Meaning and the death of architecture

"the stuff from which dreams are woven",[89] Vidler highlights the fact that the library does not provide a solution to efficient library design, rather it renders this more difficult to achieve. For it seems that the decision to divide the library catalogues into four separate towers may have satisfied a symbolic imperative, but thwarted a functional one. As such, the building is thought by regular users to be an impossible place to work, read and study. However, it appears that such goals were not adequately considered at the time of its proposal, for Perrault was able to conjure an association between his design and the ideological aspirations of the jury by the manner in which he presented his proposal. He promoted his design as "a place and not a building", "a symbolic place", "a magical place" with its "towers encased in light".[90] Yet as Vidler points out, Perrault's proposal consisted of no more than a few stylised drawings and photomontages, and a small plexiglass model. Seemingly, the architect's evocative language accompanying the presentation hit a chord, for the competition's administrators also became convinced that the four tower block design would come to symbolise open books of learning and provide a beacon of cultural enlightenment for the city of Paris. Vidler explains: "Nothing else, it seems, would explain the fixity with which the administration and its architect have maintained (perversely, against every principle of functionalist design) that the form will remain the same, no matter what changes were introduced into the program".[91] Given that there is no fixed ideal for what form a library should take, the jurors welcomed what they perceived to be 'a completely new type of library' unencumbered by the past, nevertheless reflecting the values of culture and learning. Perrault speculated that the four towers, as open books would, in his words: "Form urban beacons that valorise the book with an aleatory mode of occupation of the towers that present themselves as an accumulation of wisdom, of never-finished knowledge, of a sedimentation, slow but permanent".[92] Yet one might ask, nearly two decades after the completion of the National Library, whether such ambitions have been achieved in this project or whether they have been achieved in any other comparable project where knowledge is meant to be represented through the means of building materials? Is it at all possible that a building could ever encourage or promote such ideals, in particular, at the expense of its functional efficiency?

Vidler is critical of Perrault because despite of Perrault's modernist posturing he supplies an architectural form that bears no recognition of its function. Or in other words, the design does not better facilitate the functioning of a library, except through obvious denotive visual cues like that of a book. Perrault's adopted symbolism is nothing but what is commonly referred to as a 'one-liner' (a statement that is largely rhetorical and self referential), "framed within a dominant image that refers to its contents rather than deriving from their form".[93] All in all, the building has failed to provide Paris with the symbol of knowledge as intended, the building recedes into the Parisian skyline without any great appreciation for what it had attempted to achieve.

It might be said that Perrault's design was an attempt to reverse Hugo's assertion that the printed word had surpassed the hegemony of architecture as a cultural apparatus. According to Vidler, Perrault appears to be returning to a pre-Gutenberg sense of building as message. He writes: "For Perrault seems to have given himself the task of creating an architecture symbolic of books. In this sense, his towers, in the form of open books, belong to the category of what the Romantics of Hugo's generation scornfully called *architecture parlante* . . ."[94] The French National Library is an architecture that attempts to incorporate overt symbology in a manner that restricts the viewer's interpretation of the object. In reality, it is a feeble attempt at subjecting the viewer to a specific meaning. It attempts to prevent the viewer from finding their own significances with the building by interpreting it for them, governing the range of possible associative meanings that can be connected to the building.

Taking the example of Perrault's French National Library as an apparent failure to fulfil its designer's intentions for meaningful communication to be symptomatic of the broader built environment, it must be recognised that architecture has never inherently possessed the capacity to describe the story of humanity. In fact, it can be argued that the opposite is true, in that humanity has told the story of architecture. The examples of Perrault's Bibliothèque Nationale de France and Labrouste's Bibliothèque de Ste-Geneviève demonstrate the architect's attempt to fix meaning to form. In essence, they attempted to communicate through built form, and assumed, along with many others, that the rediscovery of meaningful architecture, in defiance of Hugo, was a matter of ascertaining the correct communicative tool. For Perrault, it was a matter of representing the building's function by rendering form in the shape of four gigantic open books. For Labrouste, it was a matter of inscribing the building's function on the exterior façade, as though the building were a text. Architecture is not a book to be read, nor did the printed word divest architecture of its cultural significance; however, it might have shifted the power relations between architecture and the people it represents.

As for Hugo, the book did not kill the building, in fact architecture is very much alive, but not in the way Viollet-le-Duc might have assumed – as an organic and evolving 'cultural object'. Rather, architecture continues to acquire various and multiple meanings, cultural, religious and otherwise, subject to the discursive practices arising within and defining a community. These associations that make for a meaningful and productive architecture are produced within a complex network of historical, social, psychological and enunciative formations, and not through any capacity inherent in the architectural object itself. To this extent, the following chapter is concerned with how discourse propagates knowledge about architecture and within the architectural profession, making particular forms predisposed to certain meanings. In accordance with the overall concerns of this book, that which is of interest here is how certain values and attitudes gain prevalence in a particular time and place, and what 'techniques' result in an architecture that

50 *Meaning and the death of architecture*

supposedly represents these values. Understanding this will enable a more precise examination of architecture as a resource for 'power', whereby buildings become the aestheticisation of particular values, like that of heritage architecture and national pride, as described through the restoration of the Notre Dame Cathedral.

Notes

1 Victor Hugo, *The Hunchback of Notre-Dame* (Philadelphia: Carey, Lea & Blanchard, 1834; reprint, London: Wordsworth Classics, 2004), 89.
2 Hugo did not approve of the English translation of the novel's title '*The Hunchback of Notre-Dame*', which leads one to believe that *Quasimodo* is the main character. The French title, '*Notre-Dame de Paris*', more accurately implicates the cathedral as the main character of the story.
3 Hugo (1834), 183.
4 Although not directly addressed in this book, it is worth mentioning recent debates relating to *Critical Architecture*, which has its origins in 1980s Deconstructionism. The issues raised by this field of architecture theory encompass a wide range of views which are seemingly relevant to broader arguments on the derivation of 'cultural' significance and meaning in architecture. The term 'critical architecture' attempts to link the criticism of architecture (or the words that surround architecture) with architectural design. [Refer to *Critical Architecture* ed. Jane Rendell et al (New York: Routledge, 2007), 2]. In an attempt to provide a brief background, this footnote will briefly outline some of the key figures who have contributed to this debate. The architectural historian Sylvia Lavin proposed that "one of the fundamental concepts of modern architectural theory is the idea that architecture is a form of language" [Refer to *Quatremere De Quincy and the Invention of a Modern Language* (Cambridge: MIT Press, 1992), X]. From this position, Lavin suggests that 'critical theory' is nothing other than a brand of literature theory and criticism that has lost its original object, namely literature. By applying the technique of literature criticism to architecture, she further concludes that 'critical architectural theory' loses its own object, namely architecture. Thus for Lavin, architectural forms are able to speak for themselves without the need for 'critical' interpretations. To the contrary, Wigley argues that literature theorists like Jacques Derrida and Mikhail Bahktin who are specialists in words, should work in parallel with architects who are specialists in images. According to Wigley, this collaboration will formulate a 'critical' understanding of the 'cultural significance' of architecture. [Refer to *The Architecture of Deconstruction: Derrida's Haunt* (Cambridge, MA: MIT Press, 1995)].

   Coming from another point of view is K. Michael Hays, who is well known for his promotion of a different kind of 'critical method'. According to Hays, *Critical Theory* is a 'mediating practice' that produces "relationships between the formal analysis of a work of architecture and its social context". [Refer to "Critical Architecture; Between Culture and Form", *Perspecta*, Vol. 21 (1984), 14–29.] This position assumes that the context and the object are one and the same, which makes for a 'totality'. This 'totality', according to Hays, is brought about through a new form of 'culture' which is no longer possessed, but rather 'constructed and deconstructed'. While Hays references Michel Foucault for his views, Hays applies his notion of constructivism to the architectural form, as opposed to the subjectification of the interpreter as Foucault would.

   Marilyn Moriarty in "The Search for Common Ground" in *Critical Architecture and Contemporary Culture* ed. William Lillyman et al. (Oxford:

Oxford University Press, 1994), claimed that any conversation about architecture "tells us something about the extent to which architecture satisfies or disappoints an array of cultural expectations" (5). Thus, for Moriarty, to ask what architecture means requires some sort of qualification with regards to its context. To this extent, Michael Stern in the same volume repositions Moriarty's claim to "what should architecture mean?" He states: "Architecture must be a reification of public values. A building must be a public act of communication: a coherent presentation, representation, reification not only of program, function, or convention belonging to the discipline itself, but also of the things that must belong to the world outside it that it must serve, honour and depict" (46–63). While Stern denies architecture's ability to be read as though a written text, he is imprecise about what might constitute 'public values'. To this extent, this book does not deny that architecture acquires meanings. However, I propose that specific meanings are not inherent in the object itself, but rather, produced in various discursive formations that produce knowledge and meanings (informing 'cultural' values) for those subjects who participate in its production.

5   Refer to Barry Mallgrave, *Architectural Theory: An Anthology from Vitruvius to 1870* (Melbourne: Blackwell Publishing, 2005), 356.

6   Bradley Stephens, 'Reading Walter Benjamin's Concept of the Ruin in Victor Hugo's Notre-Dame de Paris", *French Studies*, Vol. LXI, No. 2, (2007), 162.

7   Prem Chandavarkar, "Architecture and the Expression of Meaning", *Architecture + Design*, Vol. IV, No. 5, July (1988), 94. Refer to Judith Wolin, "In the Canyon", *JAE*, Vol. 36, No. 1, Autumn (1982), 10.

8   Quoted in Seungkoo Jo and Kwangkug Lee, "Architecture as Narrative: On Bernard Franken's Ruminations on Characterisation, Integration and Imagination", in *Journal of Asian Architecture and Building Engineering*, Nov. (2007), 213. Refer to Jennifer Bloomer, *Architecture as the Text: The (S)crypts of Joyce and Piranesi* (New Haven: Yale University Press, 2006).

9   Lewis Mumford, *Sticks and Stones: A Study of American Architecture and Civilisation* (New York: Dover, 1924), 41.

10 Hugo (1834), 94.

11 Refer to Banister Fletcher, *A History of Architecture* (Oxford: Architectural Press, 1896; reprint 12th ed. 1996), 390–394.

12 Quoted in Elizabeth Emery, *Romancing the Cathedral* (Albany: SUNY Press, 2001), 2.

13 Viollet-le-Duc advocated that the elements of beauty and honesty in Gothic architecture were not the result of its aesthetic appearance, but rather its rational approach to structural systems and constructional issues. Viollet-le-Duc's technical interests in the Gothic are repeated in twentieth-century functionalism and influenced the architects of the Chicago School. Refer to Dennis Sharp, *Twentieth Century Architecture: A Visual History* (Mulgrave: Images House, 2002), 61.

14 Millard Hearn, *The Architectural Theory of Viollet-le-Duc* (Cambridge, MA: Massachusetts Institute of Technology, 1990), 6.

15 Martin Bressani, "Notes on Viollet-le-Duc's Philosophy of History; Dialectics and Technologies", *Journal of the Society of Architectural Historians*, Vol. 48, No. 4 (Dec. 1989), 329–330.

16 *Ibid.*, 332.

17 Eugene-Emmanuel Viollet-le-Duc, *Lecture on Architecture* (New York: Dover Publications, 1987), 454

18 Achille Carlier, *Les Anciens Monuments dans la Civilisation Nouvelle* (Paris; Les Pierres de France, 1945), 469. Translation my own. For an account of the criticism directed at Viollet-le-Duc for his restoration of Notre-Dame de Paris refer to Daniel Reiff, "Viollet-le-Duc and Historic Restoration; The Western Portals of

52 *Meaning and the death of architecture*

Notre-Dame", *Journal of the Society of Architectural Historians*, Vol. 30, No. 1 (March 1971), 17–30.

19 Refer to Jukka Jokilehto, *A History of Architectural Conservation* (Oxford: Butterworth-Heinemann, 2002), 174–176.

20 Eugene-Emmanuel Viollet-le-Duc, quoted in *The Architectural Theory of Viollet-le-Duc* ed. Millard Hearn (Cambridge: Massachusetts Institute of Technology, 1990), 274.

21 *Ibid.*

22 Refer to Umberto Eco, *The Name of the Rose* (London: Minerva, 1992), 80.

23 Refer to Herbert Johnson, *Gravely Gorgeous: Gargoyles, Grotesques & the Nineteenth-Century Imagination* (2002). Avail. http://cidc.library.cornell.edu/adw/gravely/gargoyle.html (Accessed May 2008).

24 Michael Camille, *The Gargoyle of Notre-Dame: Medievalism and the Monsters of Modernity* (Chicago: University of Chicago Press, 2009), xi.

25 *Ibid.*, 16.

26 *Ibid.*, 17.

27 The Notre-Dame Cathedral is listed at number three in the top 10 'spooky' buildings in the world, refer to http://architecture.about.com/od/weirdarchitecture/tp/spookybuildings.htm (Accessed November 2008).

28 Thomas Wright, *History of Caricature and Grotesque* (London: Chatto & Windus, 1875), 73–74.

29 Eugene-Emmanuel Viollet-le-Duc, *Histoire de l'Habitation* Humaine (Berger-Levrault, reprint 1978), 26.

30 Georg Hegel, *The Philosophy of History* (Indianapolis: Hackett Publishing Company, reprint 1988), 58.

31 Hugo (1834), 148.

32 Refer to Anthony Vidler, *The Writing of the Wall: Architectural Theory in the Late Enlightenment* (New York: Princeton Architectural Press, 1996), 7–21. Martin Bressani, "Notes on Viollet-le-Duc's Philosophy of History; Dialectics and Technologies", *Journal of the Society of Architectural Historians*, Vol. 48, No. 4 (1989), 330.

33 Hugo (1834), 148.

34 *Ibid.*, 149.

35 Rob Zaretsky, *Victor Hugo and Architecture,* Lecture at the University of Houston.

36 Neil Levine, "The Book and the Building: Hugo's Theory of Architecture and Labrouste's Bibliotheque Ste-Genevieve," in *The Beaux Arts and Nineteenth Century French Architecture* ed. Robin Middleton, (London: Thames & Hudson, 1982), 149.

37 Refer to William Whyte, "How Do Buildings Mean? Some Issues of Interpretation in the History of Architecture", *History & Theory*, Vol. 45, May (2006), 154–155.

38 Keven Johnston and Nacy Gonlin, "What do Houses Mean? Approaches to the Analysis of Classic Maya Commoner Residences", in *Function and Meaning in Classic Maya Architecture* ed. Stephen Houston (Washington DC: Dumbarton Oaks, 1980), 141–142.

39 Whyte (2006), 160.

40 Roland Barthes, "Semiology and the Urban", *The City and the Sign* ed. M. Gottdiener and A. Lagopouli, (New York: Columbia University Press, 1986), 89.

41 Victor Hugo quoted in Neil Levine, "The Book and the Building: Hugo's Theory of Architecture and Labrouste's Bibliotheque Ste-Genevieve", in *The Beaux Arts and Nineteenth Century French Architecture* ed. Robin Middleton, (London: Thames & Hudson, 1982), 140.

Meaning and the death of architecture   53

42 Sigfried Giedion, *Space, Time and Architecture*, 5th ed. (Cambridge, MA: Harvard University Press, 1941), xxxiii. Refer Karsten Harries, *The Ethical Function of Architecture* (Cambridge, MA: MIT Press, 1998), 2.

43 *Ibid.*, 19.

44 *Ibid.*, 20.

45 Refer Peter Collins, *Changing Ideals in Modern Architecture,* reprint (Montreal: McGill-Queens University Press, 2000), 287–288.

46 Consider Karsten Harries who asserts: "If the main task of architecture is indeed, as Gideon claims, interpretation, architecture must possess the power of speech. But it is not at all obvious that – and if so, in what sense – architecture can be said to speak". [*The Ethical Function of Architecture* (Cambridge: MIT Press, 1998), 13.]

47 Alan Colquhoun, *Essays in Architectural Criticism: Modern Architecture and Historical Change* (Cambridge, MA: MIT Press, 1981), 12.

48 Viollet-le-Duc (1990), 116.

49 Refer to John Ruskin, *The Seven Lamps of Architecture* (St. Clair Shores: Scholarly Press, 1972).

50 Frank Lloyd Wright, *An Autobiography* (Petaluma: Pomegranate Communications, 2005), 79. Who, by the way, upon presenting his son with the writings of Viollet-le-Duc wrote: "In these volumes you will find all the architectural schooling you'll ever need. What you cannot learn from them, you can learn from me" (Quoted in Hearn, p. 14).

51 Frank Lloyd Wright, *The Art and Craft of the Machine*, address delivered to the Chicago Arts and Crafts Society, at Hull-House, (1901). Reprinted in *Catalogue for the Fourteenth Annual Exhibition of the Chicago Architectural Club* (Chicago, Chicago Architectural Club, 1901).

52 Frank Lloyd Wright quoted in K. P. Nathan "The Art and Craft of the Machine, By Frank Lloyd Wright" *Inkweaver Review* Feb. (2009). Avail. http://inkweaver-review.blogspot.com/2009/02/art-and-craft-of-machine-by-frank-lloyd.html (Accessed April 2009).

53 Wright (1901). Quoted in Paul Goldberger, *Frank Lloyd Wright at Hull House: On 'The Art and Craft of the Machine* (Chicago: Hull House Museum, 2001).

54 *Ibid.*

55 *Ibid.*

56 Daniel Libeskind, *The Space of Encounter* (New York, Universe Publishing, 2000), 180–194.

57 Ersi Ioannidou, "Humanist Machines: Daniel Libeskind's Three Lessons in Architecture", *The Role of the Humanities in Design Creativity* International Conference (2007), 2.

58 Libeskind (2000), 180–194.

59 Libeskind's design for the 'Freedom Tower' attempts to represent the values of 'democracy' in defiance of terrorism by, amongst other things, equating the height of the building (1,776 feet) with the year of the US Declaration of Independence. Yet it is highly unlikely that an unsuspecting onlooker will be able to measure the height of a building (through sight alone), and thus make any associations between such measurements as equating with a particular date in history. To this effect, Paul Goldberger adds further detail: "It was typical of Libeskind's fondness for sentimental, almost kitschy gestures – he called one of his open spaces on the site the Wedge of Light and claimed that the sun would shine there from 8:46am to 10:28am every September 11, the period representing the span between the impact of the first airplane and the collapse of the second tower. Another area was called the Park of Heroes". [*Up From Zero: Politics, Architecture, and the Rebuilding of New York* (New York: Random House Publishing, 2005), 157).

54 *Meaning and the death of architecture*

With this mind, David Simpson's enquiry is particularly pertinent. He asks: "What happens when an 'architect' (individual or collective) tells us what a building means and tries to short-circuit any discussion of the 'absolute problematical character' of the project. Libeskind has told us, lavishly and in spades, what the design was intended to mean, and I am not the first to find those meanings coercive and reductive, and perhaps also shamelessly opportunistic, whether or not they are sincere . . .". [*9/11; The Culture of Commemoration* (Chicago: Chicago University Press, 2006), 61].

60 Refer to Aaron Betsky, "Architecture in Limbo", *Archilab; Radical Experiments in Global Architecture* ed. Frederic Migayrou and Marie-Ange Brayer (London: Thames & Hudson, 2001), 32.

61 Hugo (1834), 157.

62 Ferdinand de Saussure used the term 'motivation' in order to describe 'iconic signs' – a mode in which the signifier is perceived to resemble or imitate the signified. For example; recognisably looking, sounding, feeling, etc. or possessing the similar qualities of that which the sign represents – like a portrait, model and so on. Refer to Ferdinand de Saussure, *Course in General Linguistics* (Chicago: Open Court Publishing, 1983), 130.

63 Charles Jencks, *Meaning in Architecture* ed. Charles Jencks and George Biard (London: Barrie & Jenkins, 1969), 17.

64 George Baird, *Meaning in Architecture* ed. Charles Jencks and George Biard (London: Barrie & Jenkins, 1969), 17. (Refer to note in the margins.)

65 Kevin Lynch, *The Image of the City* (Cambridge: The MIT Press, 1960), 2–3.

66 Barthes (1986), 89.

67 Refer Neil Leach, *Rethinking Architecture* (London: Routledge, 1997), 164.

68 Umberto Eco, "Functionalism and Sign: The Semiotics of Architecture", *The City and The Sign* ed. M. Gottdiener and A. Lagopoulos (New York: Columbia University Press, 1986), 56–85. Umberto Eco, *La Strattura Assente* (Milan: Bompiani, 1968).

69 Refer to Timothy Raser, *The Simplest of Signs* (Cranbury: Associated University Presses. 2004), 15–19.

70 Eco (1986), 56–85.

71 Umberto Eco, "From Internet to Gutenberg", lecture presented to The Italian Academy for Advanced Studies in America, Nov. 12, 1996, pt. 1.

72 Umberto Eco interview with Lee Marshal, "The World According to Eco," *Weird*, Issue 5.03, March (1997), 1–5.

73 Rafael Moneo, "The Solitude of Buildings", presented at The Kenzo Tange Lecture, Harvard University, March 9, 1985.

74 Richard Appignanesi, et al. *Introducing Postermodernsim* (Cambridge, Icon Books, 2004), 116.

75 Rafael Moneo, *Theoretical Anxiety and Design Strategies* (Cambridge: The MIT Press, 2004), 148.

76 Robert Venturi, *Complexity and Contradiction in Architecture* (New York, The Museum of Modern Art Papers on Architecture, 1966), 16.

77 Charles Jencks, *What is Post-Modernism?* (London: Academy Editions, 1996), 34. Jencks writes in relation to James Stirling's Neue Staatsgalerie in Stuttgart: "A Modernist would of course deny himself and us this pleasure for a number of reasons: 'truth of materials', 'logical consistency', and the ever present drive to purge and purify. By contrast Stirling, like lovers of Umberto Eco, wants to communicate more and different values".

78 Refer to Moneo (2004), 148.

79 Peter Eisenman, quoted in Thomas Patin, "From Deep Structures to an Architecture in Suspense; Peter Eisenman, Structuralism and Deconstruction", *Journal of Architectural Education*, Vol. 47, No. 2, November (1993), 91.

80 Peter Eisenman, "House VI", *Progressive Architecture*, Vol. 58, No. 6, June (1977), 59.
81 Refer to Whyte (2006), 154.
82 *Ibid.*, 167.
83 Hugo (1834), 184.
84 Henri Labrouste, "A M. Le Directeur de la Revue d'Architecture", *Revue Generale de L'architecture*, Vol. 10, (1852), 383.
85 *Ibid.*
86 Levine (1982), 168.
87 Victor Considerant quoted in Neil Levine, "The Book and the Building: Hugo's Theory of Architecture and Labrouste's Bibliotheque Ste-Genevieve", in *The Beaux Arts and Nineteenth Century French Architecture* ed. Robin Middleton (London: Thames & Hudson, 1982), 152.
88 Anthony Vidler, "Books in Space: Tradition and Transparency in the Bibliotheque de France", *Representations*, Vol. 42, Spring (1993), 116.
89 Dominique Jamet, "Du vert dans la bibliotheque," in *Bibliotheque de France: Premiers Volumes* (Paris: Carte Segrete, 1989), 23.
90 Vidler (1993), 117.
91 *Ibid.*, 116.
92 Dominique Perrault, "Une Place pour Paris", in *Bibliotheque de France; Premiers Volumes* (Paris: Carte Segrete, 1989), 106.
93 Vidler (1993), 128.
94 *Ibid.*, 126–127.

3 Statements on architecture
Meaning and determinism in the Athens Charters

This chapter examines how discourse propagates knowledge in the architectural profession. It scrutinizes two seminal documents of early 1930s modernism, both entitled, coincidentally, the Athens Charter, describing them as 'statements', a term adopted from Foucault's methods. These Charters are important to this discussion because despite subsequent revisions and multiple alternative publications the Charters continue to influence contemporary architectural practice. Both Charters promote a common belief in the ability of architectural form to convey meaning, whether as evidence for the unbroken progression of civilisation or as the validation of an 'age'. Inevitably, this attempt to prescribe the story of human civilisation as guided by a logic that stands outside of history, called 'historical determinism', must be inclusive of certain practices, traditions and values, and exclusive of others. In essence, this chapter argues that the historical monument becomes subject to a socio-political interpretation of the past which attempts to validate and legitimise cultural identities and certain ways of thinking by ascertaining their importance in the present. Or in other words, it is us, for particular reasons, who attempt to speak for these various monuments.

Of interest here is the Athens Charters' outlook towards the restoration of historic monuments and their shared directive that any new design must make use of modern techniques and materials in order to make the new distinct from the old. The principles espoused by the Charters, and subsequent documents, serve to provide a solution to a set of problematics raised by historic architecture such as preservation, restoration and/or reconstruction. With this in mind, the new additions to the historic St. Mary's Cathedral in Perth Australia demonstrates the direct influence of certain principles, found in the Charters, that attempt to tell a story about human interaction through building forms by making explicit the difference between the new and the old. In addition, the recent reconstruction of the Frauenkirche Cathedral in Dresden demonstrates a variation from such methods. While the cathedral incorporates elements of the original monument in order to tell the story of the destruction and reconstruction of the building, the project has been met with much resistance from professionals within the field of heritage architecture despite the public's appreciation of the work. These critics suggest that the commemorative capacity of the architecture was best left as a ruin, for the reconstruction provides a false representation of the building's existence. Yet both points of view attempt to manipulate the significance of the architecture for their own objectives and ends.

The Athens Charters act as 'statements' effecting knowledge about architectural form and practice, and points of reference for understanding the course of preceding debates. In effect, these 'statements' inform assumptions and expectations with relation to what monuments of the past tell us about history and how any new design should represent the 'spirit of the age'. Heritage conservation is yet to come to terms with architecture as a component of discourse which makes particular forms predisposed to certain meanings. But more importantly, this situation implies that a building's meaning is subject to change, and cannot necessarily be determined by a set of propositions, guidelines and doctrines.

The politics of the Athens Charters

The 1931 *Athens Charter for the Restoration of Historic Monuments* encapsulated the growing international concern relating to heritage practice and law. Adopted at the first International Congress of Architects and Technicians of Historic Monuments, its central tenet endeavoured to enhance the connection between the nation-state and its monuments. In so doing, the Charter assumed an innate relationship between architecture, society and history, in order to preserve the traditions, values and identities of their associated communities. Under the principles of the Athens Charter, "monuments" represented the historical progression of humankind, as though they were an unbroken link from the past to the present, whereby nations, in the act of their preservation and restoration, were declared as the custodians of such "civilising" traditions. The Charter, under the title 'Technical and Moral Co-operation', affirms: "The Conference, convinced that the question of the conservation of the artistic and archaeological property of mankind is one that interests the community of the States, which are wardens of civilisation".[1] In this way, heritage became the subject of preserving selected architectural objects based on judgements of value of the politico-nationalistic type in the attempt to define and determine the history and identity of a place. The Athens Charter sought to encapsulate a growing awareness of what was called 'cultural internationalism' which set the scene for international agreement on heritage practices. The concept of a peaceful community of nations (which brought about the creation of the League of Nations following the First World War, and was later superseded by the United Nations who in turn established the United Nations Educational, Scientific and Cultural Organisation (UNESCO) during the Second World War), supported the notion of an international consensus for the preservation of national monuments and cultures. To this end, the

58   *Statements on architecture*

Athens Charter states: "The problems of preservation of historic sites are to be solved by legislation at a national level for all countries".[2] This directive, by implication, provided each signatory nation with the legal jurisdiction for legitimising and preserving the cultural significance of their monuments in accordance with the international guidelines outlined in the Charter, rather than the application of a variety of ad hoc principles, which had previously been the case.

The 1931 Athens Conference on the restoration of historic buildings was shortly followed by the *Charte d'Athenes* (1933), which was drafted by Le Corbusier at the fourth assembly of the Internal Congress of Modern Architecture. Both Charters represented the theoretical underpinnings of the modern age and, indeed, the growing awareness of international heritage and culture. In 1957, the first International Congress of Architects and Technicians of Historic Monuments (which had already adopted the Athens Charter) recommended that any country without a central organisation for the protection of historic buildings should provide for the establishment of such an authority under UNESCO.[3] Following this the second International Congress of Architects and Technicians of Historic Monuments in Venice (1964) further solidified their authority in a series of 13 resolutions. The first resolution agreed to the adoption of the Venice Charter for the restoration of historic monuments, and the second, the creation of a new organisation called the International Council on Monuments and Sites (ICOMOS). The resolution concerning the creation of an international non-governmental organisation for monuments and sites agreed to "the necessity to creating such an organisation to coordinate international effort for the preservation and the appreciation of the world heritage of historic monuments . . . That the time had now come to implement practical measures for the creation of an international council".[4]

The International Council on Monuments and Sites extended the principles initially outlined in the 1931 Athens Charter, stressing the importance of nationalism and national identity in a global community, championing, as Emma Waterton outlined: "an ancient, idealised and inevitably relic past for the assumed universal rights of future generations".[5] For this reason, Waterton, whose research is concentrated on the conceptualisation of heritage policy which tends to privilege particular social groups, concludes that heritage was created and produced in, and as a resource for, the present, becoming more about meanings and values associated with the objects than the physical objects themselves. The Athens Charter attempted to 'freeze' historic buildings in time by turning them into 'evidence', or "concrete testimonies" as the Charter claims, of an idealised past. Although many heritage commentators and professionals disagree that heritage listed structures become frozen monuments,[6] the Athens Charter provokes the inevitable question, at which point in time should the physical fabric of a building be fixed? Given that most historic buildings have a long history of continuous occupation, which one of many conceivable meanings should take precedence over another? Raising similar doubts about the heritage principles outlined in the Athens Charter, Robert Adam argues that heritage doctrine destroys the living history of architecture. He asserts: "It [the Charter] has the effect of turning living organisms into dead specimens and takes away the life that made them worthy of study in the first place . . . To attempt to stamp out this raw edge of life for the sake of the preservation of evidence or to conserve an identification with certain moments in history, takes away a vital part of the character of a building or place; it reduces it to a specimen in the interests of academic objectives".[7] Taking Adam's reference to "living organisms" as a metaphor for meanings that are changeful, a building therefore is likely to acquire multiple meanings over the course of its history, relative to the time and values of the people who are intended to identify or who think of themselves as identifying with it. To presume that a work of architecture inherently possesses a single meaning, most likely one of national and cultural significance, is to deny the complex relations individuals might establish with built form and places over time. Inevitably, this attempt to control meaning for cultural purposes is an ideologically motivated practice that attempts to engender nationalistic pride in a country's monuments.

Along with the assumption of inherent cultural significance, the Athens Charter encourages the resolution of meanings through various techniques such as the "scientific" analysis of building materials. The Charter recommends: "That, in each country, the architects and curators of the monument should collaborate with specialists in the physical, chemical, and natural sciences with a view to determining the method to be adopted in specific cases".[8] Such analysis may be used to determine the original finishes, paint colours and other attributes of a building, whereby the possibility of "reading" the building's fabric becomes important to legitimising a valid interpretation of the site. In other words, the Charter endows "qualified practitioners", such as architects, historians, archaeologists and anthropologists, with the capacity to tell the story of civilisation through architecture. But this kind of endowment has the potential to distort the breadth and diversity of the past. Moreover, this kind of conservation ignores the multiplicity of meanings arising over time, and in response to different physical attributes, in the attempt to find one single meaning in architectural form established through these authorities. Indeed, this kind of 'historical determinism' and politically motivated explanations of the past rely on a cultural narrative that draws heavily on the idea of community to formulate a connection between territory and certain building forms. It follows, therefore, according to Brian Graham, "that if heritage is the contemporary use of the past, and if its meanings are defined in the present, then we create the heritage that we require and manipulate it for a range of purposes defined by the needs and demands of our present societies".[9] It is therefore prudent to ask why a particular interpretation of

60 *Statements on architecture*

heritage is promoted above another at a given time, and whose interests are advanced or impeded in the promotion of such values?

Consider, for example, Colonial Williamsburg in Virginia. Restored during the 1930s, the historic precinct provides an interpretation of a colonial American city at the time of the American Revolution. The town site consists of hundreds of reconstructed buildings in combination with others said to be restored to their original state. As a tourist attraction, or 'theme park' for the celebration of American patriots and the early history of the United States, the Colonial Williamsburg project has been subject to various critiques by those unwilling to accept its authority to speak as a voice for an all-encompassing American national identity. The architectural critic Ada Huxtable described Williamsburg as an "extraordinary, conscientious and expensive exercise in historic playacting in which real and imitation treasures and modern copies are carelessly confused in everyone's mind. Partly because it is so well done, the end effect has been to devalue authenticity and denigrate the genuine heritage of less picturesque periods to which an era and people gave life".[10] As part of the restoration project the architects Perry, Shaw and Hepburn demolished more than 700 existing buildings constructed after 1790 to make way for the reconstruction of new 'heritage' buildings which they thought were more representative of the desired period. Through the aid of illustrations and written descriptions, a vast variety of once-existing municipal and residential buildings were recreated in their original locations and presented as authentic representations of eighteenth-century colonial America. By such means, the Colonial Williamsburg historic site is often credited for taking the heritage movement into the realm of scientific analysis and archaeological investigation as these methods provided the documentary evidence to justify such recreations.[11] Because American heritage practices during the 1930s were influenced by internationally accepted policies and standards, such as the 1931 Athens Charter,[12] this kind of 'story telling' belongs to a broad imperative that attempts to formulate the meaning of historic monuments in relation to the interests of identity formation and the politics of nation building. It is an imperative which still seems to dominate heritage practice today. This chapter seeks to understand how.

The Athens Charter contributed towards making 'heritage' a new subject of inquiry and political concern, and initiated a long line of subsequent heritage manifestos which in one way or another continued to reinforce the principles of preceding charters. As Waterton recognises, while subsequent charters may differ by way of methodology and terms, what they all demonstrate is a "staunch unwillingness to give ground when dealing with cultural significance".[13] All subsequent charters, including the Burra Charter (1979) and its multiple revisions, the Florence Charter on Historic Gardens (1982), the Washington Charter on the Conservation of Historic Town and Areas (1987), the Nara Document on Authenticity (1994) and the UNESCO World Heritage Operational Guidelines (2005) all make reference to, or develop the framework of the Venice Charter (1964), which was based on the Athens Charter.[14] The Venice Charter, which stressed the importance of setting, respect for original fabric and accurate documentation of any intervention, states in its preamble:

> Imbued with a message from the past, the historic monuments of generations of people remain to the present day as living witnesses of their age-old traditions. People are becoming more and more conscious of the unity of human values and regard ancient monuments as a common heritage. The common responsibility to safeguard them for future generations is recognized. It is our duty to hand them on in the full richness of their authenticity.
>
> It is essential that the principles guiding the preservation and restoration of ancient buildings should be agreed and be laid down on an international basis, with each country being responsible for applying the plan within the framework of its own culture and traditions.
>
> By the defining these basic principles for the first time, the Athens Charter of 1931 contributed towards the development of an extensive international movement which has assumed concrete form in national documents . . . Increasing awareness and critical study have been brought to bear on problems which have continually become more complex and varied; now the time has come to examine the Charter afresh in order to make a thorough study of the principles involved and to enlarge its scope in a new document.[15]

Even the Nara Document on Authenticity, which deals with East Asian conservation values and rejects European conventions developed by earlier charters, states in the preamble that it is "conceived in the spirit of the Charter of Venice, and builds on it and extends it in response to expanding scope of cultural heritage concerns and interest in our contemporary world".[16] Ultimately, the Athens Charter has given rise to, or at the very least reinforced, certain ways of comprehending historic architecture as belonging to a cultural narrative that underpin the values of nationhood.

Indeed, the value of heritage architecture is a social construct, for it creates certain expectations with regards to the relationship between the built environment and cultural significance. Such values are constructed within discursive formations that inform knowledge not only in the field of architecture, but also in the community. The dimensions of this formation include, as the Charter itself represents, a valuation of the past which attempts to engender 'cultural' identity as though the past belongs to a process of 'becoming what we are today'. Thus, by treating heritage theory as a discourse and by extension the Athens Charter as a 'statement', or part of the discursive formation making heritage architecture a field of enquiry, one is better able to identify the framework that governs practice and regulates knowledge

62 *Statements on architecture*

in service of the dominant power relations within society. Heritage discourse, as Waterton explains: "promotes a consensus approach to history, smoothing over conflict and social difference".[17] In essence, it commandeers the historic monument in the interests of the nation while subverting alternative discourses which may have also occurred at the same time. In this way, the Colonial Williamsburg heritage town site has been accused of "smoothing" over, as Gable and Handler point out, "the stories about the masses, the middle classes, the tradesmen, the lower classes, and crucially, the African American slaves".[18] Colonial Williamsburg portrays the American Revolution as a triumph of democratic principles, leaving out those elements that might allude to the inequality, oppressions and exploitation of such individuals. Essentially, heritage discourse attempts to determine the cultural significance of historic monuments, one which is selectively inclusive of certain narratives, and by extension, exclusive of others.

Two years after the publication of the heritage movement's 1931 Athens Charter, the members of the International Congress for Modern Architecture (abbreviated to CIAM from the French name *Congres Internationaux d'Architecture Moderne*) met onboard the SS Patris en route from Marseilles to Athens in 1933 to formulate the principles of the modern movement on architecture and town planning. The resultant document, entitled the '*Charte d'Athenes*' and later published in 1942 by Le Corbusier, not only attempted to resolve the complex social problems bearing on modern western cities, but also played a significant role in advancing the principles and methods of contemporary heritage practices. CIAM, founded in 1928 at the Chateau de la Sarraz in Switzerland by a group of 28 prominent architects, with Le Corbusier and Sigfried Giedion foremost among them, was responsible for organising a series of symposia around Europe with the objective of propagating the principles of the modern movement. CIAM was concerned with, as Kenneth Frampton explains, "building rather than architecture" as the basic activity of humankind, which according to CIAM was directly linked to the "evolution and the development of human life".[19] Frampton further outlines: "CIAM openly asserted that architecture was unavoidably contingent on the broader issues of politics and economics and that, far from being removed from the realities of the industrialised world, it would have to depend for its general level of quality not on craftsmen but in the universal adoption of rationalised production methods".[20] Thus, for CIAM the industrial era could bring about a new economy for the building industry which it hoped would radically change attitudes towards town planning and the community.

CIAM's charter on the functional city proposed, in a series of 95 propositions, a blueprint to rid the urban environment of what the authors described as "illness", "decay" and "immorality" and called for a total remaking of the world's industrial cities by rendering them more "ordered", "hygienic" and "rational". The *Charte d'Athenes*' principles were centred on the myopic assumption that "architecture is the key to everything", the key to solving all social problems and the cure for congestion, crime and poverty.[21] Significantly, these assumptions encapsulated commonplace generalities at the time, demonstrating, as it will be argued, that the concepts which defined and shaped the modern movement and its 1933 manifesto were produced within certain ways of thinking that were particular to that era. These dominant influences, like positivism and the avant-garde (described later in this chapter), are also evident in the production of the other 1931 Athens Charter. Here it suffices to add that both documents were produced in and legitimised by discursive means, for instance, by the authors 'status' as prominent architects and experts coinciding with the declaration of propositions by way of a 'charter' for the better practice of heritage/urban architecture. These aspects served to endow their authors with the ability to speak with authority on a number of issues affecting modern city planning and the treatment of culturally significant monuments. This is evidenced, as will be shown, by the ongoing influence of both Charters on the development of current day city planning and heritage guidelines.

Formulated in response to the politics of post-war Europe, the modern movement's *Charte d'Athenes* garnered political influence as a result of decades of severe class polarisation associated with the rapid rise of urbanisation and industrialisation.[22] Following the Great Depression, strong central governments, including some fascist and communist regimes in Germany, Italy and Russia, furthered the modernist agenda to cleanse the city of illness and decay by winning popular approval for economic reform and promising raised living standards. Beyond this, CIAM saw the chaos and poverty of the city as not only a political issue but an architectural one too. In so doing, they proposed to divide the urban environment into four incontrovertible functions: living, working, recreation and circulation. The separation of these functions, if implemented by a well-disposed government, so CIAM claimed, would lead to greater social and moral improvement for the cities inhabitants – as a kind of architectural panacea.

One of the main features of the *Charte d'Athenes* was its refusal to examine works of architecture as ready-made texts for the reading of moral and historical ideas (as advocated by the heritage movement).[23] While the modernists' Charter does not dismiss the value of historic monuments, CIAM ignored their 'cultural significance' in preference of advancing the ideals of a utopian future. The Charter states:

> The whole of the past is not, by definition, entitled to last forever; it is advisable to choose wisely that which must be respected. If the continuance of certain significant and majestic presences from a bygone era proves injurious to the interests of the city, a solution capable of reconciling both points of view will be sought.[24]

For CIAM, the notion of value and meaning in architecture was more about representing the 'spirit' of the new 'age' rather than preserving certain

64 *Statements on architecture*

expectations about another age. The modernists were convinced of their ability to determine architecture's significance by reducing its elements to an identifiable language of forms and aesthetics. In this manner, CIAM proposed that if modern architecture was to be relevant in the contemporary age it required a style that was different from the past.

This deliberate attempt to invent a new style of architecture for the twentieth century was intended to represent the machine era, one of new technologies and materials. Yet, as Alan Colquhoun identifies it, the belief in an absolute connection between architectural forms and the economic and technical basis for society came from an interpretation of history which assumed the existence of a complete correlation between the objective conditions of life and the architectural style of a particular period in history. Colquhoun declares: "The fallacy of this view becomes obvious when we see that, in order to demonstrate what is supposed to be a historical determinism, it was necessary to perform an act of will, to create a 'modern style'".[25] Colquhoun argues that either the notion of historical determinism is a fact, in which case intentional acts are contemporary acts and therefore representative of the age. Or, by intentionally creating a style one attempts to symbolise history, leading one to conclude that history is not deterministic at all. This being said, it is difficult to establish exactly how much the conditions of a particular period contribute to certain architectural outcomes. To say that it leads to only one architectural style must however exclude many others, and as such, misrepresent the 'spirit' of any 'age'.

In addition, the *Charte d'Athenes* assumed that the implementation of this new style could change society and force people to follow the social program allegedly embedded within the architecture, and by extension create a new utopian age devoid of the problems of the past. But this begs the question: can such programs ever be embedded in the architecture alone? By adopting what might be described as a hardline view of physical determinism, the members of CIAM believed that people's behaviour could be modified through rational urban planning and architectural design. This having been said, it is not possible to affirm with any degree of certainty how or to what extent the conditions of the physical environment affect the way individuals behave. There is no doubt that some perceptive architects are able to enhance and manipulate certain meanings and values through various techniques. However, the question lies in whether architecture can achieve this by itself, without contribution from a variety of coincidental factors such as social, economic, political, personal and so forth. For example: if it is thought that the design of small neighbourhoods with interlinking laneways and parks between residences can create a sense of community, one denies the possibility that such strong community bonds are also the product of close family and economic ties, and may very well have little to do with the physical design of the streets.[26] The idea that the right arrangement of buildings can create social harmony has motivated many city planners and architects (as described in chapter six in relation to the creations of suburbs like Macquarie Fields in Sydney), and as a result has produced many failed visions for cohesive communities.[27] More importantly, such views misunderstand the nature of architecture and its capacities. The elevation of architecture to a 'cure-all' status that is the "key to everything" neglects appropriate consideration of a diversity of factors, of which architecture may play a role, but certainly not as a stand-alone object.

The reason for this synopsis of the two Athens Charters is not only to demonstrate the flaws in their fundamental assumptions regarding cultural significance and historical determinism, but also to show how such beliefs are brought about through ways of thinking and speaking that are particular to a certain era – in this case, the 'modern' era. By treating the Athens Charters as 'statements', or part of the discursive formation of modern architecture, one is able to appreciate that such ideas are not brought about as the culmination of a long process of developing thought culminating in an ever greater and clear understanding of 'the facts' of architecture, meaning and heritage. Rather, such propositions became normalised and validated at a particular point in time because of the way things are talked and reasoned about within a social setting. The Charters became legitimised as solutions to the problems of the day because they embodied commonly held views about the urban environment and the social responsibilities of humanity of those authorised to speak for, design and improve it. Dennis Rodwell is not alone in saying: "It is both confusing and significant that there are two Athens Charters from the 1930s. The context for both was the Modern Movement in architecture and the planning and constructional techniques and design concepts that were favoured by it".[28] The Modern Movement had its theoretical underpinnings in the dominant discursive fields of the 1930s, both of which are evident in the Athens Charters. In this sense, modernism was the combination of a nineteenth-century philosophical perspective known as Logical Positivism and the artistic avant-garde which demanded that architecture be absolutely new.[29] The 1931 Athens Charter embraced positivistic thought by its endorsement of the scientific investigation of historic monuments through "scrupulous" conservation and "thorough analysis" as the means of uncovering a "singular truth" about architecture.[30] In addition, the positivistic influence on the 1933 *Charte d'Athenes* demanded that modern architecture rid itself of decorative elements in the formulation of a functional and logical architecture. It sought to instantiate a new style of life that reflected the image of a world predicated on science and technology.[31]

This overlap of positivist thinking with the avant-garde is best exemplified by the Charters' attitude towards restoration. For example, both Charters support the use of modern materials in the development of old buildings, and recommend that new additions be designed in a modern style in order to highlight the contrast between the new and the old. This imperative clearly attempts to delineate the differences between the historical building and

66 Statements on architecture

any new 'modern' intervention. As the architect philosopher Sola-Morales Rubio recognises, the clear cut distinction between the old and new architecture has guided experts in restoration theory since the nineteenth century, and as a consequence became one of the fundamental principles laid down in the 1931 Athens Charter. He states: "Thus it can be said that the Athens Charter accepted in a generalised and standardised fashion the criteria and approaches already elaborated in that period by architects".[32] Here Rubio points out that this practice also influenced the theoretical development of the modern movement. He continues: "Architects who, whether they belonged to the world of avant-garde experimentation or the academic one of restoration, were subject to an identical historical sensibility. When the other Athens Charter, that of the men of the CIAM in 1933, also insisted on the impossibility of accepting the historical pastiche and appealed to the *Zeitgeist* to justify their demands that new interventions in historical zones be made in the language of present-day architecture, this was not in reality so far from what had been asserted two years earlier by other professionals with whom they appeared to have very few things in common".[33] Despite some obvious differences between the Charters, they are linked by a common attitude towards cultural significance and historical determination, for the architects of both parties could not avoid operating within the bounds of understanding and legitimacy of the time. Both movements desired to incorporate the new materials of the modern age into all contemporary works of architecture, including restoration work, as a means of expressing 'the spirit of the age' which personified the new developing world of the 1930s.

Fundamentally, the Athens Charters dictate that the preservation of a historic building must be fixed at a certain point in time, whereas any new work must reflect the 'age' in which it is constructed. If new materials are necessary in the intervention of any historic monument, the Charters propose that they should be made clearly distinct from the original. Here Robert Adam's observations prove useful. He suggests: "Only architecture that is obviously different from architecture of the past is an authentic representation of the present day. This theory is based on an erroneous projection of historical methodology into the present historical determinism. If you categorise history by style or artistic movement (often ignoring awkward examples that don't fit the theory) and make one style an inevitable reflection of its contemporary social, political and economic context, then you will believe that not only must new architecture be easy to identify and so quite different to what went before but that to do otherwise would not be authentic to its social, political and economic situation, it would not, to use a familiar catch phrase, be 'of its time'".[34] However, it stands to reason that whatever intervention is undertaken, it cannot be anything but 'of its time'. Adam concludes that this cannot be what is meant by "of its time". Instead, there is little doubt, by his approximation, "that what is meant is that new work must be obviously and overtly different from its historic predecessor".[35] Both Charters endeavour to determine the meaning of the architectural object and its place in society by associating past memories with the architectural object. In addition, they attempt to associate all new 'modern' architecture with the 'age', thereby enhancing its value in the present. Essentially, the Charters aim to override alternative meanings in the determination of how one should interact with and experience built form.

Despite this attempt, 'best' heritage practice is difficult to define through generic guidelines and basic principles. Every different heritage site produces a new set of 'problematics' to which there are many and varied solutions. To illustrate this I will explore some recent examples that demonstrate a differing, but critical, approach to the problem of heritage architecture; first, the restoration and additions to the St. Mary's Cathedral in Perth Australia (2009), followed by the reconstruction of the Frauenkirche (Church of Our Lady) Cathedral in Dresden Germany (2005). In so doing, this chapter will show how the different solutions have been constructed through "specific work or thought",[36] as Foucault described it, with relation to the national significance of architecture and its supposed ability to express the values and attitudes of a specific 'age'. But beyond this, the following section asks how the Athens Charters' lingering influence, as a component of discourse, subjects a variety of individuals, whether those representing government bodies, heritage professionals or academic circles, to endorse a particular mode of practice, or alternatively condemn it, regardless of the public's response to the work.

The hermeneutics of continuity

The recent refurbishment of the St. Mary's Cathedral completed in December 2009, in my home town of Perth, Australia, illustrates the influence that the principles of the two Athens Charters still have over contemporary heritage projects, and in particular, the requisite of making distinct the new from the old. Built over 20 years by Benedictine monks and completed in 1865, the small two-storey gothic church located at the top of a hill at the centre of Victoria Square accommodated the growing Catholic presence in the fledging Swan River colony. Today, as Perth Archbishop Barry Hickey proclaimed at the completion of the restoration project: "The Cathedral itself is a history lesson about the Church in Western Australia, and a lesson in Christian theology".[37] Cardinal Pell further added: "The depth of the faith of the WA people is wonderfully reflected in the architecture of the building – a mixture of the old and new, and a wonderful example of what Pope Benedict would call 'the hermeneutic of continuity', development and progress, (while) hanging on to the past".[38]

Interestingly, this attitude reflects the principles of the Heritage Council of Western Australia, which prohibits any new alteration or addition to a heritage building from mimicking the original style. This is echoed in their

68   *Statements on architecture*

design guidelines for the development of heritage places, which asks of the prospective designer:

> Is the new work easily distinguishable from the old? New work is generally permissible if it complements the building's original scale, form and massing and the original fabric is easily identifiable. New work that mimics the original should be avoided.[39]

The Heritage Council of Western Australia makes direct reference to the 1979 Australian Burra Charter which also affirms this position in Article 22, entitled New Work, which states:

> 22.1 New work such as additions to the *place* may be acceptable where it does not distort or obscure the *cultural significance* of the place, or detract from the *interpretation* and appreciation.
>
> 22.2 New work should be readily identifiable as such.[40]

Further to this, the associated notes explain:

> New work may be sympathetic if its sitting, bulk, form, scale, character, colour, texture and material are similar to the existing fabric, but imitation should be avoided.[41]

Indeed, these are clear imperatives directly attributable to the 1931 Athens Charters which permits "modern techniques and materials to be used in restoration work".[42] However, in isolation such views do not lead to the hardline view that any new intervention should be designed in a 'modernist' architectural style without the additional support of the 1933 *Charte d'Athenes*. This Charter not only supports the proposition that the new should not mimic the old, but that new work should be constructed in a modern style of architecture in both material and form.

These principles guided the Heritage Council's views with relation to the acceptability of the proposed restoration and additions to St. Mary's Cathedral. The restored Cathedral, as it stands today, is the culmination of centuries of various modifications which bring together the original 1865 building, major alterations carried out in the 1920s, and the current-day refurbishment, not to mention other significant changes over time. Although the plans to carry out a major extension of the Cathedral were never fully realised as funds were withdrawn due to the Great Depression in 1930, the partially completed works significantly altered the floor plan and façade of the original design. The alteration works transformed a long nave with an attached bell tower into a cruciform plan with the construction of an intersecting transept. A number of alterations were also completed to the front (west) façade of the Cathedral in the early 1900s, including two new additional lancet windows either side of the original centrally located window, a new entry porch and an aedicule housing a statue of the Virgin Mary. In addition, a slate clad steeple was constructed at the top of the bell tower with crenellations, pinnacles and gargoyles added too. The early twentieth-century alterations considerably modified the appearance of the original building. Significantly, the new work made no pretence at making any distinction between the old and new cathedral. Instead, it seamlessly blended into the original neo-gothic style, even enhancing it, portraying an image of a unified whole, rather than a mélange of various building stages as the contemporary interpretation of heritage guidelines would encourage.

Touted as an "architectural masterpiece" which "harmoniously blends the original 1865 structure with additions made in 1930 and *the modern new section*",[43] the recently restored Cathedral is said to "marry three centuries of history".[44] Yet whether it really succeeds in doing so is arguably a matter of interpretation, depending on one's acceptance of the validity of the heritage principles. The recent refurbishment, costing a total of $33 million, involved extensive repair work to the Cathedral's structure. For example, the entire roof was temporarily lifted so that the existing masonry columns could be replaced with steel ones. Aside from this repair work, the Cathedral received a major facelift. Underneath, a new parish centre and carpark were added, while above ground the west façade was relocated to accommodate a new curved concrete and glass structure positioned symmetrically between the nave and transept. This new feature increased the Cathedral's seating capacity from 700 to 1,050, with accommodation for an extra 500 people available in the overflow courtyard. Notably, this new floor plan breaks the traditional arrangement of pews down the length of the aisle, to an unorthodox arrangement where the pews radiate around an octagonal altar and sanctuary. A second tower was also constructed on the opposite side of the original in order to house a lift to the choir loft. However, this tower, although similar in basic form, is not aesthetically identical to the original because of the Heritage Council's stipulation that the new tower should not "shamelessly mimic" the existing one.[45]

The principle to not shamelessly mimic the original architecture is, as previously shown, directly lifted from the pages of heritage guidelines. Furthermore, the application of this directive, read in conjunction with the 1933 *Charte d'Athenes*, requires a visual distinction between the new and the old. As proposition number 70 states:

> The practice of using styles of the past on aesthetic pretexts for new structures erected in historic areas has harmful consequences . . . The masterpieces of the past show us that each generation has had its way of thinking, its conceptions, its aesthetic, which called upon the entire range of the technical resources of its epoch to serve as the springboard for its imagination. To imitate the past slavishly is to condemn ourselves to delusion, to institute the 'false' as a principle . . .[46]

70 *Statements on architecture*

Although these harmful consequences are not exactly outlined, one might assume that the members of CIAM are alluding to the potential cultural confusion that might ensue if a "false" reading of history is imparted by the mimicking of past styles. That which concerned the modern movement was new architecture, for the new was in no way to imitate the old, but rather represent the 'spirit of the age' through contemporary means. Nonetheless, the application of this principle with relation to the refurbishment of the St. Mary's Cathedral has resulted in the absurdity of the tower assuming a similar form and materiality to the original tower but without any of those elements that made it worthy of duplication in the first place. Consequently, the new tower is devoid of such gothic elements as the pointed arch windows (lancet), instead opting for rectangular windows. The tower is simply monolithic, without any of those elements that allow one to associate the architecture with that of its purpose. Most significantly, if the tower was never to function like the original (bell tower), why imitate its form and scale in the first place; is this not a type of architectural 'falsification' anyway? These potential problems appear to be contrary to one of the Heritage

Figure 3.1 The front entry to St. Mary's Cathedral following completion of refurbishment works in 2009. The new tower on the left is without any of the gothic features incorporated in the original tower constructed in 1865.

Daniel Grinceri.

Council's central tenets, which is concerned with not distorting one's 'interpretation' of the architectural work. In this manner, the Charters help map a space within which particular discriminations and value judgements about a building present themselves as acceptable solutions despite other seemingly reasonable alternatives. For instance, would it really matter to the viewing public if the new tower mimicked the old?

The authors of the modernist Charter claim that new architecture that is obviously different from architecture of the past is an authentic representation of the contemporary age. However, this theory is based on an erroneous presumption of historical determinism whereby buildings tell the story of civilisation and possess a single inherent 'truth'. Here Adam enquires: "Why should it be wrong for people to be deceived if they prefer to have a satisfying, if academically inauthentic, reconstruction rather than a bare ruin or a disfigured and incomplete building? This is not science; it is the protection of the traditions and symbolic identity of communities".[47] Adam's reference to "deception" is perhaps also constructed within the same discursive framework as the heritage profession, as there is no reason, except for those outlined in both Charters, why new architecture that imitates the old should be considered 'deceptive'. However, it is important to ask whether individuals are really concerned about being able to make clear distinctions between old and new work. Is one's 'appreciation' of a building in actuality diminished if such principles are not strictly adhered to? Such views, by necessity, must ascribe architecture the ability to inherently mean something that is naturally discerned by the viewing public. This, as argued in the previous chapter, is not within architecture's ability to control, but subject to the way knowledge is constructed within a particular social setting.

Arguably, the directive to distinguish the new from the old, which is concerned with 'authenticity' about an 'age', has become so normalised within the profession that most practitioners would adhere to such principles without a second thought. The appropriation of such requirements, like not mimicking past architectural styles in the current era, has become seemingly unconditionally accepted as natural and right. Indeed, the current discursive construct evidently regulates the practice of architects, and others in the field of heritage architecture, that the rules, norms and conventions become seemingly self-evident and incontrovertible. The "hermeneutics of continuity", as professed by Pope Benedict XVI, has no relation to the built environment, but rather to the myth of an unbroken line of continuity with relation to the Church's doctrinal, liturgical and moral traditions. However in this case, 'hermeneutics', which relates to the interpretation of texts, acts as a metaphor for the development of architecture as it seemingly progresses from one particular style to another throughout the ages. But it must be recognised that it is only in retrospect that each movement and style becomes identified as the authentic expression of their 'age', no doubt, excluding many others in the process. A reading of 1930s modernism would have us

72 *Statements on architecture*

believe that the predominant style of architecture was indeed modernist. In actuality, architecture constructed during this era typically adhered to classical rules with relation to form, proportion and aesthetics. As Adam highlights: "Inter-war architecture was almost all traditional everywhere but this is now virtually wholly ignored in favour of fledging Modernism, as this is now seen as the authentic architecture of the modern world".[48] In this way, it would seem a contrivance to suggest that the architecture of a particular era naturally followed another.

Seemingly, these heritage principles raise more questions than they answer. Does the overt contrast between the new and old really protect, as the Charters claim, the "particular and specific values . . . which a community recognises"[49] in its heritage? Which part of the historic monument does one preserve? Which elements are more authentic than others? Heritage is all about the way various material artefacts, mythologies, memories and traditions are selected in the present. In fact, there is very little continuity in the way buildings are preserved and restored. The words of Archbishop Hickey with relation the St. Mary's refurbishment – "We are preserving the best of the old and integrating it with the new" – seem to speak of a literal and selective contrast generated by present day expectations of what heritage architecture should be. This is not the product of a natural continuity between the past and the present. Instead, Hickey simply assumes what he and other like minds would like to be the case.

The declaration of Dresden

In October 2005 more than 60,000 people, along with many prominent government officials including the outgoing German Chancellor Gerhard Schroder and his successor Angela Merkel, and other international dignitaries, gathered at the steps of the Frauenkirche (Church of Our Lady) Cathedral in Dresden to celebrate its reopening after 13 years of reconstruction and nearly four decades of ruin.[50] Originally designed by architect George Bahr, the baroque-style cathedral was constructed between 1726 and 1743, and became an integral part of the Dresden cityscape and identity, with its 96m high dome dominating the skyline for more than two centuries. However, during the Second World War in 1945 Dresden was subject to incendiary bombing raids by British and US forces which obliterated the entire city, including the Frauenkirche Cathedral, and killed an estimated 30,000 civilians. To this end, W.G. Sebald examines the effect of such devastation on those German civilians who survived the war. He states that there was 42.8 cubic meters of rubble for every inhabitant of Dresden. Yet despite this, Sebald reveals that it seems to have scarcely left a trace of pain. He continues, quoting Alfred Doblin: "People walked 'down the street and past the dreadful ruins as if nothing had happened and the town had always looked like that'. The reverse side of apathy was the declaration of a new beginning, the unquestioning heroism with which people immediately set about the task of clearance and reorganisation".[51] To this effect, Sebald argues that the total destruction of German cities was, at the time and in the decades that followed, not seen as a "horrifying end of a collective aberration", but rather a stage for a "brave new world".[52]

In the decades that followed the War the East German authorities set about reconstructing Dresden, but left the ruined Cathedral untouched as a memorial to those who died in the bombings, framing the inhabitants of Dresden, as Jason James points out: "as the innocent victims of Allied cruelty".[53] Following the fall of communist rule and the reunification of Germany in 1990 pressure for the reconstruction of Dresden's Cathedral driven in the main by international fund raising gained sufficient momentum that work began in 1993. Under the direction of architect Eberhard Burger, the Cathedral was painstakingly replicated using the original plans from the 1720s, and other drawings, paintings and photographs. Where possible, the Cathedral, with exception to the dome, was rebuilt using original materials. The mountain of rubble was carefully documented and organised in such a manner that the location of each stone could be

Figure 3.2 The reconstructed Frauenkirche Cathedral in Dresden reopened in 2005.

Anja Eichler.

approximated by where it was found in the ruins. 3D imaging was used to locate 8,500 original stones in the façades of the reconstructed building according to their shape and how they fitted with other stones. As a result, the original sandstone is evidently scattered throughout the reconstructed building, made noticeable because of its dark charred colour caused by the bombings. Notwithstanding, the majority of work, including the internal paintings and sculptures are a replication, recreated in the effort to resemble the original cathedral as much as possible.

In the decades following the Second World War, German government officials, local authorities, heritage professionals and academics were embroiled in a passionate and sometimes heated debate about whether or not to allow the reconstruction of buildings destroyed by the war. For this reason the German government conducted an international symposium in conjunction with ICOMOS (International Council on Monuments and Sites) in 1982 on the subject of the 'Reconstruction of Monuments Destroyed by War', called the *Declaration of Dresden*. The meeting observed that the people of Dresden had endured "terrible suffering and losses", and proposed that the reclamation of "their treasures that had been damaged or believed lost, in particular, architectural monuments" was a significant part of their recovery.[54] In this manner, proposition number 8 of the Declaration makes the following concession:

> In the restoration of monuments destroyed by war special care should be taken that the historic development up to the present time can be traced. This applies to the elements of monuments from different periods as well as other evidence of its fate. This might include modern elements which have been added in a responsible manner. The complete reconstruction of severely damaged monuments must be regarded as an exceptional circumstance which is justified only for special reasons resulting from destruction of a monument of great significance by war. Such a reconstruction must be based on reliable documentation of its condition before destruction.[55]

Here the committee's reluctance to permit a complete abandonment of the principles defining the Athens Charters, like that of avoiding imitation of historic monuments, is clearly evident. However, in recognising Dresden's "exceptional circumstance", the Declaration conceded that because the ruined cathedral was once so integral to the 'culture' and identity of the people, it would be in the best interests of the city to reconstruct the monument on the proviso that the new work be clearly distinct from the original. To this end, computer technology and the availability of suitable documentary evidence of the former Cathedral's architecture justified such an approach. In addition, the re-use of original stone work acts as a kind of record of past damage, as if to provide an interpretation of the architecture's destruction and then rebuilding.

Notwithstanding the compromises permitted by the Declaration of Dresden, a direct counter-example exists in St. Michael's Cathedral in Coventry which was also destroyed during the Second World War by German bombings in 1940. St. Michael's Cathedral was one of England's largest gothic cathedrals until its destruction. Built during the fourteenth and fifteenth centuries, it still remains a pile of rubble with only the tower, spire and some outer walls currently standing. In 1962 a new cathedral, designed by architect Basil Spence, was constructed next to the ruins, whereby Spence insisted on keeping the ruins untouched as a 'garden of remembrance' of past atrocities. The new St. Michael's Cathedral was built in similarly coloured sandstone as that composing the ruins in order to link the new with old, but beyond this, the new work is clearly distinct from its predecessor. It does not attempt to replicate the original, but rather continue the significance and occupation of the site by installing a clearly new modern building while continuing the 'story' of the old now ruined cathedral through its conservation.

Heritage professionals argue that Coventry Cathedral better maintains the 'authenticity' of the historic site as opposed to Dresden Cathedral because, as the architectural critic for the national newspaper *Frankfurter Allgemeine Zeitung* Dieter Bartetzko argues, the former makes a clear distinction between the new and the old. He proclaims: "The new cathedral in Coventry is a striking mixture of conserved ruins and contemporary architecture – certainly not a structure that can be mistaken for its predecessor".[56] Similar arguments surrounded events following the September 11 destruction of the World Trade Centre towers in 2001, as to whether the towers should be rebuilt (although taller) in a similar style to the originals in an act of defiance against terrorism. Yet the comparison stops there; the problem lies in whether a replica can be seen as an 'authentic' piece of architecture. Can it ever replace the significance of the original? Could it be that a person's sense of place and identity is suddenly put into doubt, if the architecture that formulated such a proposition turns out to be a false original?

Indeed, apart from the discrepancy in colour between the original and new stone work, Dresden Cathedral makes no attempt to appear as though it were wholly conceived and built in the twenty-first century, but rather as though it had always existed in its original state. For this reason, the Dresden reconstruction has come under considerable condemnation from historians, architects and journalists alike, who claim that the building lacks 'authenticity' and is therefore a falsification of the past.[57] In other words, these critics claim that the reconstruction of Dresden Cathedral to its original state misrepresents the 'age' and is therefore misleading of its 'truth' and 'cultural significance'. Critics such as Jason James claim that the Cathedral should have been left in a ruined state, as though an untouched memorial to the past and to the victims of the bombings. He believes that the reconstruction will void the memorial function the Cathedral because of its lack of "authenticity".[58] Another writer, critical of the reconstruction work, described the ruins as a "witness" to the bombings. He enquires:

76 Statements on architecture

"Will the reconstructed church be able to replicate the value and power of this symbol".[59] Others argue that the reconstruction is "driven by a desire to forget the past".[60] Finally, Bartetzko expresses his serious misgivings about the reconstruction, stating: "A glimpse of something that was believed lost forever has been granted, the promise of return now takes tangible form . . . Dangerous and obliging illusions are at work here: brand new, as though untouched by time and war, the three dimensional likeness of this baroque architectural wonder presents itself as immortal".[61] Despite such claims, supporters insist that the reuse of the original stone, charred by fire, acts as "scars of an old wound",[62] which does not try to appear "immortal", but rather incorporates the damage into the features of the Cathedral. In so doing, this contrast makes distinct the reconstruction from the original.

Regardless of such debates, one wonders to what extent is the community concerned with academic arguments about architectural 'authenticity' and historical 'continuity'? Many local residents, so it is claimed, see the reconstruction as a "symbol of healing and reconciliation" that returns Dresden to its former glory.[63] Yet both positions relating to the arguments for and against the reconstruction of the Dresden Cathedral attempt to assign architecture a single definitive meaning, one that can only succeed if the viewer is provided with a 'story' of the building's existence. But meanings are interpreted from architectural form in multiple and sometimes conflicting ways. As seen, the Dresden ruins, for the communist authorities, symbolised the "barbarity" of the capitalist West, and therefore preserved the destroyed church as ruinous for their own purposes. Or, as Sebald argues with relation to Germany's reluctance to deal with the trauma of the war, the reconstruction process itself "never played any appreciable part in the discussion of the internal constitution of Germany".[64] In light of this, one fails to recognise how one particular interpretation of the ruins is more 'authentic' than another. As such, certain meanings lend themselves greater veracity depending on how discourse construct notions like identity, denial, barbarity and so forth which frame certain meanings for certain people.

Unavoidably, contradictions arise when one attempts to govern meaning or restrict the interpretation of historic monuments as though they can only mean something with relation to national identity and cultural values. For example, the Colonial Williamsburg town site can be seen as somewhat pastiche because it attempts to provide an image of national heritage by recreating a nostalgic period in history while excluding other more unsavoury memories. St Mary's too, while making the new distinct from the old, appears almost whimsical, for while the new tower provides the Cathedral with a symmetrical form, it fails to appear as though it belongs to the original structure because it does not serve the same function. Yet this principle, on the one hand, has gained unanimous support from the heritage profession because it supposedly reveals a history of built form over time and speaks of the building's interaction with the cultural community. Dresden Cathedral, on the other hand, divides opinions amongst those with an understanding of heritage principles because, despite the reuse of original stone, it does not clearly enough distinguish new work from the old. In time, they argue, the old and the new stonework will sufficiently weather as to make the contrast indistinct. In essence, it contravenes the principles outlined 80 years earlier in the Athens Charters which warn against imitating the past, for the institution of the "false" is to "condemn oneself to delusion". Yet one wonders whether architecture is really capable of inducing such a response. Like all architectural works, its meanings are subject to discursive formations that delimit one's comprehension of the thing. Meanings inevitably change. Thus to prescribe a single definitive meaning to a work of architecture is to misjudge one's ability to discern other significances. Importantly, it is to acknowledge, with relation to Dresden Cathedral, that it is a replica of an original, thus permitting individuals to reconcile the significance the object, rather than having it determined for them as heritage professionals believe is their duty to do.

Architecture and the statement

The contrasting reception and debate surrounding how to best respond to the historic monument as shown with relation to the renovations at St. Mary's Cathedral and the reconstruction of the Frauenkirche Cathedral provide a useful case study for demonstrating the continuing influence of the two Athens Charters on heritage practice. The notion that historical monuments are capable of recounting the history of a particular place or people is one advocated by the tradition of hermeneutic thought. Indeed, the practice of associating hermeneutics with architecture is typically concerned with the interpretation of meaning from built form for the discovery of truth.[65] This view suggests that architecture, as Bill Thompson explains, "is a social art with the specific task of communication".[66] Accordingly, the Athens Charters assume that the historical monument contains a 'truth of ages' that can be read hermeneutically in order to determine the correct course of action any intervention or restoration should take. Nevertheless, Jeremy Wells points out: "The problem with this concept is that it presumes the hermeneutic operation of truth finding; like a religious book, the building will 'reveal' itself and tell us how it wants to exists".[67] It therefore stands to reason that just as a book can be read in different ways, buildings too are open to a multitude of interpretations.

According to Michel Foucault, as he argues in *The History of Sexuality*, hermeneutics has not lived up to its self-proclaimed expectations that there is a hidden deep truth in all things. Dreyfus and Rabinow explain: "We think Foucault is implying that we cannot simply assume that there are deep meanings to investigate just because our culture tells us there are. This is just another way of saying that the notion of deep meaning is a cultural construction".[68] Instead, Foucault is concerned with discursive practices that he argues delimit knowledge in a particular field and prescribe how

78   *Statements on architecture*

things should mean at a given point in time. Foucault's account of discursive practices is useful to this discussion because he is concerned with how meanings are applied to objects. To this end, one can examine how meanings are applied to architectural objects and the expectations one might hold for the cultural significance of historic monuments. The Athens Charters, which, as discussed, have significantly influenced the practice of heritage architecture, may also be treated as a component of discourse. In this way, the Athens Charters become 'statements' influencing knowledge in a particular field, generating certain expectations with relation to how certain architectural forms should mean.

The principal term used by Foucault to analyse knowledge is that of "discursive formations". By employing the term 'discourse' Foucault intends to use it differently from how it is used in contemporary language. 'Discourse', in general, means a discussion or debate. However, for Foucault 'discourse' constructs objects of knowledge and this knowledge has a bearing on governing how meanings are assigned to various objects, forms of conduct, sounds, symbols, and so forth. As Stuart Hall iterates, nothing has meaning outside of discourse: "Discourse governs the way a topic can be meaningfully talked about and reasoned about. It influences how ideas are put into practice and used to regulate the conduct of others".[69] Foucault's use of 'discourse' is also tactical, in that he attempts to avoid treating knowledge in terms of 'ideas' and similar attitudes prevailing in a community.[70] In this manner, Foucault displaces the notion that 'ideas' are naturally occurring in various locations or that they have an author. Instead, Foucault treats 'ideas' as he does knowledge, in that they are produced by specific practices that include and exclude certain elements which are related to the rules and patterns that govern their formation. Thus, as Paul Hirst points out, with relation to architecture, Foucault enables us to treat the constructed object as though it were a component of discourse. He writes: "We can thus bridge the gap between theory in architecture and spatial constructs, not merely by treating constructs as examples of a theory, but by examining how discourses enter into construction and how in consequence, buildings or planned environments become 'statements'. Here is the possibility of a link between a discursive formation, the institutional conditions in which it becomes a practice and the products of that practice".[71] This formulation provides a guide for examining the Athens Charters, in that they cannot be regarded as "free products of the mind". Rather, they have what Foucault describes as "surfaces of emergence", or particular conditions of knowledge which bring about certain ways of thinking. In addition, Foucault claims that statements emerge from "enunciative modalities", whereby certain individuals are endowed with certain qualifications to speak in specific ways. As such, one can examine how the basic principles of the Athens Charters, like making distinct the new from the old, have influenced the built environment and become normalised, or part of the accepted and standard practices in architecture. To demonstrate this, I will examine some of the elements that have lent the two Charters veracity with regards to the formation of heritage guidelines by governing authorities, and the expectations one might have for meaningful architecture. This serves to highlight the fact that the Athens Charters have been taken as legitimate propositions which bear upon those endeavouring to resolve a set of problematics with relation to the treatment of historic architecture.

That which is of interest here is how we inform ourselves to accept certain meanings about architecture because they are commonly held by those in authority. In this way, the Athens Charters serve an 'enunciative function' in that the adherence of their principles endow their authors with the authority to make statements with relation to the practice of heritage architecture. Similarly, we might accept the opinion of other authorities and experts as speakers of the truth; much like a doctor may diagnose an ill patient. To this effect, the Athens Charters become 'statements' or units of discourse that are understood by an informed hearer/reader to be true because they are spoken/written with recognised authority. Furthermore, Dreyfus and Rabinow explain: "Any culture in which methods allow privileged speakers to speak with authority beyond the range of their merely personal situation and power could be the subject of an archaeological study. In any such speech act an authorised subject asserts (writes, paints, says) what – on the basis of an accepted method – is a serious truth claim".[72] When a qualified speaker speaks with authority this is described by Foucault as a "serious speech act", as opposed to a "speech act", which is day to day speech. Any speech act could be 'serious' if it is established with the necessary validation to be taken as true.

On this matter, it is not difficult to establish the authority and esteem by which the authors of both Athens Charters are held within the architectural profession. CIAM boasted as its membership some of the most influential figures in modern architecture, including Le Corbusier, Sigfried Giedion, Hendrick Berlage, Hannes Meyer, Gerrit Rietveld, Alvar Aalto and many more. The conservationist movement, now called ICOMOS, also included, and still does, many renowned architects, engineers, anthropologists and archaeologists, not to mention the backing of the then League of Nations and UNESCO. Nonetheless, the fact that both Charters were endorsed by internationally recognised organisations and prominent architects is not the only reason that their manifestos have received such notoriety, and more importantly, credibility. The language employed by the authors of both Charters also contributes to the production of a serious truth claim. Indeed, the Charters intend to impart such information for the benefit of civilisation, and so invoke what could arguably be described as a quasi-evangelical imperative with relation to the reconstruction of the past. Wells observes with relation to the 1931 *Athens Charter* that the parallel between heritage conservation theory and religious belief is not accidental. He continues: "The widely acknowledge nineteenth century godfather of historic preservation, John Ruskin, who was a staunch evangelical in his earlier

80 *Statements on architecture*

years, advocated for the preservation of buildings with a reverent fervour few authors have matched. In addition, the history of preservation rhetoric is littered with religious terms such as 'revere', 'sacred', 'desecrate', 'consecrate', 'venerate' and 'spirit'".[73] By religious, Wells intends to associate the Charter's language with a kind of unquestioned commitment to principles of belief often found in fundamentalist religious observance, but, in this case the historic monument becomes the focus of one's devotion. Moreover, this association with aspects of 'religious' belief invokes redemptory overtones, whereby the restoration of historic buildings symbolises some kind of salvation or transformation of the culture in question.

Considering this, the 1933 *Charte d'Athenes* also employs similar means to overemphasise the importance of its claims. However, rather than proclaim the transformative and venerable qualities of architecture as the conservationists did, the modernists preferred a more direct 'hell and damnation' approach. To this end, they referred to the "evil", "moral decay", "poisoned fruits" and "promiscuity" that they saw evidenced in the major industrial cities of the time.[74] Indeed, the "evil" referred to is really disorder and overcrowding, and the moral ills they supposedly cultivate. As a consequence, this use of language amounts to the Charter's ability to be accepted and implemented as authoritative documents on not only heritage architecture, but also the improvement of the moral fabric of society.

Furthermore, something as seemingly as innocuous as these documents' titles, making use of the word 'charter' (literally meaning paper document), also implies an authority to issue meaningful proclamations on a particular subject. As Gilles Deleuze claims, in reference to Foucault: "Any institution implies the existence of statements such as a constitution, a charter, contracts, registrations and enrolments. Conversely, statements refer back to an institutional milieu which are necessary for the formation both of objects which arise in such examples of the statements and of the subject who speaks from this position (for example the position of a writer in society, the position of the doctor in the hospital or at his surgery . . .)".[75] The assumed authority by which the Charters are attributed as a result of the status of their authors combined with their biased and provocative language has established a 'regime of truth' within the practice of architecture. These elements have effectively placed a hold over subsequent architectural discourses and the application of knowledge within the practices of the profession well beyond the 1930s and even into contemporary practices. This is exemplified by the directives placed over the reconstruction of St. Mary's Cathedral, and the opposition by many learned architects to the reconstruction of Dresden Cathedral.

This having been said, it must be recognised that 'statements' are produced within certain conditions that make their claims more likely to be accepted as true. In other words, the Athens Charters were born of certain conditions that made it possible for them to appear as a 'statement', having what Foucault calls "surfaces of emergence". In this way, there are multiple factors impacting on the production of the Athens Charters that no doubt resonated with their readers at the time. Here I shall concentrate on a few examples that may have influenced the acceptance of such statements.

In brief, the Charters emerged from the political turbulence of the era, in particular the political rise of socialism and the belief that technology would be the catalyst for a perfect society still affected by years of economic depression.[76] Science and technologies perpetuated the idea of a better world, whereby new medicines and discoveries were predicated on the existence of a single eternal 'truth' which lay at the heart of all matter (including architecture). These circumstances were also reflected in philosophical thought at the time, as already mentioned, logical positivism advanced the notion that all meanings could be divided into two categories of true or false. As such, the validation of truth, even in architecture, was subject to the measurable and quantifiable analysis of scientific principles.

The combination of such factors led many architects of the emerging modernist movement to associate the dominant discourses of the time with that of architecture. In particular, the Bauhaus is renowned for merging the principles of science with architecture, referring to their workshops as "laboratories" for "advanced technologies". As Hannes Meyer, one time head of the Bauhaus proclaimed: "Building is not an aesthetic process . . . Architecture which continues a tradition is historicist . . . the new house is a product of industry and as such is the work of specialists: economists, statisticians, hygienists, climatologists . . ."[77] Instead of backward-looking 'historical' buildings, the modernists advocated a new style that put engineering before aesthetics. In so doing, new architecture, so the modernists claimed, also reflected the 'age'. In addition, the application of such principles, as Meyer continued, would "reorganise the material world" and reform people's lives. In reality, the modernists' claims to 'truth' and 'fact' were really hiding their own subjective value judgements about architecture which informed the aesthetic imperatives of the modern movement.

These ways of thinking shaped the style of writing, the methodological approach, the philosophical assumptions and the emergence of the Athens Charters. Indeed, they are the product of specific discursive practices particular to the modern era. Wells goes so far as to conclude: "The Athens charter[s] is the discursive formation, or groups of statements explained by the limits of discourse relations as described by Foucault, that created a regime of 'truth' that absorbed the ejected matter of modernism".[78] Indeed, it is no coincidence that the popularisation of the Athens Charters and their contribution to the further professionalisation of architecture as a discipline parallels the rise of modernism in mainstream western culture. This, however, begs the question: if the Athens Charters are the product of their era why have they retained their relevance for today? This query does not intend to imply that the discursive formation of heritage architecture has not changed in 80 years. Rather, it seeks to highlight the issues explicit in this book that 'statements', like the Athens Charters, have the potential to

82 *Statements on architecture*

inform practices within the profession. This has not come about because of some kind of inherent connection between the principles of the Charters and 'truth', but rather, because heritage professionals and architects have continued to apply its principles, for a lack of any dominant alternative, to the practice of architecture.

As shown, the Charters arose out of a dogmatic way of thinking that is arguably no longer relevant to the current day. Yet they continue to bear influence on the practice of architecture by the way they portray architecture as a meaningful form of communication capable of recounting the story of humanity or representing the spirit of the age. Architects and urban planners are seemingly reluctant to give up on the notion that the principles espoused by the Athens charters can enhance cultural values. As Eli Rubin speculates with relation to the recent global financial crisis: "For all the obvious flaws contained within the Athens Charter . . . It is not clear that a better solution has in principle yet been found . . . It may very well be that the flaws of the Athens Charter are not so fundamental that some of its basic ideas cannot be usefully adapted to the post-2008 world".[79] How these "basic ideas" might be adapted is not entirely clear, yet such comments epitomize the 'power' that such discursive forms, like those encompassed by the principles of the Athens Charters, continue to have on the practices of the profession.[80]

There is no logical reason why one particular style of architecture should be promoted over another as a more authentic representation of the age. Or, for that matter, why new restoration work should be made overtly distinct from the original, except that these form part of the principles outlined in the Athens charters and have been accepted as 'true' through discursive means. In this way, the Charters as 'statements' have added to the already substantial amount written on architecture, and in addition lent weight to that which has followed, regarding the cultural significance of architecture. The Athens Charters play a role in subjecting individuals to certain ways of thinking, and as a consequence, one is more likely to accept certain explanations and traditions because they are a normalised part of practice. Effectively, the Charters delimit knowledge in the field of heritage and architecture by excluding other possibilities that do not subscribe to or share similar interpretations of the past.

Indeed, the possibility of determining the value of historic monuments has a productive social benefit in communicating messages about place and identity.[81] Certain interpretations of the past and their association with historic monuments can play a role in validating and legitimising certain beliefs and national traditions. As Brian Graham outlines: "This is particularly associated with identity in which language, religion, ethnicity, nationalism and shared interpretations of the past are used to construct narratives of inclusion and exclusion that define communities and the ways in which they are rendered specific and differentiated".[82] The interpretation of historic monuments can lead to the validation of the present by conveying the illusion of an unbroken narrative of what are assumed to be timeless values.

As shown, the restoration of St. Mary's Cathedral, under the guidance of the Western Australian Heritage Council, supposedly reveals the continuation of those values and mores typically associated with Christianity which are then projected onto the community. The distinction between the historic architectural features of the Cathedral with the new ones attempt to provide a tangible representation of an unbroken trajectory from the past to the present and into the future. In essence, it allows the occupant to associate such ideals with their own personal beliefs in the validation and legitimisation of their own personal identity. In addition, the reconstruction of the Frauenkirche Cathedral in Dresden attempts to speak of the past by recording the damage which befell the city during the Second World War. Supporters, on the one hand, argue that its reconstruction again provides the city's inhabitants with a sense of identity and place, while healing the wounds of the past. On the other, critics suggest that the commemorative capacity of the architecture was best left as a ruin, for the reconstruction misrepresents the past by providing a falsification of the building's real existence. Either way, both parties attempt to manipulate the possible significance of the architecture for their own objectives and ends.

There is no doubt that certain traditions, narratives and memories tend to be associated with and located within culturally defined spaces. In these constructs, the city, particular monuments and buildings become part of the national landscape, becoming representative of the national ethos and character. The past is integral to both individual and national representations of identity, whereby the interpretation of such meanings from architecture has the potential to reinforce the national image and subject individuals to particular beliefs and traditions. Statements like the Athens Charters, and subsequent associated manifestos, serve to reinforce opinions and knowledge in fields of practice like heritage conservation. These principles present themselves as solutions to the many challenges raised by the conservation of historic buildings. Yet, by acknowledging that meanings and/or cultural significances are produced within discursive formations, one is better equipped to comprehend the "cultural machinery"[83] by which people are formed as perceptive and discriminating beings for whom buildings convey meanings. Heritage conservation is yet to come to terms with architecture as a discursive object, and, more importantly, that a building's meaning is subject to change, and cannot necessarily be determined by a set of propositions, guidelines and doctrines.

This notion is further addressed in the following chapter which examines the attempted association between certain forms of architecture and specific ideologies during the dictatorship of Nazi Germany. The fourth chapter will examine the role architecture played in the propagation of particular attitudes, like racism, amongst the general population. To this end, the case study of the Königsplatz in Munich will follow its transformation from an historic community square to the ideological centre of National Socialism, and then the attempted removal of such significances following the Nazis'

84 *Statements on architecture*

defeat in 1945. This chapter will show that even seemingly ideologically loaded structures are capable of change and adaption subject to a complex set of discursive forms, relating to the memory of the past, which governs identities, acceptable forms of behaviour and our understanding of things.

Notes

1 ICOMOS, *The Athens Charter for the Restoration of Historic monuments*, (Adopted at the First International Congress of Architects and Technicians of Historic Monuments: Athens 1931), VII.
2 *Ibid.*
3 Refer to ICOMOS, *Historic Background*. Available at http://www.international.ico mos.org/hist_eng.htm (Accessed October, 2011).
4 ICOMOS, *The Venice Charter* (Adopted at the Second International Congress of Architects and Technicians of Historic Monuments: Venice 1964), Document 2.
5 Emma Waterton, Laurajane Smith and Gary Campbell, "The Utility of Discourse Analysis to Heritage Studies: The Burra Charter and Social Inclusion", *International Journal of Heritage Studies*, Vol. 12, No. 4 (July 2006), 341.
6 Timoticin Kwanda, "The Interpretation of Cultural Heritage: The Living Authenticity and the Sense of Place", *Architectural History & Conservation* (Academia.edu).
7 Robert Adam, "How Heritage Dogma Destroys Living History", *Byens Fornyelse*, March (2003), 3.
8 ICOMOS (1931), V.
9 Brian Graham, "Heritage as Knowledge: Capital or Culture?", *Urban Studies*, Vol. 39, Nos. 5–6, (2002), 1,004.
10 Ada Huxtable, *Will They Ever Finish Bruckner Boulevard?* (Berkeley: University of California Press, 1989), 232.
11 Refer to Jeremy Wells, "The Plurality of Truth in Culture, Context and Heritage: A (Mostly) Post-Structuralist Analysis of Urban Conservation Charters", *City & Time*, Vol. 3, No. 2 (2007), 7.
12 W. Brown Morton, *Ethics in Preservation,* Lectures Presented at the Annual Meeting of the National Council for Preservation Education, (Indianapolis: October 1993), 14.
13 Waterton (2006), 349.
14 Refer to Neza Cebron Lipovec, *Preventive Conservation on the International Documents: From the Athens Charter to the ICOMOS Charter on Structural Restoration* (November 2008).
15 ICOMOS (1964).
16 ICOMOS, *The Nara Document on Authenticity* (drafted by 35 participants at the Nara Conference on authenticity in relation to the world heritage convention: Nara 1994).
17 Waterton (2006), 339.
18 Eric Gable & Richard Handler, "After Authenticity at an American Heritage Site", *American Anthropologist*, Vol. 98, No. 3 (1996), 569.
19 Kenneth Frampton, *Modern Architecture a Critical History* (London: Thames & Hudson, 1980), 269.
20 *Ibid.*
21 Le Corbusier, *The Athens Charter* (New York: Grossman Publishers, 1973), 103–104.
22 Alan Colquhoun, *Modern Architecture* (Oxford: Oxford University Press, 2002), 218.

23 Alan Colquhoun, *Essays in Architectural Criticism: Modern Architecture and Historicity* (Cambridge: MIT Press, 1981), 13.
24 Le Corbusier (1973), 86.
25 Colquhoun (1981), 18.
26 Refer to Cliff Moughtin, "The European City Street", *Town Planning Review*, Vol. 62, No. 1 (1991), 56.
27 Refer to John R. Gold, The Practice of Modernism: Modern Architects & Urban Transformation, 1954–1972 (New York: Routledge, 2007).

Consider the city of Birmingham, which was rebuilt after the Second World War. At the time of its reconstruction its high rise apartment towers were seen as the solution to housing shortages whereby the strict adherence to the modernist planning principles of functional segregation connected by freeways was seen a symbol of mobility and freedom. As Sandercock and Lyssiotis explain:

> In the rebuilding and expansion of European and New World cities after World War II, freeways were that mandatory symbol of social progress and individual freedom. . . City centres thus became ringed with a concrete neck-lace, or collar, like Birmingham's. The project of modernising cities was always both a physical and a symbolic project, expressing and conveying speed, democratisation, dynamism, change, moving on to better worlds in which technology would set us free. (Leonie Sandercock & Peter Lyssiotis, *Cosmpolis II* (London: Continuum, 2003, 14)

Over time, these same apartment towers began to deteriorate, turning the buildings from their idealised pristine whiteness to a dull dirty grey. Despite the initial enthusiasm for modernist design principles perceptions soon began to change. An increasing number of tower blocks became associated with such poor living standards and poverty that they were described as 'slums in the sky'. By the 1980s those that remained in the deteriorating modernist housing projects were generally the underprivileged and unemployed, resulting in the 'ghettoisation' of the tower blocks and a rapid increase in social dysfunction and poverty. The architects and planners had intended to create vibrant communities of social harmony. Instead, residents became the victims of vandalism and muggings, aided in part by the dark internal corridors that were once thought to provide the centre of social activity. As Burrell remarks:

> The modernist tower blocks envisaged by Le Corbusier were designed to free the inhabitants from the poverty of the 'ghettos'. . . What they succeeded in doing was to replace one form of imprisonment with another. (Gibson Burrell, "Eco and the Bunnymen", *Postmodernism and Organisation* ed. John Hassard and Martin Parker (London: Sage Publications, 1993, 73)

28 Dennis Rodwell, *Conservation and Sustainability in Historic Cities* (Oxford: Blackwell Publishing, 2007), 12.
29 Refer to Colquhoun (1981), 12.
30 Refer to Wells (2007), 8.
31 Refer to Peter Galison, "Aufbau/Bauhaus; Logical Positivism and Architectural Modernism", *Critical Inquiry*, Vol. 16, No. 4 (1990), 711.
32 Ignasi De Sola-Morales Rubio, "From Contrast to Analogy", *Lotus International*, No. 46 (1985), 37–45.
33 *Ibid.*
34 Adam (2003), 6.

86 Statements on architecture

35 Ibid.

36 Michel Foucault, Ethics; Essential Works of Foucault 1954–1984 Vol. 1 ed. Paul Rabinow (London: Penguin Books, 1994), 118.

37 Anthony Barich, "God is Back as a Cathedral Re-Opens", The Record, 6 January (2010).

38 Ibid.

39 The Heritage Council of W.A. Guide to Developing Heritage Places, December (2003), 8.

40 ICOMOS, The Burra Charter (Burwood: Deakin University Press, 2000), 7.

41 Ibid.

42 ICOMOS (1931), I.

43 Joseph Catanzaro, "Hallelujah, a Long Journey Ends in New-Look Cathedral", The West Australian, 5 December (2009).

44 Dawn Gibson, "Christmas Re-Opening Date for Cathedral", The West Australian, 4 July (2009).

45 Ibid.

46 Le Corbusier (1973), 88–89. Refer also to The Athens Charter (1931) resolution No. 5: "Modern techniques and materials may be used in restoration work. . .".

47 Adam (2003), 7.

48 Ibid. 8.

49 Ibid. 7.

50 Refer to "Dresden Cathedral Reopens, 60 Years After the Bombs", Associated Press, 31 October (2005).

51 W.G. Sebald, On the Natural History of Destruction (New York: Random House Publishing, 2003), 5.

52 Ibid. 6.

53 Jason James, "Undoing Trauma; Reconstructing the Church of Our Lady in Dresden", Ethos, Vol. 32, No. 2 (2006), 246.

54 ICOMOS, The Declaration of Dresden, 18 November (1982).

55 Ibid.

56 Dieter Bartetzko, "Dresdner Frauenkirche; Dem Schatten entronnen", Frankfurter Allgemeine Zeitung, June 23 (2004), 33.

57 Refer to Mark Jarzombek, "Disguised Visibility: Dresden/Dresden", Memory and Architecture ed. Elani Bastea (Albuquerque: University of Mexico Press, 2004), 56.

58 Jason James, "Undoing Trauma; Reconstructing the Church of Our Lady in Dresden", Ethos, Vol. 32, No. 2 (2006), 246.

59 Refer to Wiederaufbau Frauenkirche, Electronic document, http://www.wieder aufbau-frauenkirche.de (Accessed June, 2010).

60 Ibid.

61 Dieter Bartetzko, "Der erste Blick; Dresdens Frauenkirche luftet den Schleier", Frankfurter Allgemeine Zeitung, May 16 (2002), 43.

62 Refer to Reconstruction Frauenkirche Dresden, Electronic document, http:// www.frauenkirche-dresden.de/wiederaufbau+M5d637b1e38d.html (Accessed June, 2010).

63 Quoted in James (2006), 246.

64 Sebald (2003), 4.

65 Refer to Dalibor Vesely, Architecture in the Age of Divided Representation (London: MIT Press, 2004).

66 Bill Thompson, "Hermeneutics for Architects", The Journal of Architecture, Vol. 12, No. 2 (2007), 184.

67 Wells (2007), 7.

68 Herbert Dreyfus and Paul Rabinow, Beyond Structuralism and Hermeneutics (Chicago: University of Chicago Press, 1982), xxv.

Statements on architecture 87

69 Stuart Hall, *Representation: Cultural Representation and Signifying Practices* (London: Sage Publications, 1997), 44.
70 Mark Cousins and Athar Hussain, *Michael Foucault* (London: MacMillan, 1984), 78.
71 Paul Hirst, "Foucault and Architecture", *AA Files*, Vol. 26 (1993), 53.
72 Dreyfus and Rabinow (1982), 48.
73 Wells (2007), 4.
74 Le Corbusier (1973), 49.
75 Gilles Deleuze, *Foucault* (London: Continuum, 1988), 9.
76 Refer to Wells (2007), 6–9.
77 Quoted in Peter Galison, "Aufbau/Bauhaus: Logical Positivism and Architectural Modernism", *Critical Enquiry*, Vol. 16, No. 4 (Summer, 1990), 717.
78 Wells (2007), 6.
79 Eli Rubin, "The Athens Charter", *Themenportal Europaische Geschichte*, 2 July (2009), 7.
80 Refer to Waterton (2006), 349.
81 David Lowenthal, *The Heritage Crusade and the Spoils of History* (Cambridge: Cambridge University Press, 1998).
82 Graham (2002), 1004.
83 Refer to Ian Hunter, "Setting Limits to Culture", *New Formations*, No. 4, Spring (1988), 106.

4 Aesthetics and politics
The building of Nazi Germany

Following the previous chapter, which dealt with the practices of heritage architecture and attempts to depict history in a manner that validates and legitimises cultural identities and certain ways of thinking in the present, this chapter will further examine the representative capacity of architecture. In particular, how building form might be utilised to portray specific social and political goals. In doing so, three questions become central to this chapter: how do certain buildings become associated with specific meanings, can these meanings be removed and what role do architects play in this process? This chapter focuses on the National Socialists and their deliberate use of architecture as a way of symbolising and promoting the power of the Third Reich and the cultural superiority of the German race. Moreover, it examines the means by which the Nazis' attempted distortion of history, race and culture was facilitated by the many thousands of architects who willingly provided their services to the Nazi regime.

At the centre of this discussion is the Munich Königsplatz, a prominent city square commandeered by the Nazis and assigned a quasi religious status as a site for party rallies and ceremonial displays during Hitler's dictatorship. The Königsplatz served a significant ideological and political function for the Nazis by interweaving their story and 'struggle' against the Jew into the traditions and fabric of the German past. Considering this intention, upon the defeat of the Nazis the local community found themselves grappling with the dual problem of whether or not the Königsplatz would forever serve as a reminder of the atrocities of National Socialism and if not, how could such associations be removed? This chapter recounts the course of this attempted process of removal in order to demonstrate that even such seemingly ideologically loaded structures, when governed under a completely different set of values and ideals, are capable of adaptation not only within the urban environment but society too.

In conjunction with the case study of the Königsplatz, this chapter argues that the architecture constructed by the Third Reich did not impose certain practices and attitudes onto the population. Rather, they were accepted through participation in the prevailing practices (discursive, behavioural and conceivably others) of the time. In so doing, the chapter describes the

Aesthetics and politics   89

manner in which architecture contributed to the subjectification of individuals producing certain ways of thinking and behaving, rather than, for instance, merely acting as a conduit for ideas, either promoting or repressing them. Moreover, this chapter denies claims that Nazi architecture is inherently 'evil'. Rather, it argues that it was made to function for the fulfilment of specific aims. For this reason, every architect who contributed towards the construction and propagation of National Socialism should be held accountable, in some way, shape or form, for Nazi atrocities.

Nazi 'evil' and the 'ordinary'

At the time of their publication in *The New Yorker*, the series of articles written by the political theorists Hannah Arendt concerning the 1961 trail of Nazi war criminal Adolf Eichmann provoked a great deal of debate and controversy about how the Holocaust should be remembered. Nonetheless, Arendt's depiction of the SS Lieutenant Colonel, who organised and managed the mass deportation of Jews to the ghettos and extermination camps, provides a useful foundation for analysing the means by which ordinary individuals facilitated the pervasion of National Socialism in every aspect of German society. In particular, as it relates to this book, the thousands of architects who provided the means for propagating a highly aestheticised image of National Socialism through built form.

Since the collapse of the Nazi regime, many historians and theorists alike have attempted to explain the actions of ordinary German citizens, in particular the persecution of the Jews that culminated in the Holocaust. Most notable amongst them is William Shirer, whose bestselling book puts forward the proposition that the Holocaust occurred as a result of the people's "blind obedience" to Germany's leaders to whom they placed a "premium on servility".[1] Another prominent writer, Karl Dietrich Bracher, suggests that Germans were persuaded by the "power of German ideology",[2] while others put it down to the people's complacency and "indifference",[3] their fear of punishment, oppression and peer pressure. More recently, the historian Richard Evans in his trilogy of books on Nazi Germany justified the speed and enthusiasm by which so many people came to identify with National Socialism as the result of some kind of "predisposition" which had been engrained in the German culture prior to the rise of the Nazis.[4] These theories seemingly indicate that ordinary German citizens were somehow steered through various historical developments, from Protestantism, the unification of Germany, defeat in WWI, the depression and so forth, towards the inevitability of the Holocaust. Contrary to these opinions, recent publications like Daniel Golhagen's *Hitler's Willing Executioners* and Christopher Browning's *The Origins of the Final Solution* posit that the Holocaust was brought about as a direct result of the German people's widespread and virulent hatred of Jewish people, whose extermination became not only justified but also

90   Aesthetics and politics

just.[5] Goldhagen goes so far as to state: "Many thousands of 'ordinary' Germans had been appropriately positioned to slaughter Jews. Not economic hardship, not the coercive means of a totalitarian state, not social psychological pressure . . . but ideas about Jews that were pervasive in Germany, and had been for decades, induced ordinary Germans to kill unarmed, defenceless Jewish men, women and children by the thousands, systematically and without pity".[6] It is likely that this kind of extreme thinking with relation to race outwardly coerced others, to some degree, to adopt similar attitudes. But Goldhagen's position, read in conjunction with Foucault's writings on discursive formations, suggests that there is not one single explanation for the Holocaust. Rather, its derivation can be examined by analysing the everyday thought, speech and conduct typical to the German population. To this end, which concerns this chapter is how those elements, seemingly deeply engrained in the German psyche at the time, like anti-Semitism, territorial expansion, military conquest and so forth were discursively formed. But beyond this, this chapter examines the role that architecture, and by extension, architects, played in providing physical form to the political aspirations of German citizens as encapsulated by the dictates of National Socialism.

With this in mind, the built structures of the Third Reich, it has been proposed, played a strategic role in propagating Nazi ideologies. Peter Adams, in *Art in the Third Reich*, went so far as to claim that Nazi art and architecture was "in some measure responsible for the atrocities".[7] Adams puts forward the proposition that 'evil' regimes produce 'evil' buildings. He further adds: "The art of the Third Reich is difficult, complex, and controversial. Whether it be in the form of fine arts, architecture, film, literature, or music, it cannot be considered in the same way as the art of other periods. It must be seen as the artistic expression of a barbaric ideology. One can only look at the art of the Third Reich through the lens of Auschwitz".[8] Here it is difficult to disagree with Adams, for the art and architecture of the Third Reich should not be abstracted from its context. However, Adams' claim that the architecture of the Third Reich was the perfect medium for "directing desires and dreams", and programming the people's emotions and behaviour, is highly questionable. "The result", Adams concludes, "was the people's total submission to a state aesthetic: stifling to the eye and their sensibilities".[9] No doubt the built structures of the Third Reich participated in and facilitated the slaughter of millions of people (and the ethical implications of the architects' involvement in the procurement of such buildings will be discussed later in this chapter). Yet it is not within architecture's capacity alone to direct the minds of ordinary individuals to commit 'evil'. Architecture, as stated in previous chapters, must be accompanied by an associative discourse – relating to culture, race and power in the case of the Nazis – for such meanings to take hold.

Overlapping Adams' depiction of Nazi architecture as inherently 'evil' is, as a point of worthwhile comparison, Arendt's character assessment of Adolf Eichmann during his trial in Jerusalem 15 years after the war, although Arendt believed that the public trial was an attempt to engender a sense of national unity among a mass of demoralised new immigrants to Israel. Her main reason for attending was to understand Eichmann's mind and somehow try to comprehend the reasons for the moral collapse of ordinary German people. After her first day in court, Arendt is seemingly struck by Eichmann's mediocrity and insipid character, describing him as a "banal" yet a "diligent bureaucratic criminal". She wrote in a letter to Karl Jaspers: "He isn't even sinister . . . he had a cold and was sneezing inside his bullet proof glass cage".[10] The fact that Eichmann appeared "ordinary", stumbled his words, and exhibited a less than average intellect, led Arendt to believe that most tyrants, when "out of power", are simply ordinary and harmless individuals. Consider, for example, Saddam Hussein's capture in 2003. Discovered in a tiny cellar at a farm house outside of Tikrit, he appeared bewildered and dishevelled-looking, far from the maniacal dictator everyone believed him to be.[11] Similarly, Arendt came away with the disconcerting impression that Eichmann, one of the most brutal criminals in history, was really just an ordinary man. Even the Israeli court psychiatrist who examined Eichmann found him "completely normal", he commented, "more normal, at any rate, than I am after examining him".[12] For Arendt, Eichmann personified neither hatred or madness, nor "an insatiable thirst for blood, but something far worse, the faceless nature of Nazi evil itself".[13] The fact that such a seemingly ordinary man could mete out such cruelty to hundreds of thousands of people[14] explodes our conception, Arendt concludes, of how such events are allowed to take place. Accordingly, Eichmann was not a deranged psychopath, but caught up in practices that at the time seemed normal and necessary in German society.

The legal order under the Third Reich (as discussed in the next chapter with relation to Giorgio Agamben's notion of the 'exception'), became transformed from what most people would recognise as wrong and malevolent into the foundation of the new "righteousness". Accordingly, Arendt explains: "In the Third Reich evil lost its distinctive characteristic by which most people had until then recognised it. The Nazis redefined it as a civil norm".[15] With this in mind, this chapter is not necessarily concerned with what constitutes 'evil', but rather how certain meanings and behaviours become normalised in a particular society, and more importantly, the role architecture played in such pogroms. Moreover, it is asked, how are the surviving buildings of the Reich regarded today? Are they still sinister and evil or ordinary buildings within a redefined social and political network? To this end, the case study of the Königsplatz in Munich will be important in demonstrating that even such seemingly ideologically loaded structures are capable of adaptation within the urban environment when governed under a completely different set of values and ideals.

Arising from the proceeding queries is the additional ethical question of whether such buildings can be appreciated for their artistic merit alone.

92 *Aesthetics and politics*

Despite some claims that Nazi architecture simply does not stand up to artistic scrutiny because it demonstrates, as Nerdinger argues, "a massive degree of incompetence and ineptitude",[16] one cannot deny that its procurement was intended to serve the military and genocidal ambitions of Nazi Germany. In light of this, the architectural historian and neo-classicist, Leon Krier, argues that there is no inherent link between the social and political demands of the architecture and the architects themselves. Krier declares: "There is neither authoritarian nor democratic architecture, no more than there are authoritarian or democratic Wienerschnitzel. It is just as childish to read a particular colour or the immanence of a political system into a row of Doric columns as it is to accept a kidney shaped table and tensile structure as the authentic expression of a libertarian and democratic regime. Architecture is not political; it is only an instrument of politics".[17] Such a statement might sit comfortably alongside some of the earlier arguments of this book if one fails to take into account the context and the purpose for which the buildings are designed. Thus with relation to the architecture of the Third Reich, Krier further adds: "The very fact that I have been looking at the buildings and monuments of Albert Speer without the declared ambition of condemning them outright has made me in the eyes of many otherwise sound minds an objective ally of sordid crimes".[18] Nonetheless, Krier seems to ignore the fact that the Nazis' passion for building was related to the criminal capabilities of the regime, and thus provided the Nazis with the means by which to communicate their message and propagate an image of power.[19] Moreover, such architecture was not limited to a symbolic representation of power alone, but also facilitated the workings of the regime to carry out genocide and war, not to mention the use of forced labour camps for the supply of materials such as stone and brick. This does not suggest that Nazi architecture was inherently evil, or that it induced people to conduct themselves in certain ways. Rather, the buildings of the Third Reich were designed for morally repugnant purposes and functioned to serve those ends.

Neo-classicism and National Socialism

It is clear that the buildings constructed by the National Socialists were not intended to be 'ordinary' buildings. Their colossal scale and unified aesthetic make the buildings of the Third Reich some of the most recognisable and studied objects in the world. Over the past few decades, numerous architects and scholars have published books analysing the architecture of Nazi Germany. In the main, these publications have attempted to implicate the architecture as part of the massive propaganda machine that communicated the social and political ideologies of National Socialism.[20] The Nazis were so successful in generating an overwhelming and unified image of the Reich that it is not uncommon to ask whether the buildings played some role in persuading the population to adopt Nazi ideologies. To this end, one cannot flatly deny that the buildings had a role to play. No doubt, they become a component of the discursive formation of Nazism and its ideologies, and furthermore, played a significant role in the facilitation of Nazi atrocities. Nonetheless, it is highly questionable whether the buildings can be attributed with the capacity to inculcate specific beliefs and attitudes amongst the populations as a whole. As Jelavich contends, such a proposition not only "attributes excessive power to the aesthetic sphere, but also exculpates the citizenry from responsibility for accepting Nazi values".[21]

Many of the public and government buildings constructed by the Third Reich are easily identifiable as a result of their adherence to a particular brand of 'stripped back' neo-classical architecture. These buildings are typically out of scale with other surrounding buildings and distinguished by their stone masonry structures. This brand of neo-classicism was intended to link the National Socialist movement with the imperial power of Athens and Rome, and present the Reich as indomitable and all-powerful. However, the Nazis were not the only governing authority to embrace this architectural style. Although coinciding with the rise of modernist architecture, the neo-classical style was widely accepted and adopted by many architectural practitioners at the time. Consider, for example, the US Supreme Court building in Washington DC, designed by architect Cass Gilbert in 1935, who employed neo-classicism as a means of reflecting American democratic ideals.[22] Other prominent neo-classical works at the time include the Shanghai Exhibition Centre in China, which was influenced by Soviet communism. To this end, Ockman explains: "There is a well established linkage between . . . the tradition of classicism and a calculating and cold instrumentality . . . It is precisely this inherent aspect of order in classicism which renders it so potent a political instrument".[23] Perhaps because classical architecture is reliant upon order, symmetry and hierarchy, it more easily lends itself, metaphorically speaking, to the aspirations of a governing body, regardless of its ideological makeup. Nonetheless, the physical qualities of the architecture cannot simply induce similar qualities in a government or group of people. Rather they are brought about through various discourses which construct associations between building form and the aspirations of a group of people.

Similarly, such metaphors are not limited to classicism alone, but may also be equated with other forms of architecture too. Consider the dictatorial regimes of Italy and Russia, which coincided with the rise of Nazism in Germany. While all three shared an obvious desire to address the population through various media such as architecture, art, film, radio, newspapers, rallies and so forth, they all differed in their preferred style and content. Italian fascism, on the one hand, was much more open to modernism, as exemplified by the linearity and minimalism of Giuseppe Terragni's *Casa Del Fascio*. On the other hand, Russian communism tended towards the 'industrial' aesthetic, as exemplified by the Constructivists.[24] Nevertheless, the Third Reich, under the dictatorship of Adolf Hitler, had a preference

94   *Aesthetics and politics*

for classicism and placed a ban on all other forms of art, calling them 'degenerate', 'Bolshevik' and 'Jewish'. To this end, the Propaganda Ministry even assembled a travelling exhibition of unacceptable forms of art in order to 'educate' the people, where audiences were encourage to laugh at the so-called 'degenerate' exhibits on display.

Despite this, the preference for classical architecture did not necessarily fully embody the views of every individual aligned with the Nazi party. Modernist architects like Walter Gropius, Hans Poelzig, Ludwig Mies van der Rohe and others from the Bauhaus demonstrated their support by signing pro-Nazi manifestos and removing Jewish students from the school. Having said this, it is difficult to determine exactly where Mies van der Rohe's allegiances lay, as it seems he was prepared to lend his services to anyone willing to pay regardless of their political views. His design for the Communist monument to the November Revolution in 1926 is a case in point. The fact that Mies had designed one of the most significant monuments to Germany's fallen Communists seemingly did not prevent him from later attempting to acquire work from the National Socialists.[25] Mies van der Rohe submitted proposals for the German Pavilion at the International Exposition in Brussels in 1934 and participated in the Reichbank competition in Berlin, which he won. Speaking of his design, Mies highlights the functionality of the proposed design without necessarily revealing his own personal political allegiances. He claims: "This clear and striking language corresponds with the essence of German work . . . it serves to accommodate the national emblems and the representations of the Reich".[26] Despite Mies' efforts, his winning design was later overruled by Hitler himself because it did not suit the Führer's personal tastes. By 1937, Mies van der Rohe, Walter Gropius and others had left Germany in order to pursue opportunities in the United States. However, as Boyd Whyte points out, many modernist architects continued to design buildings for the Third Reich, in particular factories, which better suited their aesthetic leanings.[27] Yet one might speculate, had Hitler been more accommodating of modernist architecture would those buildings be attributed with the same ability to oppress and indoctrinate as many have claimed of their neo-classical counterparts? In response, one would suggest that they would have to be subject to the same sort of scrutiny. Yet modernist architects like Giuseppe Terragni and Mies van der Rohe have seemingly avoided the same sort of criticism that has been applied to various neo-classicists like Albert Speer and Paul Ludwig Troost.

These examples show that the link between an architectural aesthetic and a particular political ideology is very tenuous indeed. The modernist style simply did not suit Hitler's architectural imagination. For Hitler, modernism represented the failure of Weimer democracy.[28] But the association between neo-classical architecture and National Socialism may have been brought about simply because Hitler preferred classical buildings. For Hitler, neo-classical architecture provided the means to distort history by providing a tangible link between the past and the future of Germany. Hitler was drawn to the classical architecture of the Ringstrasse in Vienna, where he spent much of his young adult life painting these buildings. Richard Evans, in his history of the Third Reich, explains that Hitler had a strong interest in architecture. He writes: "From the very beginning, buildings interested Hitler mainly as a statement of power. He retained this interest throughout his life. But he lacked the application to become an architect".[29] Hitler was often derided for his taste in art and architecture by members of the educated aristocracy. Yet his "appalling taste in art, his ignorance of wine and clumsy table manners", were seen as the reason for his appeal amongst the masses.[30] The wealthy and the educated did not necessarily see eye to eye with the Führer – even Joseph Goebbels was an advocate for modern art – but they all eventually fell into line with Hitler's preferences. Jelavich argues that Goebbels would have opted for the Italian policy because he realised that the flight of Germany's best-known artists and architects in 1933 was a public relations disaster; "he also believed that Germany could benefit from drawing upon the services of the . . . architectural modernists, with their faith in technology. But Hitler was convinced that his own aesthetic preferences, mired as they were in the nineteenth century, were infallible".[31] Many of the prominent modernist architects at the time were far more accomplished and experienced than those who rose to fame under Nazism. Albert Speer, for example, was an unknown, and up until his association with National Socialism had completed very few, and only minor, architectural projects. Similarly, Paul Ludwig Troost, who died in 1934, although more experienced than Speer, did not belong to the leading group of German architects when he was appointed Hitler's chief architect.[32] Nonetheless, Hitler was fully aware that his tastes, rooted in the German working class, were shared by thousands of conventional architects and importantly, the population in general. For this reason neo-classical architecture, for the National Socialists, best represented the people. It became symbolic of a nostalgic past that invoked the legacy of Bismarck and the Kaisers, and provided evidence of a new regime, one capable of restoring Germany's national pride following its defeat in the Second World War and the humiliation of the Treaty of Versailles. Neo-classicism set the stage for what was to come. The propagation of Nazi beliefs such as anti-Semitism, blood and soil, living space, military conquest and so forth were constructed through discursive means. Architecture was thus a component of these discourses to which it provided representative form.

Words in stone

When people are silent, the stones speak. By means of the stone, great epochs speak to the present so that fellow citizens are able to uplift themselves through the beauty of self-made buildings. Proud and self-assured, they should be able to look upon these works erected by their

96   *Aesthetics and politics*

own community . . . The stones have not spoken in vain . . . the fields are German again. Buildings are always erected by people. People are children of their blood, are members of their race. As the blood speaks, so the people build . . . (Heinrich Himmler, 1941)[33]

Hitler believed that architecture defined the collective and embodied the 'spirit' of the *German* community. By design, it was supposed to represent uniformity and strength, and was intended to project the indomitable power of the Reich centuries into the future. Hitler, the self-proclaimed 'supreme master builder', declared in 1938: "Every great era finds the concluding expression of its values in its buildings. When people inwardly experience great times, they also give these times external expression. Their word is then more convincing than the spoken: it is the word in stone".[34] Hitler saw architecture as extrinsically linked to the expression of Nazi values. Yet as argued previously in chapter 2 with respect to Hugo's similar proclamation, architecture is not capable of such a task. Nevertheless, the totalitarian propagation of Nazism and their associated 'discourses' on architecture and power resulted in a connection between certain aesthetic representations and National Socialist values. This is a connection which, even today, is very difficult to put aside.

These discursive regimes constructed specific associations between the words of Nazi ideology and the built forms of architecture. For example, anti-Semitism, which by the late nineteenth century was still very much on the fringes, began to enter the political mainstream when new ways of speaking about Jews entered into everyday vocabulary. Advances made by German medical science in the late nineteenth century brought about a widespread 'medicalisation' of society in which ordinary people adopted hygienic practices such as washing and cleaning.[35] Moreover, it furnished Germans with a whole new vocabulary with which to refer to the Jewish race; these terms included 'disease', 'plague' or 'cancer' on society.[36] In addition, the idea that there existed a 'Jewish spirit' which propelled Jews towards areas of influence, such as law, banking and journalism, reinforced perceptions of a 'plague' and coincided with a view that portrayed Jews as 'greedy' and 'subversive'. This standpoint, common amongst the German working class, enhanced the idea that ordinary citizens were somehow outnumbered and impeded from receiving their entitlement to higher wages, better living standards and so forth. It was believed that the people's 'struggle' would require a united commitment against the 'eternal Jew'. Indeed, Germans became partial to the view that the nation required a saviour. Speaking of the popular beliefs at this time, Evans states: "Germany required the restoration of a hierarchical society led by a 'secret Kaiser' who would one day emerge from the shadows to restore Germany to its former glory".[37] In this way, the colossal architectural forms of the Reich provided evidence of this "restoration". These new buildings, along with the grand motorways, bridges and other infrastructure, not only increased the demand for labour, but provided the physical evidence of Germany's return to power and its triumph over it suppressors.

The discursive formation of architecture and other art forms under the Third Reich played a significant role in aligning the values and attitudes of the people with the aspirations of the Nazi dictatorship. The Nazis managed to adapt and distort popular cultural ideals, like traditional craftsmanship, Germanic history, music and philosophy, to name a few, to accord with their ideologies relating to race and nationalism. This section will further highlight these associations.

Consider the extensive use of natural stone in Nazi structures. Not only did it provide a visual representation of national solidarity, but it also enhanced the socialist ideals of traditional craft techniques. Furthermore, stone provided a link, both racially and visually, between the present and a glorified and nostalgic past. But beyond this, stone buildings projected an image of the future, one that was supposed to last not only thousands, but tens of thousands of years into the future. Hitler reaffirmed this attitude at Nuremburg in 1937: "Never throughout all of German history have greater and nobler buildings been planned, begun, and completed than our own time [. . .]. This is why these buildings are not intended for the year 1940, or for the year 2000, but rather, they should reach out, like cathedrals of our past, into the centuries of the future".[38] To this end, Nazi architects abandoned the modern constructional techniques typical of 1930s technologies because they believed that such buildings would not appropriately dignify and communicate the glory of the Nazi regime to future generations. Albert Speer wrote in his essay *Theory of the Value of Ruins*: "My theory was designed to solve this dilemma. I wanted to give up using modern materials found in metallic and concrete constructions. By respecting certain laws of statics, buildings could be constructed that after thousands of years, would clearly resemble Roman models".[39] Indeed, the use of stone was not seen as the act of a regressive culture, but rather, that of a progressive nation capable of controlling its own destiny. Stone not only linked Germany with the power of the Greek and Roman empires, it projected an image of durability and strength centuries into future.

The emergence of the Third Reich, following the humiliation of defeat in the Great War, provided evidence of Germany's emerging prosperity and 'cultural' ascendancy. This emerging 'culture', although heavily based on a distorted view of history, served the Nazis' vision for the future, one of Aryan dominance and racial purity. According to Herman Glaser, the classical period was an extremely fruitful period in Germany intellectual and 'cultural' life, and so became "flagrantly abused as façades of German culture". Glaser continues: "Elements of German culture, especially classicism, were perverted, distorted and twisted into opposites and yet nominally retained. What remained was lifeless, resentful words

98 *Aesthetics and politics*

deprived of their meaning. Culture became a façade, it was destroyed and replaced by a confused myth".[40] Not only did classical architecture become an essential aesthetic image of Nazism, but equally, notions of traditional Germanic architecture were applied to the domestic context too. Consider the mountain lodges of Hitler's inner circle in Obersalzberg consisting of traditional Alpine timber structures.[41] In addition, military structures, in particular those used by the SS, borrowed elements from medieval fortifications to invoke, in contrast to Hitler's pronounced interest in classical architecture, the Ottoman Empire. Jaskot reveals that this ideological projection influenced the education, military training and institutional identity of SS members as a "new caste of German Knights". Jaskot concludes: "Of course, Himmler's vague and distorted notion of the Germanic past was not the only guiding beacon for SS ideology. But his faith in the relationship between ideological goals and political power, each of which could be expressed and enacted architecturally, defined a key component of SS enterprises in the early war years".[42] In other words, the Nazis managed to select various elements of the past in order to represent the contemporary attitudes and ethos they wanted to assume of the people. In many cases, architecture provided the vehicle by which to achieve this.

Similarly, other forms of art and media were distorted in order to promote certain Germanic myths. For example, the music of Richard Wagner, although capable of being interpreted in multiple ways, was used to cultivate anti-Semitism. Following his death, members of the Wagner family, for one reason or another, did their best to interpret the composer's operas as pitting Nordic heroes against Jewish villains.[43] Even the work of Friedrich Nietzsche, whose writings argued for the emancipation of the individual against the conventional moral restriction of his day, was used to support Nazi views on nation and race. Concepts such as the "will to power" and the "ideal human" came to justify a form of social Darwinism, whereby the strong would triumph over the weak. Taken to the extreme, the distortion of Nietzsche was used to validate controlled breeding according to racial and eugenic criteria.[44]

Taking into account the Nazis' distortion of science, history, race and culture (all of which were brought to accord with specific national goals and values and provided tangible forms in mass rallies, military displays, architecture and so forth), what does one interpret when viewing the architectural works of the Third Reich now that time has distanced us from such events? Do these buildings "reach out" as Hitler intended? How do they now sit within the contemporary context of re-unified Germany? How do, or should, Germans respond to such reminders of a shameful past? And how have these structures been modified or suppressed, in order to dissociate the past from their current function? Architecture as a discursive object is produced within certain historical moments. As such, the passing of time is likely to alter the social and political construction of a building. It therefore becomes prudent to enquire just what do these monuments, created under Nazism, represent today.

The Königsplatz

By way of examining the representative capacity of buildings under a particular discursive regime, and the Nazi-lead distortion of the past, the Königsplatz in Munich provides an interesting example of how meanings may change, but not without some constraints that can be historically located and logically explained. Following the First World War the Bavarian capital city was a key centre of political unrest where certain individuals played a major part in the development of the views of the young Adolf Hitler. Hitler, who arrived in Munich from Austria in 1913, became involved in various political movements, eventually gaining influence and recognition for his oratory talents in the National Socialist German Workers' Party (NSDAP, later abbreviated to Nazi from the German pronunciation of *Nationalsozialistiche*). In 1923 the city staged the failed Hitler-led uprising against the Weimar Republic known as the 'Beer Hall Putsch', in which 16 of Hitler's supporters were killed. Hitler's arrest and subsequent trial gained a national audience and proved a watershed moment in his rise to power in 1933. As a result of Hitler's affection for the city, Munich occupied a central position in Hitler's goal of territorial expansion as the *Hauptstadt der Bewegung* (Capital of the Movement). Writing while imprisoned in what later became his autobiography *Mein Kampf*, he states referring to Munich: "The geo-political significance of a focal centre for a movement cannot be overemphasised. Only the presence of such a place, exerting the magic spell of Mecca or a Rome, can in the long run give the movement a force which is based on inner unity".[45] To this end, Munich, during the dictatorship of the Third Reich, provided a place of symbolic significance because of its associations with Germany's cultural heritage and antiquity and became the central location for what could be best described as the Third Reich's "political religion".[46]

Central to Munich's importance as the Capital of the Movement was the Königsplatz. Having come into existence well before the advent of Nazism it formed a large part of Munich's identity as a city serving to celebrate the cultural legacy of antiquity. For these reasons, Hitler was drawn to the Königsplatz and sought to transform the square into the ideological and architectural centre of the city and an expanded German empire. It was to become the embodiment of Hitler's notion of "community" by creating a gathering point for the population and a place for active participation in rituals underlying state identity and power. The neo-classical square was originally planned to celebrate the ancient cultures of Athens and Rome and incorporated two complimentary structures to the north and west sides of the square, both designed by Leo von Klenze. On the north side was

100 *Aesthetics and politics*

located the Glyptothek, a museum of ancient sculpture constructed between 1816 and 1830, and on the west, the Propylaen, a monumental stone gate constructed between 1843 and 1862 (modelled on the entrance gates to the Athens Acropolis). To the south stands the Neue Staatsgalerie, an exhibition hall built from 1838 to 1845, positioned as the mirror of the Glyptothek. Klenze's design for the Königsplatz deliberately left the east side vacant in order to open the square towards the centre of Munich. The buildings were separated by lush lawns bisected by a main boulevard on the east/west axis. The square became known as one of Munich's most attractive sites and acquired cultural significance as the location for numerous ceremonial parades and political demonstrations. In addition, the buildings are world renowned for their display of ancient Greek artefacts and statues, in particular the Aegina room of the Glyptothek containing the pedimental sculptures from the temple of Aphaia at Aegina.[47] Indeed, the Königsplatz provided a readily useful and amendable site, materially and conceptually, for Nazi ceremony and spectacle. Moreover, the site more easily lent itself to the Nazis' distortion of history and the association between race and nation.

Hitler had already conceived of the potential for the Königsplatz to be a backdrop for political demonstrations and military rallies, having developed plans for remodelling the site while in prison and then in collaboration with architect Paul Ludwig Troost in 1931. Following Hitler's ascent to power, the plans were put into effect. Hitler attempted to draw upon the cultural significance of the site and weave the public's perception of the place into the Nazi ethos by building into the site additional and complementary monuments that were supposed to impress upon the public the majesty of Nazism. The Königsplatz was dramatically overhauled, all vegetation was removed and the grounds were resurfaced in 22,000m² of granite slabs. Traffic was diverted around the square so that each building became integrated into the whole of the space. Hitler focussed on enhancing the site's monumentality by constructing at the east end two new administration buildings, the Führerbau (which housed Hitler's office and the offices of his closest staff) and the NSDAP party headquarters. These two buildings are externally identical but stand out from the rest of the square because of their size and dimensions. Significantly, the Führerbau was the site of the Munich Accord meetings in 1938 in which the French and English governments agreed to Hitler's demands that the Sudetenland in Czechoslovakia should be ceded to Germany. The addition of these Nazi administrative buildings attempted to equate the history of the square with the National Socialist government, thus lending the Nazis a greater sense of grandeur and authority, whereby the discursive formation of the past seamlessly blended into the Nazi ethos of the present.

In addition, Troost located two 'Temples of Honour' (*Ehrentempel*), built between the Führerbau and NSDAP headquarters. Again these temples served to enhance the cultural and political significance of the site. The temples (demolished after the war as subsequently explained), again identical, consisted of 20 rectilinear fluted marble columns of the Doric order on a three stepped podium. The columns supported a heavy architrave with the roof open to the sky. The temples were treated with reverent sacredness, with the bodies of the 16 'martyrs' killed in the 'Beer Hall Putsch' displayed in sarcophagi recessed in a central well. On each sarcophagus was inscribed the words '*Der letze Appell*' (the last roll call), and "here", the dead's imagined response. Each year on the anniversary of the Putsch large crowds marched the route from the Beer Hall to the Königsplatz where the names of the dead were called; after each name the crowd shouted "here".[48] As one observer commented: "Something new had been created . . . Here the organised masses would gather to swear allegiance to the new order. The whole ensemble was ideology become stone".[49] The Nazi discursive formation of military conquest, and the memorialisation of those who gave their life for the nation, was transposed onto the structures of the Königsplatz. Once again, the past became distorted and confused, whereby moments significant to the cult of Nazism were blended into the history of the German nation through the association of the word and the stone monument.

The Königsplatz served a significant ideological and political function for the Nazis, who referred to the site as the new 'Acropolis Germainiae'. The site, having already contained cultural significance prior to Nazism, became interwoven into the story of National Socialism and the struggle for reformation, and associated the national body with that of its ancient traditions. Joseph Goebbels wrote in his diary with relation to the

Figure 4.1 'Ehrentempel' and 'Führerbau' (background) on the Königsplatz in Munich, circa 1937.
Willi Ude, Wikimedia Commons.

102   *Aesthetics and politics*

Königsplatz: "Here the Führer wrote his will in stone".[50] Albert Speer, with the Nazis facing defeat, drew upon the architecture of the Königsplatz for inspiration, writing in 1944: "Our faith in victory is unshaken. The buildings of Paul Ludwig Troost, the first, strong stone symbol of the movement, are part of this. It is they, as much as anything that strengthen our belief in victory and fortify our will to attain that victory".[51] More than merely representative, however, or simply 'written in stone' as material ideology, the temples, their architecture and sculptural scheme, figured in the broader formation and enactment of Nazism. In the Königsplatz, the military, government, culture and architecture were presented as "complementary components", as Jaskot points out, "in the destiny of the German People".[52] The Königsplatz presented itself as the embodiment of Nazi ideology, it emerged from a discursive field that associated architectural grandeur with German culture, racial superiority and military might. The Königsplatz provided, as Hirst calls it, "a setting for politics as theatre",[53] in other words, the visual display of German values embodied by the State.

Not surprisingly, the Königsplatz, following the defeat of the Nazis in 1945, became a mixed record of the past, perhaps provocative in ways its previous authors had not envisioned. While the original buildings suffered extensive damage during the war, the Nazi buildings somehow remained intact. Ostensibly, the architectural legacy of the Third Reich provided a highly visible reminder of an era that most citizens now preferred to forget; thus, in the months immediately following the war the suppression of any Nazi association with the city became urgent.

'Denazification'

In the period immediately following the defeat of the Nazis, German citizens were faced with the challenge of suppressing or removing altogether the meanings that had become associated with numerous public buildings during the Reich. However, the effort to purge the Königsplatz of its Nazi past proved highly problematic. In reality, such associations could not be so easily removed from the place while the atrocities of the Third Reich and the recovery from the war preoccupied people's minds. Local residents were said to be haunted by the sound of thousands of voices shouting '*Here*' supposedly resonating from the square.[54] As a consequence of the German defeat, the city became burdened by such literal reminders of a shameful past (for some) or failed aspirations (for others), whereby local residents called for the immediate removal of such buildings from the city and in particular from the Königsplatz.

Nonetheless, demolition was not necessarily feasible, for these buildings were useful structures and easily adapted to suit other functional requirements. The Americans had already taken possession of the Fuhrebau and replaced the Nazi symbols on the façade with that of the American eagle. (They also held military parades in the Königsplatz, in an obvious attempt to display the authority of the new power following the defeat of the Nazis.) Later the buildings were given to the Bavarian government and were eventually used for cultural functions. The local authorities, while desiring to erase such tangible evidence of the past, weighed the economic cost of demolition and rebuilding against the possibility of the continued and profitable use of the buildings, albeit in modified form. In very few cases were Nazi-era buildings demolished. In the most part, attempts were made to 'normalise' the buildings and integrate their architecture into the community by urban camouflage and by removing all Nazi insignia and symbols from the façades.

For the Königsplatz, the attempted 'denazification' occurred on various levels; the original buildings (constructed during the 1800s) damaged during the war were repaired and reopened according to their previous purpose as museums to antiquity. The granite was removed from the square and replaced by lawn and gardens, with the boulevard again intersecting the square. In addition, a new road was constructed perpendicular to the boulevard literally isolating the Nazi buildings from the Königsplatz by, in effect, removing their visual connection with the square. Slowly, the existing buildings began to acquire their previous association by functioning as originally intended as a museum and gallery.[55]

Figure 4.2 The Führerbau, view from the intersecting roads of the Königsplatz with the remains of one of the Ehrentempels in the foreground, 2007.
Daniel Grinceri.

104   *Aesthetics and politics*

However, what of the fate of new buildings constructed by the Nazis? Somehow they remained intact after the war, and their very presence evoked a complex set of emotions, perhaps foremost among them shame and guilt. Pointedly, the architectural critic Hans Eckstein remarked: "It is feared that the pretentious monumental buildings of Troost will be a heavy burden on the Munich cityscape for a long time, if not forever".[56] The Ehrentempel proved the most significant reminder of the horror of Nazism. The sarcophagi of the putschists were immediately removed and the bodies buried in unmarked graves, while the steel coffins were melted down and used in the city's reconstruction. Following this, numerous conflicting proposals were put forward with regards to how to deal best with the stone structures, which in effect served only to prolong the outcome and existence of the temples. As Rosenfeld recounts, proposals coming from these debates ranged from "physically altering the structures and giving them new functions . . . to a complete break from the past by order of demolition".[57] Various authorities argued that the memory of the Reich would be best suppressed by altering the building's function. One particular initiative proposed transforming the Ehrentempels into art galleries, suggesting: "The radical elimination of the temples would awaken memories of brutal Nazi methods that one wants to avoid, while the preservation of a few buildings given new function would be more effective at preventing the immortalisation of Nazism".[58] The argument here hinged on the idea that an empty space, where the temples stood, would invoke memories of the past far more than their integration. However, some scepticism remained with respect to the proponents' motivations, as they seemed to advocate their retention for the sole purpose of transforming the buildings to fulfil their own commercial ends. As such, the public continued to demand the complete elimination of the Ehrentempel, as expressed by the journalist Bernhard Pollak: "The curse that weighs upon us will only be removed once the last cues of Nazi evil in our public life and disposition are covered up".[59] Following more than a year of debate, the demands of the public won out, and in January 1947 works were carried out to demolish the two temples. However, complications arising during the demolition process, and concerns for safety and expense, resulted in the retention of the temples' two-meter high podium and underground bomb shelter. Instead of the desired complete 'denazification' of the Königsplatz, traces of an architecture from the Nazi period remained. In the ensuing months, all the rubble was removed and the sunken interiors where the sarcophagi had been located were in-filled with earth. The absence of a suitable proposal for utilising the podium resulted in the erection of a timber fence to obscure the view of the temples' remnants from the public. The fence remained in place, hiding the Ehrentempel for more than a decade. However, as the fence began to deteriorate and gaps appeared in the wall, attention was once again drawn to its unwanted presence. Further architectural competitions were held with few suitable outcomes. Finally, the absence of an appropriate proposal resulted in the eventual acceptance of the status quo and the temples' podiums remained untouched. Today, the remnants still remain, although covered by thick vegetation and consequently somewhat disguised from the unassuming observer. Nevertheless, the site is now memorialised by a plaque and a brief description of the buildings that once stood there, acting as an obvious reminder of the past.

The fate of the other two buildings constructed by the Nazis on the Königsplatz, the Führerbau and the NSDAP headquarters, were the focus of significantly less debate probably because they were less symbolically charged to begin with. While the public desired a complete purge of Nazism from the Königsplatz the buildings themselves proved too useful to government officials to be demolished. Nonetheless, the buildings underwent the process of 'normalisation', involving the removal of all Nazi insignia and symbology. Today the Führerbau is home to the local University's School of Music, and the NSDAP headquarters currently functions as a museum. Interestingly, these very same buildings today invoke a completely different response from that during the Nazi regime, and contain little reference to their Nazi past. However, some astute observers might notice the presence of patched hooks for supporting the Nazi eagle and swastika on the front façade over the balconies.

Today, a visitor without any prior knowledge of the Nazi acquisition, appropriation and redesign of the Königsplatz, is highly unlikely to recognise its aesthetic features as essentially Nazi. Regardless of Hitler's intentions, the neo-classical aesthetic does not inherently signify the supposed glory of the Third Reich. With the passing of time these buildings bear little obvious association with their Nazi past, having been consumed into the Munich cityscape. However, it must be acknowledged that the Ehrentempel remained associated with the Nazi regime for the short time that they existed following the war, for the buildings were unable to acquire new functions and meanings while the media continued to cover the debate relating to the proposals for their renovation or demolition. Today the Königsplatz serves a memorial function to those who died during the 12-year reign of National Socialism. The recent opening of a Documentation Centre adjacent to the Führerbau to commemorate the seventieth anniversary of Munich's liberation from the Nazis illustrates the city's ongoing attempts to reconcile the past. To explain the long delay between the end of National Socialism and the construction of the Documentation Centre, the centre's director Winfried Nerdinger said: "In general, it can be said that Munich has carried a heavy guilt, more so than other cities in Germany because it was more burdened with history than any other city. It all began here".[60] While the Königsplatz continues to be integrated into normal Munich life, the associations pertaining to the square, with relation to its Nazi past, may never entirely dissipate as a result of the square's new memorial function and people's ongoing fascination with associated Second World War sites. Nonetheless, it is evident that even buildings riddled with associative meanings can acquire alternative meanings and come to represent completely divergent ideals by way

106 *Aesthetics and politics*

of their normalisation into the fabric of the urban environment, and most importantly, people's changing perception of built form.

Culpability

While it might have been over presumptuous to assume that certain buildings will "reach out" and propagate the "spirit" of National Socialism thousands of years into the future, what should never be denied is the sinister purposes for which these buildings were made to function. During the reign of the Third Reich an unprecedented number of new buildings were planned and constructed as part of Hitler's strategy for a renewed Germany. But what drove the agenda for new construction? In his examination of the building boom under the Nazis, Jochen Thies highlights that new building plans were generated not only from within the National Socialist organisation, but also from local city and town councils that lobbied Berlin to have their own plans approved for state support. He highlights that architects, anxious not to be passed over by the boom, began to compete with each other for the numerous available projects. In effect, this rapid growth in building construction placed an increasing demand on the supply of materials and labour with which the current market could no longer keep pace. Quarries and brickworks were suddenly in high demand and unable to supply the required quantities of materials. The Nazis therefore established the German Earth and Stone Works (DEST), headed by the SS, to enable the production of building materials. As a consequence, new concentration camps were established at stone outcrops and at disused quarries where forced labour was used to satisfy work shortages. Jaskot explains: "While the SS established Flossenburg like other camps to punish political and ideological enemies of the state, it also adapted the process of punishment to the massive demand for stone in the monumental building economy. Thousands of prisoners lost their lives in the forced-labour quarries, realising the political function of the camp".[61] The exploitation of forced labour was not only driven by the massive bureaucratic architectural offices of Speer and Giesler, but also buildings by numerous other lesser-known architects. All architects working in the service of the Third Reich served to increase the demand for stone and by extension the SS controlled labour camps. Thies concludes: "It is clear that all these architects and engineers, local politicians, and administrative and party officials, technical draughtsmen, stone masons and skilled workers, sculptors and painters, formed a group many thousand strong; they should now face a wide range of questions which hitherto Speer alone has had to answer. And even he is only one among a collection of star architects, all of whom, have hitherto remained silent".[62] Indeed, the Auschwitz survivor Primo Levi goes so far as to state that anyone who sought to gain in one way or another and refused to acknowledge the repercussions of their labour should be condemned.[63] Thousands of architects benefitted from the privileged status awarded to the profession generally by the Führer. As a result, they, along with others, were complicit in the propagation of National Socialism amongst the German people, which resulted in the exploitation of slave labour, and amongst other things, war and the murder of millions of people.

With this in mind, one might ask; against what performative standard should not only the numerous members of the Nazi party, SS guards and soldiers, but also the others, including architects, be measured? For it is clear that not only were Hitler's most favoured and decorated architects, like Albert Speer, Hermann Giesler and Paul Ludwig Troost, complicit in the facilitation of the Nazi regime, but so too was every architect, draughtsperson and engineer who participated in the procurement of Nazi buildings. The architect as a professional is not immune to basic moral principles and standards of decency, even when they must risk a great deal. Indeed, the participation of architects cannot be simply justified, as Krier claims, as an aesthetic interest in neo-classical architecture to which Nazism provided the opportunity for its practice.[64] Nor can one accept the argument, as outlined by Hochman, that these architects were simply following the Führer's orders.[65] Rather, architects played a key role in the propagation of National Socialism, to which they provided the knowledge to bring about the facilitation of certain objectives.

Albert Speer freely admitted, following his trial at Nuremburg, that his architecture deliberately attempted to impose the political values of the state onto the people. In retrospect, Speer commented with relation to his body of work under Adolf Hitler: "Beyond the representation of political might, the modern viewer can recognise a psychological intention in the buildings and projects of the Third Reich, an attempt to achieve effects through architectural means . . . I believed in the claim to absolute domination and my architecture represented an intimidating display of power".[66] To what extent Speer's opinions reflect those of all architects working for the Third Reich is difficult to say. Needless to say, architecture under National Socialism attempted to aestheticise Nazi ideologies by creating an association between the characteristics of the architecture and that of the government. Indeed, this architecture participated in the discursive formation of race, culture and history which permitted individuals to behave in ways that would not have been tolerated by normal standards. Nonetheless, such atrocities were not brought about as a consequence of the architecture alone, but rather, the discursive association between the object and its meaning. This, as the example of the Königsplatz demonstrates, is unfixed and capable of adaption to new and diverse meanings.

For this reason, the architecture of the Reich was not inherently 'evil', nor did it induce people to commit 'evil', but rather it formed a component of discourse on race and culture which made what would normally be considered morally repugnant seem just. During the Nuremburg Trial, Speer argued that his interest in National Socialism was solely architectural and that he cared little for its core beliefs and ideologies.[67] Speer was at

108 *Aesthetics and politics*

pains to qualify his position when appointed Minister for Armaments and Munitions in 1942. He stated: "I am an architect".[68] By depicting himself as an artist, who was just following orders, Speer succeeded in focusing his trial at Nuremberg solely on his managerial skills as an architect in order to make the distinction between his architecture and other political concerns. To this end, Speer refused to acknowledge the political and social implications of his work, preferring only to recognise its artistic value instead. Similarly, Mies van der Rohe, whose architectural career was stifled under Nazism, protested at the closure of the Bauhaus that modern architecture was entirely 'un-political'. By contrast, Richard Evans declares: "But art was anything but un-political in Germany at this time, for the radical modernist movements of the Weimer years, from Dadaism to the Bauhaus itself, had propagated the view that art was a means of transforming the world".[69] The denial of any political interest attempts to absolve the architect from the ethical responsibilities for their work. As Mary Devereaux points out, in her investigation of Leni Reifenstahl's Nazi propaganda film *Triumph of the Will*, the standard solution to questions of ethical responsibility is to look at the work, from an "aesthetic distance". She continues: "The aesthetic distance allows us to set aside the practical concerns of everyday life, including questions of the work's origins, its moral effects, and so on, and concentrate exclusively on the work of art itself".[70] Devereaux explains that when one assumes the posture of aesthetic distance we deny the work's historical realities; in effect, disconnecting the intended message from the means used to convey it. Architects like Troost, Speer, Mies van der Rohe and no doubt many others, regardless of their stylistic preferences, were keen to provide Germany with an aestheticised image of National Socialism. To this end, the artistic qualities of the work stand secondary to the purpose for which the architecture was intended, being the attempted subjectification of individuals to certain ways of thinking and behaving. Indeed, Speer tirelessly went about performing his 'duty' because he was driven by the desire to elevate himself above others. His successful articulation of Hitler's architectural ambitions provided him with the means to achieve this. Moreover, his refusal to acknowledge the repercussions of his work paved the way for his rise to the top echelons of the Nazi administration.

Likewise, Eichmann, who also refused to acknowledge the products of his labour, was desirous to rise through the ranks of the SS. To this end Arendt reveals: "Based on the Führer's order; whatever he did (Eichmann), he did, as far as he could see, as a law abiding citizen".[71] During his trial in Jerusalem Eichmann pleaded his innocence, stating: "With the killing of the Jews I had nothing to do. I never killed a Jew, or a non-Jew – I never killed any human being".[72] Yet such a pronouncement does not absolve Eichmann of their death, for no doubt his facilitation of Nazi orders, as one who organised the mass transportation of Jews from the ghettos to the extermination camps, resulted in the death of many millions of individuals. Indeed, Eichmann and Speer both claimed to be doing their duty. They may not have murdered with their own hands or witnessed such events with their own eyes, but they did provide a form of endorsement of the Nazis' grotesque political aims by devising a means for its performance.

More than 70 years since the fall of Nazism many of the buildings constructed during this era remain. But these buildings have been adapted to accommodate functions other than those originally intended. They reveal little to nothing about the atrocious political purposes for which they once served. Despite this, those architects who participated in the design of such buildings, intending to serve National Socialism through the provision of their services, must be held accountable for their contribution to the discursive construct of Nazi ideologies. To this effect, the conviction of Aryan superiority, the perceived threat imposed by the Jews, the belief in eugenic planning and racial hygiene, military conquest and the restoration of a nostalgic past were not brought about by a single event – being the appointment of Adolf Hitler to the Reich Chancellor. Rather, they belonged to wider and deep rooted sentiments that had been circulating amongst citizens since the last quarter of the nineteenth century.[73] Architects effectively gave representative form to such discursive regimes, thus further perpetuating Nazi ideologies throughout 'normal' German society. Indeed, architecture not only contributed towards the further propagation of particular discourses relating to race, culture, history, power and so forth, but also, as the next chapter will demonstrate, provided means for defining the population through the inclusion and exclusion of certain individuals from an imagined ideal called nation.

Notes

1 William Shirer, *The Rise and Fall of the Third Reich* (New York: Touchstone, 1959), 1,080. Shirer is typical of the *Sonderweg* thesis, which proposes that the Holocaust was the culmination of a 'special path' of German historical development, from Luther to Hitler.
2 Karl Dietrich Bracher, *The German Dictatorship* (London: Penguin Books, 1991).
3 Ian Kershaw, *Hitler* (New York: W.W. Norton Company Inc. 1998).
4 Refer to Richard Evans, *The Third Reich in Power* (London: Penguin Publishing, 2005), 114, 459, and Richard Evans, *The Third Reich at War* (London: Penguin Publishing, 2008), 177.
5 Refer to Daniel Goldhagen, *Hitler's Willing Executioners* (New York: Alfred A. Knopf, 2002), and Christopher Browning, *The Origins of the Final Solution* (London: Arrow Books, 2005).
6 Goldhagen (2002), 9.
7 Peter Adam, *The Art of the Third Reich* (New York: Harry N Abrams, 1992), 305. Quoted in Paul Betts "The New Fascination with Fascism; The Case of Nazi Modernism", *Journal of Contemporary History*, Vol. 37, No. 4 (2002), 548.
8 Adam (1992), 9.
9 *Ibid.*, 10.
10 Hannah Arendt, *Eichmann in Jerusalem* (London: Penguin Books, 1977), xii.
11 Refer to "Saddam Hussein Arrested in Iraq", BBC News, 14 December (2003).
12 Arendt (1977), xiv.

110 *Aesthetics and politics*

13 *Ibid.*, xiii.
14 Adolf Eichmann is responsible for sending an estimated 430,000 Hungarians to their deaths in the gas chambers.
15 Arendt (1977), xiii.
16 Winfried Nerdinger, *A Hierarchy of Styles: National Socialist Architecture between Neoclassicism and Regionalism* (Munich: 1993), 324.
17 Leon Krier, "Vorwarts, Kameraden, Wir Mussen Zuruck", *Oppositions*, No. 24 (1981), 37.
18 Leon Krier, *Albert Speer Architecture 1932 – 1942* (Bruxelles: Archives d'Architecture Moderne, 1985), 217.
19 Refer to Paul Jaskot, *The Architecture of Oppression* (London: Routledge, 2000), 67.
20 Refer to Peter Adam, *The Art of the Third Reich* (New York: Harry N. Abrams, 1992), 38. Ian Boyd Whyte, *Art and Power: Europe under the Dictators* (London: Thames & Hudson, 1995). Kim Dovey, *Framing Places: Mediating Power in Built Form* (London: Routledge, 1999), 55–70. Stephen Helmer, *Hitler's Berlin: The Speer Plans for Reshaping the Central City* (Ann Arbor: UMI Research Press, 1980). Paul Jaskot, *The Architecture of Oppression* (London: Routledge, 2000). Steven Lehrer, *The Reich Chancellery and Führerbunker Complex: An Illustrated History of the Seat of the Nazi Regime* (Jefferson, North Carolina: McFarland, 2006). Jonathon Petropoulos, *Art as Politics in the Third Reich* (Chapel Hill: University of North Carolina Press, 1996). Peter Hans Rasp, *Eine Stadt für tausend Jahre: München—Bauten und Projekte für die Haupstadt der Bewegung* (Munich: Süddeutscher Verlag, 1981). Gavriel Rosenfeld, *Munich and Memory: Architecture, Monuments, and the Legacy of the Third Reich* (Los Angeles: University of California Press, 2000). Alex Scobie, *Hitler's State Architecture: The Impact of Classical Antiquity* (University Park: The Pennsylvania State University Press, 1990). Albert Speer, *Architecture, 1932–1942* ed. Leon Krier (Brussels: Archives d'Architecture Moderne, 1985). Deyan Sudjic, *The Edifice Complex: How the Rich and Powerful Shape the World* (London: Penguin Books, Allen Lane, 2005), 87–114. Robert Taylor, *The Word in Stone: The Role of Architecture in the National Socialist Ideology* (Los Angeles: University of California Press, 1974).
21 Peter Jelavich, "National Socialism, Art and Power in the 1930s", *Past and Present*, No. 164 (Aug. 1999), 245.
22 Refer to Sharon Irish, *Cass Gilbert, Architect* (New York: The Monacelli Press, 1999).
23 J. Ockman, "The Most Interesting Form of Lie", *Oppositions*, No. 24 (1981), 38–47.
24 Consider the 1934 Narkomtiazhprom (NKTP) architectural competition for the People's Commissariat of Heavy Industry to be constructed Red Square Moscow, which included designs by such notable constructivist architects as Ivan Leonidov, Konstantin Melnikov, Vesnin Brothers and Ivan Fomin.
25 Refer to Terence Riley and Barry Bergdoll, *Mies in Berlin* (New York: Museum of Modern Art, 2002), 63–64, 218.
26 Quoted in Elaine Hochman, *Architects of Fortune; Mies van der Rohe and the Third Reich* (New York: Weidenfeld and Nicolson, 1989), 226.
27 Boyd Whyte, *Art and Power; Europe under the Dictators* (London: Thames & Hudson, 1995), 266.
28 Refer to Jelavich (1999), 257.
29 Richard Evans, *The Coming of the Third Reich* (London: Penguin Books, 2003), 163.
30 *Ibid.*, 187.
31 Jelavich (1999), 257.

32 Although Albert Speer is the most well known of the Nazi architects, Paul Troost was extremely influential in the development of Adolf Hitler's architectural tastes. Speer in his memoirs speaking of Hitler's relationship with Troost, states: "His relationship to Troost was somewhat of a pupil to his teacher . . . Hitler, who felt himself to be an architect, respected the superiority of the professional in the field. He would never have done that in politics . . . One could only assent; it is ghastly to think what his (Hitler's) architectural taste would have been like without Troost's influence" (40–41). He further writes:

> Paul Ludwig Troost was a Westphalian, extremely tall and spare, with a close shaven head. Restrained in conversation, eschewing gestures, he belonged to a group of architects such as Peter Behrens, Joseph Olbrich, Bruno Paul and Walter Gropius who before 1914 led a reaction against the highly ornamented Jugendstil and advocated a lean approach, almost devoid of ornament, and a Spartan traditionalism with which they combined elements of modernity. Troost had occasionally won prizes in competitions, but before 1933 he was never able to advance into the leading group of German architects. There was no 'Führer's style' for all that the party press expatiated on this subject. What was branded as the official architecture of the Reich was only neoclassicism transmitted by Troost; it was multiplied, altered, exaggerated, and sometimes distorted to the point of ludicrousness . . . . (Albert Speer, *Inside the Third Reich Memoirs*, New York: Simon & Schuster Paperbacks, 1970, 42)

In an essay on the Fuhrer's building ambitions in 1936, Speer further remarks:

> At the proper time, fate introduced him [Hitler] to Paul Ludwig Troost, with whom a close friendship soon developed. Professor Troost had an architectural impact on him similar to the influence Dietrich Eckart had on his political thinking. . . For years he [Hitler] visited Professor Troost in his free time. There, free from his political duties, he was able to submerge himself fully in the plans. The Führer was interested not only in the general plans, but also in every detail, every material used, and much was improved as the result of his suggestions. The Führer has often said that these hours of common planning were his happiest hours and gave him the deepest satisfaction. They gave him new strength for his other plans. Here he had the chance to devote himself to his buildings in the few free hours that his political duties left him. In the years before the takeover, Hitler discussed the buildings he planned to build with Troost. During the winter of 1931/32, they discussed the future work on Munich's Königsplatz, resulting in many beautiful proposals. Before the takeover of power, the final layout of the square had been decided. Until his death, Paul Ludwig Troost was the Führer's irreplaceable architect. Troost understood how to give his ideas the proper architectural form. In his major speech at the cultural session of the at the 1935 Reich Party Rally, the Führer gave Professor Troost the highest praise a contemporary architect could receive:

> We should be filled with pride that the greatest German architect since Schinkel has built his first and unfortunately only monuments for the new Reich and for Germany. They will stand as stone memorials of a noble and truly Germanic architecture. (Albert Speer, "Die Bauten des Führers", *Adolf Hitler. Bilder aus dem Leben des Führers*, Hamburg: Cigaretten/Bilderdienst Hamburg/Bahrenfeld, 1936, 72–77)

112   *Aesthetics and politics*

33 Heinrich Himmler, "Deutsche Burgen im Osten", *Das Schwarze Korps* Vol. 4 Jan. (1941), 4. Quoted in Jaskot (2000), 114.

34 Quoted in Evans (2005), 181.

35 *Ibid.*, 37.

36 Refer to Robert Proctor, *Racial Hygiene; Medicine Under the Nazis* (Cambridge: Harvard University Press, 1988), 290.

37 *Ibid.* 32.

38 Quoted in *Fascination and Terror*, Exhibition catalogue of the Documentation Centre, Nazi Party Rally Grounds Nuremberg (Nurnberg, Dokumentationszentrum Reichsparteitagsgelande, 2006), 47.

39 Quoted in Paul Virilio, *Bunker Archaeology* (New York: Princeton Architectural Press, 1994), 56.

40 Herman Glaser, *The Cultural Roots of National Socialism* (London: Redwood Burn Limited, 1978), 9.

41 Refer to Geoff Walden, *The Third Reich in Ruins*, Available at http://www.third reichruins.com/bgaden.htm (Accessed March 2007).

42 Jaskot (2000), 115.

43 Refer to Evans (2005), 33.

44 *Ibid.*, 39.

45 Adolf Hitler, *Mein Kampf* (Munich: Zentralverlag der NSDAP, 1937), 347.

46 Gavriel Rosenfeld, *Munich and Memory: Architecture, Monuments and the Legacy of The Third Reich* (Los Angeles: University of California Press, 2000), 85.

47 Refer to William Diebold, "The Politics of Derestoration: The Aegina Pediments and the German Confrontation with the Past", *Art Journal*, Vol. 54, No. 2 (1995), 60–66.

48 Refer to Jay Baird, *To Die for Germany: Heroes in the Nazi Pantheon* (Bloomington: Indiana University Press, 1990), 41–72.

49 Evans (2005), 182.

50 Quoted in Klaus Backes, *Hitler und die bildenden Kunst* (Cologne: Dumont, 1988), 152.

51 Albert Speer, "Paul Ludwig Troost", *Die Baukunst: Kunst im Dritten Reich 8* (1944), 3.

52 Jaskot (2000), 114.

53 Paul Hirst, *Space and Power; Politics, War and Architecture* (Malden: Polity, 2005), 215.

54 Refer to Winfried Nerdinger, *Bauen im Nationalsozialismus* (Munich: Klinhardt und Biermann, 1993), 9.

55 Rosenfeld (2000), 87–88.

56 Hans Eckstein, "Zur Neugestaltung des Münchner Königsplatz", *SZ*, 25 January (1947), 5.

57 Rosenfeld (2000), 88.

58 *Ibid.*

59 Bernhard Pollack, "Nazismus auf Abbruch" *SZ*, 16 November (1946), 4.

60 Quoted in "Nazi Documentation Centre Opens in Munich", *Deutsche Welle*, 27 February (2015), Available at http://www.dw.de/nazi-documentation-center-opens-in-munich/a-18285359 (Accessed April 2015).

61 Jaskot (2000), 1.

62 Jochen Thies, "Hitler's European Building Programme", *Journal of Contemporary History*, Vol. 13, No. 3. (1978), 428.

63 Refer to Primo Levi, *The Drowned and the Saved* (London: Abucus, 1986), 5.

64 Refer to Krier (1985), 217.

65 Refer to Hochman (1989), 738–739.

66 Quoted in Krier (1985).
67 Albert Speer, *Inside the Third Reich* (Ney York: Simon & Schuster Paperbacks, 1970), 507.
68 F.C. DeCoste and Bernard Schwartz, *The Holocaust's Ghost: Writing on Art, Politics, Law and Education* (Alberta: University of Alberta Press, 2000), 161–162.
69 Evans (2003), 416.
70 Mary Devereaux, "Beauty and Evil: The Case of Leni Riefenstahl's Triumph of the Will", *Aesthetics and Ethics* ed. Jerrold Levison (Cambridge: Cambridge University Press, 1988), 242.
71 Arendt (1977), 135.
72 *Ibid.*, 22.
73 Refer to Evans (2003), 450.

5 The camp and the resort

Exclusion and inclusion associated with 'bare life'

This chapter is concerned with the methods by which the biopolitics of space produced the racial inclusion and exclusion of people under the Third Reich, and the extent to which architecture might contribute to and bear witness to this process. In so doing, it explores the policies that produced the 'power over life' and the 'right to kill' – both notions associated with the theory of the biopolitical – and their subsequent architectural manifestation in the 'resort' at Prora on the island of Rugen in the Baltic Sea (1936–1939) and the 'camp' at Auschwitz (1939–1945). This chapter examines how architectural aesthetics are implicated in the horror of the Auschwitz death camp and the supposed 'joy' purported to be obtained by visitors to the Prora resort. It prescribes the term 'aesthetic' to be more appropriately applied to the exploitation and self-justification of a certain biopolitics that created the need for such buildings, rather than to the physical architectural structures that constituted the camp and the resort. Both the camp and the resort reveal the space in between the politics of production and that of the disposability of life, a space marked by the marginalisation of people and the constitution of an outside and inside in relation to the social body or 'body politic'. As such, the camp and the resort are remnants of institutional spaces that demonstrate, in the extreme, that the inclusion of individuals into a political community is only made possible by the exclusion of 'others'. Without Prora, it is impossible to understand how Auschwitz happened, in the sense that both were instituted to produce similar outcomes, being the normalisation of racial characteristics that defined the national community.

This chapter is important to the overall concerns of this study because it highlights the manner in which space and architecture become appropriated to produce particular outcomes. Building upon the discussion of the previous chapter with relation to the Nazi aestheticisation of specific ideals like race, culture and history, this chapter seeks to explore further the various ways in which architecture may come to represent the values and beliefs of the national body. It is concerned with the processes by which individuals are made subject to particular discursive practices

The camp and the resort   115

which define identities and regulate conduct, and how architecture might be implicated in such a practice.

The zone of indistinction

Auschwitz survivor Primo Levi would never have considered himself a writer by natural inclination, but undertook the task as a matter of responsibility in order to bear witness, by proxy, on behalf of "the drowned, the submerged and the annihilated". Racked with shame and tormented by guilt for having survived Auschwitz, Levi eventually committed suicide as a final comment on his 'right to death' and assertion of the limits of the National Socialists' 'power over life'. He writes: "I was waiting to file past the 'commission' that at one glance would decide whether I should immediately go into the gas chamber or was instead strong enough to go on working. For one instant I felt the need for help and asylum; then, despite my anguish, equanimity prevailed . . . I know that otherwise were I to survive, I would have to be ashamed of it".[1] Levi proclaimed that as the true witnesses – the victims – can no longer speak, the survivors must speak in their stead, in that they saw the events at close hand but did not die. Thus, their fate is to testify to life. With this responsibility in mind, Levi tells the story of a three-year-old boy from the camp, described as a "nobody, a child of death, a child of Auschwitz", who could not speak, possessed no name (except for Hurbinek, which had been given to him by the internees), and was paralysed from the waist down. Levi recalls lying awake at nights, listening and attempting to decipher the repetitious moans that emanated from Hurbinek's corner of the barracks. He recounts: "No, it was certainly not a message, it was not a revelation; perhaps it was his name, if it had ever fallen to his lot to be given a name, perhaps it meant 'to eat', or 'bread' . . . Hurbinek, who was three years old and perhaps had been born in Auschwitz and had never seen a tree; Hurbinek, who fought like a man, to the last breath, to gain entry into the world of men, from which a bestial power has excluded him; Hurbinek, the nameless, whose tiny forearm – even his – bore the tattoo of Auschwitz died in the first days of March 1945, free but not redeemed. Nothing remains of him; he bears witness through these words of mine".[2] As for Levi's own survival, it provides a voice for those who cannot speak, bearing testimony for those whom history has forgotten.

Levi, through his body of work, speaks for those who are nameless, highlighting what he describes as the "zone of indistinction", a space where the "right to death and the power over life"[3] is blurred, revealing the living/dead. Hence, for Levi the power and horror of National Socialism is best represented by the concept of the "Muselmann" (the living/dead): a person in a state of absolute desensitisation, without consciousness, yet alive (however compromised). By this concept, Levi describes how the implementation of the Nazis' extermination policies brought about a zone of existence

116 *The camp and the resort*

in between the living and dead, for which no one felt any compassion and "thought only of their elimination".[4] This chapter is concerned with this marginalised zone, "the state of exception that produces the rule", the space in between that constructs an architecture where people are produced as subjects both outside and inside the rule of law that governs human rights and liberties. Both the camp and the resort reveal the space in between the politics of production and the politics of disposability, a space marked by marginalisation and the iteration of biopolitics. While the architectural products themselves belong to this discussion, that which is of main concern is the aestheticisation of the principles that led to the operation of the camp and the resort. In this sense, 'aesthetics' not only refers to the appearance of things, but also to the art of 'self fashioning'. According to this second understanding 'aesthetics' entails the rules by which people not only govern themselves as subjects, but also seek to transform themselves according to the particular standards and practices by which a population comes to associate itself.[5] This process is inevitably entwined with the technological apparatus of inclusion and exclusion, to which buildings may play a key role in achieving one or the other or both states of being.

Of chief concern here is the manner in which bodies are positioned in space so as to permit one group of people power over another. The camp and the resort are remnants of institutional spaces that demonstrate, in the extreme, that the inclusion of individuals into a political community is only made possible at the exclusion of 'others'. Accordingly, Giorgio Agamben recognises: "At the beginning of all politics we find the establishment of a borderline and the inauguration of a space that is deprived of the protection of the law: 'The original political relation is the ban'".[6] In this case, the "ban", for Agamben, is the state of exception or the zone of indistinction that presupposes a sovereign who posits law and constitutes the "sphere of the political".[7] Consider, for example, the suicide attacks in the London Underground in July 2005. Two weeks after the event, a Brazilian electrician, noticing that he was being followed by plain clothes police in the Underground, panicked and fled. Upon his capture, the police shot him five times in the head killing him instantly. According to the London Police, his clothing was much too heavy for the warm London weather, thus rendering him a suspect; this coupled with his attempted escape justified his death by police without committing homicide. In the days that followed, the police issued their apologies to the family, while at the same time pressing their mandate to do everything necessary to prevent further attacks on British citizens. As Claudio Minca points out: "Jean Charles de Menezes, apparently marked out by his heavy clothing, was killed to protect the body of the population/citizenry – of which he, in that particular time and place, ceased to be part of".[8] In that moment, the police had absolute sovereign power over him. But above all, his death was a product of his location, for the London Underground, the scene of a recent suicide attack, had become a space of 'exception'. In this space, the police were granted the extraordinary

The camp and the resort 117

and arbitrary decisional power, in effect, constituting the 'ban' whereby the rule of law ceases to exist.

From this account, and many others like it, it is possible to draw parallels between the idea of a camp as a place of exception and a resort as a place of insertion in contemporary cities; both make for spaces that are marked by inside and outside, exclusion and inclusion from the social body. The camp defines those who are excluded and outside the rule of law, whereas the resort, seemingly distinct in consequence to the Nazi death camps, defines those inside the rule of law, or those who construct the border. Through the implementation of such mechanisms individuals are 'produced' outside the rule of law, rendering them nameless/faceless. In effect, the inauguration of the exception serves to protect the interests of the citizen 'inside' the state at the expense of those who cease to be part of it.

In the camp, Auschwitz exemplifies more than just the utilisation of built structures for the enactment of the politics of the 'Final Solution'. According to Agamben: "The camp is less a physical entity surrounded by fences and material borderlines, [more importantly it] symbolises and fixes the border between bare life and political existence".[9] "Bare life" (the living/dead) is life with no qualities other than merely being alive, or life without any determinates other than not being dead.[10] In this manner, the camp does not refer only to the Nazi death camps, but also to other spaces that produce 'bare life'. As Agamben further asserts: "The stadium in Bari into which the Italian police in 1991 provisionally herded all illegal Albanian immigrants before sending them back to their country, the winter cycle-racing track in which the Vichy authorities gathered Jews before consigning them to the Germans . . . or *zones d'attentes* in French international airports in which foreigners asking for refugee status are detained will then eventually become camps".[11] In these apparently innocuous spaces, the order of the state has been temporarily suspended, seemingly justified by the law that produces the exception. As there is no prerequisite for these spaces to function for the purpose of detention and incarceration, the carrying out of such atrocities depends, as Agamben recognises, "not on law but on the civility and ethical sense of the police who temporarily act as sovereign".[12] Thus, the camp is the paradigm for the social and historical site of rendering life bare and the constitution of the biopolitical. According to Foucault, biopolitics defines the mechanism by which life is called into question through the process of exclusion,[13] thereby producing the exception, being individuals subject to exploitation by the sovereign, or in this case, the sovereignty of the state.

Here too, the resort at Prora, seemingly vastly different in consequence to the death camp as Auschwitz, exemplifies more than just the utilisation of a built structure for the activation of the politicised notion of 'Strength through Joy'. Yet, they are both (Auschwitz and Prora) manifestations of policies that permitted, on the one hand, the exclusion of 'others' outside the rule of law, and on the other, the inclusion of the racially 'superior'. The Prora resort, spanning some five kilometres along the Baltic coast, was designed

118 *The camp and the resort*

to represent, manifest and manufacture the collective joy and enthusiasm of holiday makers for the Nazi regime. Nonetheless, while the structure would have provided, had it been finished, a destination for holiday makers, the actual architecture, per se, could not have conjured such emotions except by way of the people's sense of inclusion in the regime's economic policies (in which 'leisure' had value) and the tangible reward of a beach holiday. The resort itself is a colossal structure and was, at the time, the largest construction project of the Third Reich. The design provided all ten thousand rooms with a view of the ocean and included several restaurants as well as cinemas, sports halls and spaces for other entertainment activities. The *Kraft durch Freude* (KdF – Strength through Joy) programme, which funded and commissioned the project, was an overt attempt at winning over the working class citizens of the Reich by creating the illusion of their inclusion and participation in the Nazi regime's wealth and strength, and social and material progress. However, as the historian Richard Evans remarks: "Strength through Joy aimed to organise worker's leisure time rather than allow them to organise it themselves, and thus to make leisure serve the interests of the racial community and reconcile the divergent worlds of work and free time".[14] Leisure, in this 'reality', was a means of producing greater productivity and more focussed workers. Thus, by providing the working class with a cheap holiday, one they could never have previously afforded, the resort provided further opportunities to strengthen the ideals of the racial body through the people's immersion into Germany's cultural life and associated leisure activities.

The camp and the resort turn into the architectural aestheticisation of the production of differences and the manifestation of the biopolitical subjectification of individuals and subsequently the population. As a point of distinction, Agamben describes this process as the fulfilment of juridico power as the result of the imposition of repressive laws. He attributes the power to impose laws to a centralised sovereign governing body, rather than the population. By comparison, Foucault recognises that biopower operates in all aspects of social life, producing normality, and as such, gives the impression that there is an autonomous centre of sovereign power. That is to say, although the mechanisms for the operation of the camp and the resort were instituted by the Nazi government, the ends were arguably endorsed by the individuals that constituted the population, if only through their ambivalence towards Nazi atrocities, rather than their active participation. Biopolitics refers to the 'power over life' brought about through self-imposed and normalised disciplinary techniques, like adhering to certain social rules that prescribe acceptable forms of behaviour. As a consequence, these rules become imbedded and normalised by a population when endorsed by political authorities and experts, bearing influence on how one should conduct one's life. Here the work of Rose and Miller proves useful to describe this situation. They claim: "The self regulating capacity of subjects as autonomous actors have become key resources for present forms of government that rely in crucial respects on forms of scientific expertise and knowledge".[15] In this manner, the endorsement of the racial community underscoring National Socialism was propagated through educational, scientific and medical technologies (all of which are tools of biopolitics) that enabled the fulfilment of social racism. However, it must be recognised that along with the tangible architecture of the regime, the technico-legal apparatus that followed did not produce widespread hatred and the genocide of millions of Jews. Rather, these results were brought about through the desire to advance oneself – and by extension one's people – above another, and the Jews were seen as an obstacle in achieving this. The camp and the resort represent these two extremes, the inclusion of the self and the disposal of the other, both for the express purpose and goal of achieving some distorted concept of national unity and racial heritage.

In this vein, Foucault asserts that the power to kill, which was evident in all aspects of Nazi society, was normalised when the value of life became dependent on an arbitrary demarcation of racial heritage. He asserts: "The power of life and death, was granted not only to the state but to a whole series of individuals, to a considerable number of people (such as the SA, SS, etc). Ultimately, everyone in the Nazi state had the power of life and death over his or her neighbour, if only because of the practice of informing, which effectively meant doing away with the people next door, or having them done away with".[16] Contrary to popular representations, the Nazis, in particular the Gestapo, were not all-knowing, all-powerful and omnipresent, for they were limited by inadequate resources and a smallish number of agents and spies within their ranks. Yet the practice of denunciation from within the civilian population came to mean that Germans had just as much to fear from each other as they did the governing body. In this way, the idea that the national citizenry adhered to certain principles and values was not necessarily carried out by force, although this too did exist, but by the disciplinary techniques carried by the population itself.[17] Thus the camp, often defined by fences and barbed wire, came to establish itself within 'normal' society through the disciplinary practices of denunciation and informing.

In this way, the power to eliminate the other was held by the individuals that constituted the racial community and the power to enact such processes was thereby harnessed by the governing body as representative of the state. From this perspective, Foucault describes racism as a 'vital technology' in the functioning of the power over life and death. Indeed, 'technology' for Foucault refers to the structured forms of action by which we exercise power over ourselves through widely accepted forms of behaviour.[18] Andrew Feenberg suggests that according to Foucault, power/knowledge is a web of social forces and tensions in which everyone is caught as both subject and object. Feenburg explains: "This web is constructed around *technologies*, some of them materialised in machines, architecture, or other devices, others embodied in standardised forms of behaviour that do not so much coerce and suppress the individuals as guide them toward a more productive use of their

120 The camp and the resort

bodies".[19] In this manner, racism advanced the status of the national body through the systematic elimination of the degenerate and contaminated. Of the architectural 'machinery' involved in advancing racism the gas chambers, the concentration camps, medical experiments and so forth became justified as necessary for the protection of the life and health of the national body.

The analysis of biopolitics is not limited to those who are deprived of their legal rights, such as the condemned or exterminated Jews, or even refugees or asylum seekers; rather it also includes all those who are implicated in social processes of exclusion. Lemke points out: "More and different segments of the populations are effectively excluded not only from labour and the working process but from education, housing and social life".[20] These phenomena, where "different segments of the population" are spatially excluded from the population as a whole, are those, in accordance with Agamben's description, that constitute a 'camp'. In addition, those participating in the enactment of such political technologies constitute the 'resort' as an opposing 'place' for the included. The 'camp', being the architectural/spatial manifestation of exclusionary politics, includes a range of facilities from those such as the Nazi death camps, at one extreme, to basic spaces of detention or confinement, like the Australian detention centres or even the socio-economic structure of suburbia (discussed in the following chapters). At the same time, the 'resort' constitutes the utilisation of architectural spaces that attempt to define the collective, being the Nazi holiday resort at Prora in this case, but including other examples, like the demarcation of territorial borders, such as the 'peace wall' in Israel,[21] or the reconstruction of the World Trade Centre site as a symbol of 'freedom'.[22] To this end, appellations like 'peace' or 'freedom' to certain building structures seek to define a population through the very people they exclude. Equally, they attempt to segregate and divide, for the identification of difference is essential to the production of a community. As such, the link between the national body and the geographic territory is defined by the demarcation of spatial zones and physical borders, whereby the definition of space, both physically and philosophically, becomes integral to the production of identity and non-identity. Concepts like 'blood and soil', 'volkloser Raum', the Nuremberg laws, 'Strength through Joy', and the 'final solution' (discussed in this chapter), illustrate the Nazis' sense of 'rightful' dominion over the land which seemingly justified the propagation of physical force and violence against others, and inevitably the tangible architecture where such events took place.

The buildings that constitute the camp and the resort are significant because they not only defined spaces for the inclusion and exclusion of certain kinds of people, but they also better facilitated the performance of certain activities that physically segregated individuals from each other, and/or merged others based on racial grounds. However, it is important to ask: to what extent do these buildings now bear witness to this process? To all outward appearances they give little hint of the millions of people who died, yet both the camp and the resort facilitated such activities. According to Levi, the Nazi death camps and the attempted annihilation of the Jews was a horror unique in history. He submits: "For the first time we become aware that our language lacks words to express this offense, the demolition of man".[23] Indeed, if words are seemingly inadequate to appropriately testify of the dead, then to what extent might the buildings of the Third Reich bear witness as an "archive" or record of the past? For this reason Agamben is significant to this debate. He claims: "The problem of the historical, material, technical, bureaucratic, and legal circumstances in which the extermination of the Jews took place has been sufficiently clarified. However, when it comes to the significance, discursive, ethical, political, moral, of the extermination, not only do we lack anything close to a complete understanding; even the sense and reason for the behaviour of the executioners and the victims, indeed very often their very words, still seem profoundly enigmatic".[24] By extension, one may argue that just as language is seemingly opaque to the Holocaust so too are the archival monuments and architecture of National Socialism. Here, Agamben concludes that the "zone of indistinction" between inside and outside, inclusion and exclusion could not have led to a comprehensible structure of testimony, hence why so many survivors find it so hard to speak, or why so many individuals remained silent at the time. For the 'exception' is not 'aesthetic'.[25] In this regard, it is not the components that make for a visible architecture that are important, rather the discursive constructs that made subjects of individuals to permit such events to occur.

Volkloser Raum

The power over life and the right to death underlying the concept of biopower was manifest spatially and at different scales, such as the camp and the resort, and the territory constituting the nation. Under the Third Reich, space and territory were intrinsically linked to the racial community. It was believed that the German race had reached the height of human evolution and was therefore superior to all others. Representing this school of thought was the anthropologist Ludwig Woltmann, who claimed that "the German race had been selected to dominate the earth".[26] To this end, in October 1936, Hitler announced a new economic programme for Germany dedicated entirely to preparing the economy for war. The 'Four-Year Plan', a product of this programme, signalled a growing urgency in Hitler's megalomaniacal drive for European and subsequent world domination and focused on economic planning, military technology and arms production. Thus the plan marked a significant escalation in the state's intervention in the economy, for priority was now given to the fulfilment of the plan rather than an overall concern for German industry as a whole. As part of this plan the State laid down the foundations for stripping the Jews of their finances and assets, as previously the Nazis were reluctant to do so for fear of destabilising economic growth. Significantly, new laws dispossessed

122 *The camp and the resort*

those classified as racially and socially inferior of their rights to citizenship in order to rid the state of the supposed financial burden imposed by their living amongst a simultaneously 'cleansed' population. Yet, the Four-Year Plan was a monster in the making. Hitler consistently argued that the enormous strain placed on the economy by an industry dedicated to rearmament could only be alleviated by the "conquest of living space in the east"; in the meantime the German people would have to make sacrifices.[27] In this manner, the state's increased interference in the lives of the German people was presented as an absolute necessity, for the reclamation of Germanic territory, and the Aryanisation of the population was presented as the patriotic duty and right of modern Germany. Both of these aims, as described by Agamben, "required an unprecedented absolutisation of the biopower to *make live* to intersect with an equally absolute generalisation of the sovereign power to *make die*".[28]

Hitler's desire for greater territorial expansion coincided with the German people's desire for improved 'living space'. This focus on territory made up the conceptual and practical dimensions of space for the Nazis. To this end, space, as Paul Hirst recognises, is configured by power and becomes a resource for power. He explains: "At different scales and under different social and technological conditions, spaces interact with and are constructed by forms of political power, armed conflicts and social control".[29] This ascent to power via territorial expansion in order to take control of its natural resources, extant infrastructure and architecture inevitably required war and the oppression of those currently occupying the desired territory. However, the conquest of new territory, while providing greater resources and wealth, also presented the Reich with greater numbers of 'degenerates' and thus a greater threat to the health of the national body. Thus, the Nazi Reich conflated and then promoted the twin goals of conquest and elimination as essential for the protection of the hereditary health of the German people, while at the same time this belief was also aligned with the individual's desire to become encompassed by the national body. From this perspective, the power to 'let live' was held by the people and the power to 'make die' was passed to the state-governed institutions for the benefit of the people. Foucault explains: "In the biological continuum of the human species, the opposition and hierarchy of races, the qualifications of certain races as good and others, by contrast, as inferior, are all ways to fragment the biological domain whose care power had undertaken; they are ways to distinguish different groups inside a population. In short, to stabilise a caesura of biological type inside a domain that defines itself precisely as biological".[30] These biological and economical relations were construed as a means for focusing governmental strategies for the inclusion and exclusion of certain kinds of people. Thus the management of the health of the national body required at its most basic level first, the control and elimination of all things foreign, and second, the spatialisation of the national body as belonging to a specific territory. At this caesura Agamben explains: "The

The camp and the resort   123

non-Aryan passes into the Jew, the Jew into the deportee, the deportee into the prisoner, until biopolitical caesuras reach their final limit in the camp".[31]

It is within this formulation that Hitler claimed the need for a *volkloser Raum* (literally a space without people); however, what Hitler intended was not simply a deserted site or a geographical location devoid of inhabitants. Rather, it was a space in which people pass into populations. In other words, the *volkloser Raum*, by extension, is a place where the population is transformed into 'bare life'. Hitler intended that every life would transcend its political existence and become motivated solely by the Leader, effectively transforming the population into 'bare life', the living resources of the government. In this space, life is without value, and death, at this point is a simple 'epiphenomenon',[32] for the value of one's life is therefore measured by their contribution to the total body and, by contrast, without value unless totally subsumed. The plan to achieve this attempted to propagate the people's unbroken connection, by blood, to the soil, as though the native German was endowed with rightful dominion over the land. It must be recognised, however, that this is not a process unique to the Nazis. Various forms of the *volkloser Raum* can be identified as functioning within many contemporary political/geographical landscapes today. Take for example, the overreaction to 'boat-people' entering Australian waters from Indonesia, where armed navy war vessels are used to intercept and turn around rickety leaking boats; or the *Strategic Defence Initiative* (or so-called *Star Wars*) proposal by US President Ronald Reagan in 1983 to use ground and space based technologies to protect the United States from the threat of nuclear attack on 'home soil'. In this manner, the formulation of the resort finds itself operating in various incarnations when the identity of the people is linked to that of the land, where borders are clearly defined and the population is defined by spatial concepts of territory and living space.

When the territorial limits of the nation and the desires of people converge, the 'exception' is produced. According to Minca: "It is precisely on the basis of the intimate relation that the sovereign invents and invokes between geometry and emotional life that the nation-state is able, at once, to mobilise hearts and minds and to translate citizens into statistics, into 'population', into a *biopolitical residual*".[33] In this way, the citizens become a member of the national body, to be managed, organised, contained, regulated and consolidated within specific geographical confines. Under National Socialism this included public health measures to control reproduction and marriage, increased policing powers, and specific educational standards designed to promote the values of the state, amongst other measures. Minca argues that this process was necessary not only for characterising people in order to render them 'identical', but also for reducing their subjectivity to a unit of measure. He adds: "'the People' thus progressively becomes 'the population', that is, a pure spatial-political abstraction".[34] Accordingly, Agamben robustly declares: "every 'people' is doubled by a 'population' every democratic people is, at the same time, a demographic people".[35]

124   *The camp and the resort*

This so called "doubling" of the population, where a social group is both characterised and quantified, becomes the 'biopolitical threshold', that "third space" described by Agamben as the zone of indistinction or the point between a life worth living and a life that is expendable. Indeed, Minca declares that this process is put into effect when individuals begin to identify themselves as belonging to a particular cartography or to a specific geographical location, thus "marking the original spatialisation of sovereign power".[36] Agamben argues that the convergence of the "zone of indistinction" is found operating at the intersection between Foucault's notions of "political technologies" – described as the care of natural life assumed by the state, and "technologies of the self" – enabling the individual to link his identity to that of the state. In this manner, the actions of the state are perceived to be an extension of one's consciousness, which must be spatialised and constituted by an 'inside' and 'outside'. As such, the subjectification of a people requires a tangible space: "Space that is indistinct though not indescribable, merely exceptional . . . and works on the concurrent putative inclusion of all subjects within a prescribed order".[37] In this manner, one begins to realise the process by which a concept, in the case of the 'final solution', originally promulgated by extremists within the political system, gradually begins to contribute to social norms. Here Foucault's concept of the biopolitical explains how ideas situated on the margins of a social entity begin to take hold over individuals and potentially the populace at large. This occurs because they enter into the everyday discursive formations and have modalities of enunciation (like that of pseudo science) that place notions like racial superiority into the very speech acts of the population. In so doing, they enter into a "zone of irreducible indistinction" as a result of their dependence on exclusion and inclusion, outside and inside, *bios* (biological life) and *zoe* (non-biological life). Hence the process of identification, the recognition of oneself as belonging, aligns those as inclusive at the expense of the exclusive. It is at this juncture that Agamben finds 'bare life', in its totality, represented in the built structures of the 'camp'.

Indeed, the rise of the Nazi concentration camp engaged with both the economic desires of the people to improve living standards, and the political rationale of the governing body. This historical phenomenon grew out of certain circumstances that came to coincide with specific norms promulgated by the Nazis. The concentration camp was a space that embodied the increasing convergence of democracy with totalitarianism, thereby imposing specific rules and norms circulated within the mainstream society upon others deprived of rights. As Levi recognised, never before have human beings been so deprived of rights to such an extent as in the Nazi concentration camps. He concludes that this was only ever made achievable because exception became the rule.[38] The privileges of inclusion into the national body and the rights of citizenship came at the expense and deprivation of others, whereby their exclusion was made possible by the literal abandonment by the sovereign state and disconnection from the territorial limits constituted by the nation-state.

The Nuremberg Law

The link between humankind and place, Agamben observes, is commonly defined and privileged by birth. In this way, it is often assumed that one has greater claim to the land one inhabits if one is bound to it by blood, or in other words, by lineage and ancestry. Thus by proximation one is perceived to be born of one's identity and connection to the land, and by extension, the privileges of nationhood and citizenship. Agamben states: "The fiction implicit here is that *birth* immediately becomes *nation* such that there can be no interval of separation between the two terms. Rights are attributed to man (or originate in him) solely to the extent that man is the immediately vanishing ground of the citizen".[39] In fact, the word nation is derivative of the Latin verb '*natus*', which means to be born. Thus, when individuals have been led to determine their right to any particular topography, it is no doubt typical that they begin to feel threaten by the appearance of 'others' – to the point that the dislocation from one's place consigns to identity a state of crisis. Hence, the preservation of the borders, inside and outside, inclusion and exclusion, demarcation and redefinition are vital to the stability of identity. The presence of difference as encompassed by the immigrant, for example, is more often than not, associated with the decline of national character and a threat to the social and economic fabric of society. The privilege of nativity is the inheritance of nationality. However, the acceptance of anything foreign is subject to the demonstration and judgement of worth.

The introduction of laws to 'denationalise' the citizen (not only Jews, but 'degenerate' others) had their origin in France in 1915, when efforts to delegitimize the citizen were linked to perceptions of their 'enemy origins'. In 1922 Belgium revoked the citizenship of individuals who had committed 'anti-national' crimes during the war. The Italian fascist government in 1926 passed legislation regarding the unworthiness of Italian citizenship, and Austria continued the trend in 1933, until in 1935 the Nuremberg Law divided Germany into full citizens with political rights and those without based on race – namely Jews.[40] Agamben comments: "These laws – and the mass statelessness that resulted – marked a decisive turning point in the life of the modern nation-state and its definitive emancipation from the naïve notions of 'people' and 'citizen'".[41] It was within this stateless domain that the Nazis were able to introduce the Nuremberg Law, which defined citizens of the Reich as people of German or kindred blood. Crucially, the new law declared that only someone who "through his conduct, shows that he is both desirous and fit to serve the German people and Reich faithfully was entitled to citizenship".[42] All others, notably the Jews, but even those who were not, but opposed the regime, were denationalised, deported and/or eventually eliminated. As Göring declared at the introduction of the

126 *The camp and the resort*

Law in 1935: "We know that to sin against the blood is to sin against the inheritance of a people. We ourselves, the German people, have had to suffer greatly because of this hereditary sin. We know that the final root of all Germany's decomposition came in the last analysis from these sinners against heredity. So we have to try to make a connection again to the chain of heredity that comes to us from the greyness of history . . . and it is the duty of every government, and above all it is the duty of the people themselves, to ensure that this purity of the race can never again be made sick or filled with rottenness".[43] By this reasoning, once an individual, either by race or conduct, had brought sickness to the health of the body nation their fate was eradication, as though they were a disease, and they were literally stripped of their rights to citizenship, 'denationalised' and eliminated.

The Nuremberg Law provided the legal means within the German judiciary to enable the conduct of the 'Final Solution'. As such, the Nazi death camps became the "pure space of exception",[44] its detainees a threat to the national body and therefore outside the protection of the state. As Hannah Arendt pointedly remarks, when people are 'denationalised' they become the detested 'other', the "detritus of the world".[45] Consequently, the non-citizen breaks the perception of a natural link between man and nation. Similarly, a refugee entering the sovereign territory of another state is an individual devoid of rights, so that incarceration and detention become justifiable responses in order to protect the state from the non-citizen. In the case of the Jews living under Nazi domination, they were first denationalised and stripped of all rights of citizenship as a result of the Nuremberg Law, which effectively removed their status as legal subjects. Agamben adds: "One of the few rules the Nazis faithfully observed in the course of the 'final solution' was that only after the Jews and the Gypsies were completely denationalised could they be sent to the extermination camps. When the rights of a man are no longer the rights of the citizen he is truly . . . destined to die".[46] Following such precedents, there have been numerous examples where the rights of humans have been denied as a result of their non-citizenship (as discussed in later chapters on Australian detention centres). Other examples include the 'US Patriot Act', which in 2001 authorised the "indefinite detention" and "trial by military commission" of non-citizens suspected of terrorism. In so doing, any alien suspected of activities that endangered "the national security" of the United States of America could be taken into custody. The individual targeted by this legislation, under the Bush administration, became stripped of their legal status, thus producing, according to Agamben, an "unnamable" and "unclassifiable" being. "Not only do the Taliban captured in Afghanistan not enjoy the status of POWs as defined by the Geneva Convention, they do not even have the status of persons charged with a crime according to American laws. Neither prisoners nor persons accused, but simply 'detainees', they are the object of a pure de facto rule, of detention that is indefinite not only in the temporal sense but in its very nature as well".[47] The Guantanamo Bay detention camp is thus the architectural means to divest certain individuals of their legal status as prisoners of war. The facility, known for its alleged cruel treatment of 'detainees', is located outside the United States' legal jurisdiction and therefore not entitled to protection under the Geneva Convention and the US Supreme Court. In 2001 President George W. Bush signed an executive order that allowed the military to indefinitely detain any non-citizen believed to be an enemy of the state, thereby withholding the detainee from the law by which they are held captive.

Agamben draws parallels between the legal status of detainees and that of the Jews during the Holocaust, who, in addition to losing their citizenship, were also stripped of their legal identity. In this manner, the state no longer becomes the institution protecting human rights but becomes intrinsically involved in the enforcement of legal violence. In this ambiguous socio-legal space the individual who is suspended from the rule of law becomes the 'state of exception'. As Julie Browning highlights, this makes for "a nightmarish version of western modernity in which the condition of exception is said to inhabit every power structure".[48] Here, the citizen becomes the subject of rights encompassed by the state and the 'exception' is withheld those very same rights because they hold no claim to citizenship.

Carl Schmitt, perhaps in support of National Socialism's legal aims, argues that the sovereign is distinct in its ability to constitute the exception, for only the sovereign can determine the point at which the law can be withheld from certain subjects.[49] In this sense, biopower becomes indistinguishable from the sovereign. Yet for Foucault, biopower is not held by the sovereign but rather by the people whose governmental representation responds to the predominant forms of disciplinary discourse. In this manner, power is not possessed but exercised, existing in a network of relations held by anyone and any group, not solely by the sovereign. Thus, the power to institute a state of exception which constitutes the camp is produced within the framework that locates the citizen in relation to the state. In this manner, Agamben perceives the presence of the camp as a suspension in the juridico order in which norms become indistinguishable from the exception. In other words, the exception introduces instability within the legal order, whereby the state of exception becomes an "anomic space in which what is at stake is a force of law without law".[50] In effect, the lines between logic and praxis become blurred, and violence becomes the only possible outcome.

The introduction of the Nuremberg Law legalised discrimination against minorities such as homosexuals, Gypsies, the mentally ill or handicapped, and in particular, the Jews, in the attempt to 'purify' the German race. In the early years of the regime this discrimination ranged from a lack of employment opportunities, through public humiliation to compulsory sterilisation. The effect of such actions, which were wilfully carried out by the German people, arguably demonstrated to the Nazis how much they could get away with and led to the introduction of more stringent laws which effectively sanctioned physical violence against Jews. Indeed, these individuals

128   The camp and the resort

became subject to a systematic increase in state-sponsored violence. At the introduction of the Nuremberg Law, anti-Semite violence broke out throughout Germany, aided in part by a proliferation of anti-Semitic propaganda initiated by the Nazi government which affected all forms of media, including film, music, newspapers, magazines, painting and other means. This violence served to define the territory of the included as belonging to a certain kind of individual, while the degenerate was denied access, not only to common law, but also to public space. During this period, signs were erected at the boundary of many towns and villages stating: "Jews are not wanted here", or "Jews enter this locality at their own peril!".[51] In addition, Jews were prevented from using the city library, local shops and other public spaces. If Jews were found walking the streets they were required to walk in the gutters, and to identify themselves with a yellow Star of David sewed onto their clothing. By this point, such individuals were basically confined to their own homes. However, this space too was to become progressively more precarious.

The increased spatial confinement and isolation of Jews within German cities and towns produced a state of exception with defined spatial dimensions, whereby the dislocation of certain individuals outside the state served to locate others within. Agamben argues that the camp is a portion of territory that is placed 'outside' of the normal juridical-political order. However, it is not simply an 'external' space, but rather a space in which "not only is law completely suspended but fact and law are completely confused".[52] In this space anything is possible. Once the state of exception takes hold the complete removal and eventual elimination of the 'other' is achieved. Before the concentration camps Jewish people were herded up and cordoned off within specific areas of the city. The eventual ghettoisation of cities like those established in Łódź and Warsaw in Nazi-occupied Poland were governed by laws that called for the better facilitation of control over Jewish people in preparation for their eventual deportation. The concentration of Jews within certain quarters of the city divested Jewish people of all their property, including their homes, for no longer were they entitled to the protection of the state. In this manner, the main motivation for the ghettos was to remove Jews totally from the German sphere of influence and control. It was intended as a transition, a temporary and ad hoc measure in preparation for their eventual deportation to the death camps. Accordingly, the German ghetto commissioner Heinz Auerswalde stated: "Ghettoisation was decisive for it was first of all the desire to segregate the Jews from the Aryan environment for general political and ideological reasons".[53] But mere segregation was not seen as the permanent solution, as Christopher Browning points out: "ghettoisation was still a way station to a final solution".[54]

The genocide of the Jews, along with the euthanasia of the 'feeble minded' and 'morally congenital', enabled the state to make political use of their segregation and eventual murder, in that these acts were justified as necessary for preserving the life and health of the national body. In fact, the population became so committed to the protection of the national body that any act against the 'other' was no longer considered a crime, but instead a benefit to 'life necessity' and, by extension, the population. As Foucault affirms: "Entire populations are mobilised for the purpose of wholesale slaughter in the name of life necessity . . . It is as managers of life and survival, of bodies and the race, that so many regimes have been able to wage so many wars, causing so many men to be killed".[55] During the reign of the Third Reich, biopolitics constructed the need to eliminate all Jews, 'degenerates' and others so classified for the vitality and health of the nation. This desire was advanced by a state of exception that was grounded in the geographical imagination of the state, whereby certain individuals were stripped of rights and confined to a space designed for their exclusion and eventual elimination.

Ironically, the power to kill exerted a productive influence over life making subjects of individuals as a result of their desire to be included into the national body, and in effect, stay alive. Foucault explains: "It was the coincidence between a generalised biopower and a dictatorship that was at once absolute and retransmitted throughout the entire social body by this fantastic extension of the right to kill and of exposure to death".[56] The 'power over life' and the 'right to kill' becomes essential to the classification and identification of the national body as belonging to a particular territory and the protection of all that it values. In this way, the protection and care of the national body is passed over to the state for the 'better' management of the population. Here Rose observes: "This is what enables the sovereign alone to make legitimate political use of their death".[57] Rose, further expanding this view, states: "The thanatopolitics [the use of death to mobilise political life] of population purification is immanent within the very project of biopolitics: to manage the health of the 'body politics' inescapably requires the control and elimination of 'foreign bodies'".[58] The National Socialists assumed a mandate for the administration of life and the execution of death. Life itself became the prevailing method for the application of political authority which required the implementation of programmes to enhance the national body, both physically and mentally, and likewise, institutionalised methods for the elimination of the weak, idle, criminal, degenerate and insane.

Fritz Lenz, leading German geneticist and advocate of 'scientific racism' during the Third Reich, declared at the introduction of the Nuremburg Law that finally "Germany had a government that was prepared to take such issues seriously and do something about them".[59] Yet this necessary intervention into the lives of the population ranged from compulsory education of racial hygiene in school and university curricula, involuntary sterilisation of the congenital feeble-minded and the moral feeble-minded including alcoholics, criminals and the unemployed, the requirement for approval of marriages and/or encouragement for divorce from infertile partners, and ultimately the extermination of those who threatened the health of the racial community. These policies and practices re-energised the

130   *The camp and the resort*

capacity of buildings (the schools and universities, the hospitals and asylums, the workplace and home) and physical spaces to make a community of a certain kind (heterogeneous and segregated, dispersed and manageable). In this community life could be equated with a value and rendered calculable, whereby some lives have less value than others. Accordingly, Rose determines: "Such a politics has the obligation to exercise this judgement in the name of the race or the nation. All the eugenic projects of selective reproduction, sterilisation and incarceration follow".[60]

In addition to the elimination of the racially and morally degenerate, Nazi eugenics also necessitated the improvement of the racial community in order to strengthen the health of the nation and therefore relieve the government of the economic burden and social responsibility of caring for defective life. In this way 'positive eugenics' included financial reward and other accolades for meeting certain targets and outcomes. For example, a mother who gave birth to and so contributed more than ten healthy children to the national population was awarded the title "Mother of the Reich" along with the gold Honour Cross personally presented by the Führer. This entitled her to jump queues at grocery stores, and in addition, the privilege of having Hitler as godfather of the tenth child, which meant in the case of males naming him Adolf.[61] Positive eugenics favoured reproduction and the right to life, while negative eugenics exercised the power to kill by preventing the possibility of certain individuals from breeding,[62] permitting medical experimentation on prisoners and psychiatric patients and the extermination of lives 'not worth living'. With this in mind, such strategies were endorsed and carried out by the medical profession, whether voluntarily or for fear of punishment, whereby their participation enabled the 'scopic' assessment of the racial community which was justified as necessary for the health of the nation. Rose declares: "Here one might agree with Agamben that the sovereign has extended his powers over the living bodies of his subjects by entering into an alliance with 'the jurist . . . the doctor, the scientist, the expert and the priest".[63] The fact that such activities were sanctioned by so-called experts engaged the already prejudicial minds of individuals, thus entangling the aspirations of building and strengthening the association of the racial homeland with that of the German nation.[64]

When 'political sovereignty' is established over a territory, not only through law but also through various agents, and through ways of defining and manipulating space and the population, the value of life becomes a measure by which the state sanctions the elimination of degenerate elements and the protection or expansion of borders. In this way, the judgement of life worth living as opposed to the political expediency of life not worth living is completely determined along the lines of inclusion and exclusion in which the constitution and fabrication of sovereign territory is absolutely necessary for the maintenance of such identities. The existence of the camp, a space reserved for the politically expendable, thus produces 'bare life' on a national scale. The very act of exclusion inside the confines of the camp provides those outside with the means to elevate themselves above the detainee for inclusion into the national body and the rights of citizenship. The biopolitical power that requires the qualification of individuals along biological and territorial predeterminates by necessity requires the usurpation of rights to the territorial sovereign and its governmental institutions for the implementation of politically motivated apparatuses for the protection of the national body at the expense of all those who threaten to weaken it.

Strength through Joy

Formed in 1933 ten months after Hitler's ascent to power, Strength through Joy's (KdF) mission was ostensibly geared to providing for the population's leisure, but was also simultaneously directed to cultural production, and aimed at providing middle class cultural practices to the working class at subsidised costs. KdF organised concerts, plays and art exhibitions, provided tennis, horse riding and sailing lessons, and most significantly provided vacation travel to those who would otherwise not be able to afford it. The Nazi-run organisation specifically targeted people's leisure time in order to provide them with worthwhile activities for the building of the nation. The KdF programme served the interests of the racial community by merging the divergent worlds of work and leisure, as Evans describes: "Between factory and home, production line and recreation ground. Workers were to gain strength for their work by experiencing joy in their leisure".[65] Strength through Joy demonstrated the Nazi regime's ability to promote the values of National Socialism by appealing to, forming and responding to the desires of the people and by providing them with the tangible evidence of the increased wealth and prosperity delivered by the Reich to all 'racially valuable' and compliant citizens. As testament to the organisation's popularity, by the year 1938 over 13.5 million people had attended its staged cultural activities, performances, concerts, exhibitions, educational evenings, sporting events and tours. More importantly, however, the organisation attempted to consolidate the working classes' enthusiasm for race and nation by making them a participant in the prosperity and wealth under the Reich and by providing them with a sense of inclusion in the national community as exemplified by the Prora resort.

Strength through Joy guided its low cost, budget enterprises in ways that would provide the German citizens with a vision of future prosperity under the Reich. Strength through Joy promoted travel destinations to politically sympathetic locations which presented travellers with evidence of local poverty. Travel to destinations such as Portugal and southern Italy and overseas to north Africa were designed to provide the tourist with an appreciation for their own material possessions back home and the prosperous livelihood provided under the Third Reich. In addition, the programme allowed the German traveller to elevate themselves above the 'other' by attributing poverty to racial difference. On this subject, the work of Shelley

132   *The camp and the resort*

Baranowski is important. She observes: "*Tourism* emerged as a significant means of negotiation between the Nazi regime and its racially 'valuable' citizens which was acknowledged as a crucial component of the regime's legitimacy. In a less direct but subtler way than popular denunciations to the Gestapo, KdF's management of *tourism* exacerbated the exclusions that defined the Third Reich".[66] The inclusion of workers in the KdF program provided racial acceptance to the underclasses and provided them with advantageous circumstances such as entertainment, diversions and cultural education previously only available to the wealthy, culturally aware and educated.[67] Nonetheless, the fellowship of the worker was necessarily contrasted with the racially excluded and a-social 'other' who was prevented from sharing in the regime's prosperity. It is necessary to note that the conventional social history of the Third Reich has, more often than not, depicted German citizens as terrorised, submissive people forced to participate in unimaginable crimes due to the Nazi leadership's control over their lives. However, it must be recognised that the exclusion and ultimate elimination of the racially inferior was made possible by contrasting them against the racially superior, in the sense that the former were perceived as a threat to the health of the nation. Those who felt aggrieved or threaten by the presence of racial 'undesirables' and 'deviants' found acceptance amongst those of the same cultural and racial heritage. Strength through Joy managed to harness people's desire for belonging and provided them with tangible evidence of self worth and affirmation. In this way, the KdF contributed towards the Nazi ambitions of territorial expansion and racial purity by capturing people's leisure time for the benefit of the state, not so much for mindless indoctrination but for pedagogical purposes.

The Nazi regime's goal of expanding Germany's 'living space' required the social and racial purification of the homeland prior to expansion into foreign territory. "Only a *Volk* united against the social distinctions of the past, particularly that of class, and cleansed of 'undesirable' genetic traits, could become a 'master race' capable of defeating its enemies and ruling the empire".[68] With racial cohesion as the precondition to territorial expansion, Strength through Joy deliberately attempted to bring Germans of different classes and regional backgrounds together in a spirit of unity in order to build the racial community of the Third Reich. Hitler, who dreamed of the '*volkloser Raum*' as the destiny of Germany's global domination, conceived a 'super' resort/vacation complex so large that it would dwarf all others in existence. The resulting Prora resort, situated in the Prora bay on the island of Rugen in the Baltic Sea, designed by architect Clemens Klotz and overseen by Albert Speer, was designed to accommodate twenty thousand beds, as was five kilometres long and six storeys high.

Construction began in 1936 (the year the four-year plan was announced) and halted in 1939 at the outbreak of war with Poland. During its construction the resort consumed as many resources as Hitler's grand motor highway scheme. The resort consisted of ten thousand identical rooms each with

Figure 5.1 Prora, building complex, view from sea side, 2008.
Unukorno – Wikimedia Commons.

a view of the sea, and consisted of more relaxed living spaces or outbreak areas including dining halls, theatres, gymnasiums, indoor swimming pools and spaces accommodating a plethora of other activities, all connected by a central avenue kilometres long.[69] At the resort's core was a gigantic convocation hall capable of seating all twenty thousand guests at one time (not constructed). The hall was to be four thousand square meters in size with the capacity to stage mass rallies, parades and other forms of military demonstrations, and in addition, provide sufficient flexibility for the performance of concerts, plays and art exhibitions. The resort also included housing for workers, a rail station and all other necessary infrastructure such as electrical power stations, water works and a post office. A large quay was built at the centre of the complex with moorings for KdF cruise ships, with a seawall promenade dividing the complex from the beach. Upon arrival visitors were to proceed to one of two reception halls to be assigned rooms and then transported to their rooms via light rail. The Prora resort was the first of many others of its type to begin construction and featured heavily in the Strength through Joy publications and promotional material. Despite the overt attempt to educate the people during their subsidised leisure activities, the Prora resort was promoted as the ideal location for providing "a family with children the vacation that they seek in nature, in the sun, and in the air, which in the interests of the Reich's healthy family policy they simply must have".[70]

134 *The camp and the resort*

It was planned that each vacationing worker would stay for 10 days, during which they were to participate in physical activities like sports, hiking in nature or relaxing on the beach in the sun. In addition to this, equal priority was placed on improving the mind by attending lectures or movies on history, eugenics and other themes favourable to Nazi propaganda. Loudspeakers would ensure that every guest was kept informed of their daily routine and impending activities. The resort, located by the sea, fell into line with Nazi ideas on racial hygiene of "improving the race" by 'relaxing' in nature,[71] providing physical and mental nourishment, and, as intended, a better more productive worker. In addition, its design, a monolithic structure rising six storeys above ground and spanning kilometres along the coast, served to overawe and reduce the individual to feeling as though they were part of the larger whole. In this sense every room was to be identical to every other so as to imply, as Stelter points out, that the "life of the people as a whole was superior to individual lives".[72]

Prora's location, beyond the German mainland but within German territory, was close to Hitler's future 'living space', which "curiously blended", as Shelley Baranowski claims: "The overseas dimension of German imperialism with the continental . . . and underscored the global scale of German desires".[73] The Nazis' merger of pedagogical leisure and tourism enabled the politics of racism to take hold of a population by providing them with a sense of elitism over those 'inferior' to themselves. To this end Baranowski concludes: "KdF's fostering of a *tourist* imagination with its promise of future abundance, so evident at Prora, was arguably its most significant contribution to the Nazi's culture of exclusion".[74]

The Prora construction site was abandoned at the outbreak of war with Poland and never actually operated as a resort. During the war, parts of the complex was used for police training and as a military hospital. It was also utilised to shelter thousands of displaced residents during the RAF bombings of Hamburg. The East German army occupied some of the building from 1945–1991, during which they used it for armed combat training which destroyed large sections of the structure. Since reunification several symposia have been convened to discuss whether the building should be completely demolished or preserved, although no clear direction has been decided. Some parts are currently used as a youth hostel, dance club, restaurant and a documentation centre and museum on Nazi history with guided tours. More recently a group of private investors have begun plans to transform the largely dilapidated building into luxury condominiums, half of which have already been sold.[75]

The Prora complex is a fascinating reminder of the worst of times. In reality, the KdF programme acted as a cheap travel agency and instigator of leisure activities. In effect, as historian Detlev Peukert points out, participants found the combination of de-individualisation and regimentation somewhat overbearing. Yet in saying this, Peukert recognises that the programme succeeded, in a way, if only producing a "non-political" ambivalent individual. He posits: "Although the National Socialists went all out in the direction of the 'aestheticisation' of politics, in order to indoctrinate their *Volksgemeinschaft* ideal into existence, the result of the stage-management of public life was only to render it empty and to provoke the retreat into non-political privacy – though this was indeed enough to secure passive consent and approval for the 'normality' that was achieved".[76] This "retreat into non-political privacy", as Peukert calls it, had the express aim of securing the people's "passive consent and approval" for the regime, whereby any real communal activities and voluntary social interaction became replaced by prefabricated 'leisure' activities. Without the Nazis' productive culture of inclusion as exemplified by the aestheticisation of the resort, the racial exclusion of degenerates and their attempted genocide would not have been made possible. Cook makes this abundantly clear in his own travel log of the region: "Prora is the largest remaining monument to the worst of times, the flip-side of the Final Solution. Tragically, for the majority of Germans, Rügen was more real than the concentration camps. Without Prora, it's impossible to understand how Auschwitz happened".[77]

'Ethica more Auschwitz demonstrata'

With relation to Levi's life work of bearing witness, it is important to recognise, as he did, that one can only recount one's own reality. Yet Rousset also recognised: "To leave even a seemingly small element out of the document is, in a sense, to fall short of one's duty as a survivor, for that detail might symbolise the reality of a thousand dead".[78] Hence, as Agamben describes, "the anguish and shame of survivors",[79] for they will never be able to adequately account for those who died. Thus, it must never be said that the Holocaust was an unspeakable act. For those like Theodor Adorno, who assert that "to write poetry after Auschwitz is barbaric";[80] Paul Virilio, who in agreement considers that our over-exposure to the Holocaust has resulted in a form of desensitization to its reality;[81] and Nikolaus Pevsner, who claimed that any word devoted to Nazi architecture is one word too many,[82] have by their pronouncement of the camp's 'unsayability', "surrendered to silence". In this way, Alvin Rosenfeld remarks: "The camp inmates witnessed cruelty, deprivation, and terror on a scale that so far surpassed anything previously known as to make writing about it a next to impossible task".[83] Yet to remain silent is, as Lynn Gunzberg argues, "by implication a concession to the very forces that had created Auschwitz".[84]

Agamben proposes that almost none of the ethical principles recognised by 'our age' could withstand the horrors of Nazi Germany. He writes: "We can enumerate and describe each of these events, but they remain singularly opaque when we truly seek to understand them".[85] Similarly, Lawrence Langer recounts: "It has been said that the human mind had never been confronted before with such a reality on such a massive scale: a situation in which no basic human needs were satisfied; in which perception,

136 *The camp and the resort*

planning and coherent living were forcibly displaced by the all-pervasive imminence of death; in which ambition and incentive were replaced by the desire to disappear in the face of beatings and selection and in which so many formerly civilised people set aside, or forgot, their fundamental human principles in the attempt to survive".[86] Thus, at this threshold, the 'zone of indistinction', people desired to let live or make die. Levi's shame for having survived Auschwitz, prompting his eventual suicide, was not derived from a sense of personal insignificance in the face of such enormous power. Rather, by surviving, life demanded that he bear witness of the dead to whom he felt he was unable to and could never have provided the means for appropriate justice.[87]

Agamben provides a basis from which to examine the "ethical territory" of testimony by invoking an "Ethica more Auschwitz demonstrata", or a way of examining the morality of Auschwitz. In so doing, he describes a new ethical relationship with regards to the biopolitics of space and the aestheticisation of the roles of victim and executioner. From this perspective, he explores how bodies were positioned within a spatial domain so as to permit one group the power over life and the other's death. Conceivably, one could refer to the architecture used by the Reich to manifest and justify such claims. However, the extent to which the architecture bears witness to the dead is, as Levi laments, hardly adequate, for the true witnesses of such crimes can no longer speak. Thus, it is we who attempt to speak for them.

That which bears witness to the activities of the Reich, including its architecture, must be examined, not for the purpose of providing commentary on how politics was indoctrinated and imposed onto the private lives of the people, forcing them to commit unimaginable crimes.[88] Rather, National Socialism must be seen in the context of biopower that was enacted through the institution of programmes like the 'Final Solution' and 'Strength through Joy'. Their tangible representations, like the camp and the resort, demonstrate the people's desire to identify themselves as the nation's included, at the expense of the 'other'. The buildings that constitute the Auschwitz concentration camps were largely disused barracks and stables: in isolation they suggest nothing of the horrors there conducted without prior knowledge of the history and means by which they were made to function. As Nigel Taylor, with effected naivety observes, the buildings "for all the world looked like a pavilion hospital, and indeed, they could have been".[89] For this reason, it is through the use of language, although inadequate, that history bears witness to how such buildings were made to operate under National Socialism. Thus, it is only through the testimony of survivors that we are able to come to some sort of comprehension of what took place.

From May 1940 to January 1945 more than a million Jews were transported by train to the Auschwitz-Birkenau camp. On the railroad sidings children, the elderly, the sick and large numbers of able-bodied men and women were randomly selected for death and marched directly to the gas chambers. Following this, their bodies were immediately incinerated in the

The camp and the resort 137

camp's crematoria. The remaining arrivals were registered as prisoners, tattooed and shaven, and used for slave labour. Of these individuals hundreds of thousands died of malnutrition, exhaustion and disease, or at the hands of the SS guards.

The Auschwitz camp site was selected to make use of 16 single storey buildings (later converted to double storey) which had previously served as army barracks outside the nearby Polish town of Oświęcim. As the camp rapidly expanded the local population was evicted from the area. Zone after zone was added to the camp compound, which included the entire town site, forests, farmland and swamps. This so called 'zone of interest', which occupied approximately 40 square kilometres, was surrounded by concrete walls, watchtowers and double-depth, electrified barbed-wire fences that were illuminated at night.[90] Construction of the Auschwitz-Birkenau camp began in October 1941, necessitating the draining of the swamp. The camp consisted of rows of timber barn structures originally constructed as horse stables, repeated en-masse. Yisreal Gutman states that "setting foot on the soil of Auschwitz marked a radical and irrevocable departure from one's previous existence".[91] Prisoners who had experienced the harsh living conditions of the ghettos were perhaps better prepared. However, those unable to adapt soon sunk into apathy and dejection, becoming what Levi describes as the "Muselmann". According to Gutman's account; "such prisoners hovered in the twilight zone between life and death. Before long, their bodies lost their shape, becoming little more than skeletons covered with dry yellowish skin. Gazing aimlessly with their lifeless eyes, they moved slowly, unperturbed by the savage cries in German . . . ".[92] The Auschwitz concentration camp system truly spawned a reality in which all beliefs, values and norms of behaviour adhered to on the outside world were suspended. The camp made 'indistinct' the living from the dead, not only by the fact that it produced the 'Muselmann', but also that the value of life became necessitated by the politics of death.

The camp provided the means, under Nazi ideology, for 'protecting' the racial body. Yet its structures make visible the underlying formulation of a particular 'political constellation', whereby the ends justified the means. In this manner, the Nazi-instituted Auschwitz death camp and the Prora resort were the physical manifestation of a biopolitics that constituted the racial community imagined by National Socialism. While the architecture of the Reich was pervaded by particular meanings, it served to enable the functioning of specific beliefs that aestheticised the interests of the German population. Thus, the question of what role did the buildings play in the attempted extermination of certain people, and do the remnants provide adequate witness of the events that occurred there, remains largely unanswered when one examines the architecture alone. The response as provided by Levi is no: the buildings were a means to an end and did not cause nor motivate the carrying out of such hideous crimes. Instead, such crimes were carried out by the citizens that constituted the body politic,

138 *The camp and the resort*

thus requiring the buildings to function for a particular purpose. Indeed, the control of how the buildings functioned was integral to the capabilities of the Nazi regime.

Notes

1 Primo Levi, *The Drowned and the Saved* (London: Abacus, 1989), xvi.
2 Primo Levi, *If this is a Man. The Truce* (London: Abacus, 1979), 198.
3 Refer to Michel Foucault, *The History of Sexuality Vol. 1: The Will to Knowledge* (London: Penguin Books, 1976), 133–159.
4 Quoted in Giorgio Agamben, *The Remnants of Auschwitz: The Witness and the Archive* (Brooklyn: Zone Books, 1999), 43.
5 Refer to Ian Hunter, "Aesthetics and Cultural Studies", in *Cultural Studies* ed. Lawrence Grossberg et al., (New York: Routledge, 1992), 348. Michel Foucault, *The Use of Pleasure* (New York: Vintage Books, 1988), 10. Refer to Alan Milchman and Alan Rosenberg, "The Aesthetic and Ascetic Dimension of an Ethic of Self Fashioning: Nietzsche and Foucault", *Parrhesia*, No. 2 (2007), 44–65.
6 Giorgio Agamben, *Homo Sacer: Sovereign Power and Bare Life* (Stanford: Stanford University Press, 1995), 181.
7 Refer to Astrid Deuber-Mankowsky, *Agamben as Master Thinker* (Ruhr Universitat Bochum), 6. Available at http://www.ruhr-uni-bochum.de/adm/weiter/Agambentranslation.pdf (Accessed October 2009).
8 Claudio Minca, 'Giorgio Agamben and the New Biopolitical Nomos', *Geografiska Annaler*, Vol. 88, Issue 4 (December 2006), 387.
9 T. Lemke, "A Zone of Indistinction", *Outlines – Copenhagen*, Vol. 7, No. 1 (2005), 5.
10 The term 'bare life' comes from Walter Benjamin's "Critique of Violence", in *Selected Writings Vol. 1* (Belknap: Harvard Press, 1996), 1,913–1,926. Translated by Edmund Jephcott into English as 'mere life'.
11 Agamben (1995), 174.
12 *Ibid.*
13 Refer to Giorgio Agamben et al., *Means Without Ends* (Minneapolis: University of Minnesota Press, 2000).
14 Richard Evans, *The Third Reich in Power* (London: Penguin Books, 2005), 465–466.
15 Nikolas Rose and Peter Miller, "Political Power Beyond the State: The Problematic of Government", *British Journal of Sociology*, Vol. 43 (1992), 173–205.
16 Michel Foucault, *Society Must Be Defended* (London: Penguin Books, 2003), 259.
17 Refer to Eric Johnson, *Nazi Terror: The Gestapo, Jews and Ordinary Germans* (New York: Basic Books, 1999), 253.
18 Refer to Jim Gerrie, "Was Foucault a Philosopher of Technology?" *Techne*, Vol. 7.2, Winter (2003), 14.
19 Andrew Feenberg, *Critical Theory of Technology* (New York: Oxford University Press, 1991), 71.
20 Lemke (2005), 10.
21 Refer ro Eyal Weizman, "Hollow Land", *Against the Wall* ed. Michael Sorkin (New York: The New Press, 2005), 224–253.
22 Refer to Paul Goldberger, *Up From Zero* (New York: Random House, 2005), and David Simpson, *9/11: The Culture of Commemoration* (Chicago: Chicago University Press, 2006).
23 Levi (1979), 8.

The camp and the resort 139

24 Agamben (1999), 11. Refer to Ronit Lentin, "Postmemory, Unsayability and the Return of the Auschwitz Code", *Representing the Shoah for the Twenty-first Century* (Oxford: Berghahn Books, 2004), 1.
25 Agamben (1999), 36.
26 Quoted in Richard Evans, *The Coming of the Third Reich* (London: Penguin Books, 2003), 34.
27 Refer Evans (2005), 410–411.
28 Agamben (1999), 83.
29 Paul Hirst, *Space and Power; Politics, War and Architecture* (Cambridge: Polity Press, 2005), 3.
30 Foucault (2003), 227.
31 Agamben, (1999), 85.
32 *Ibid.*, 86.
33 Minca (2006), 87.
34 *Ibid.*, 88.
35 Agamben (1999), 84.
36 Minca (2006), 79.
37 *Ibid.*, 83.
38 Quoted in Yisrael Gutman "Auschwitz – An Overview" *Anatomy of the Auschwitz Death Camp* ed. Yisrael Gutman and Michael Berenbaum (Bloomington: Indiana University Press, 1998), 5.
39 Agamben (1995), 127.
40 Refer to Evans (2005), 543.
       One is reminded of the situation under the Howard government which involved a person who came to Australia from Yugoslavia in the 1960s as a child but had his permanent residence cancelled after the introduction of the strengthened provisions for citizenship based on character and conduct. He sought refugee status to prevent being deported to Croatia, where he claimed he would be punished for not having returned to the country to do military service and would have no means of making a living since he did not know the language, but his application was rejected. Unable to find employment and completely unfamiliar with his new environment, he camped outside the Australian consulate until, due to media and public pressure, the Australian government permitted his entry back into Australia.
       Refer to Glenn Nicholls, *Deported: A History of Forced Departures from Australia* (Sydney: UNSW Press, 2007), 196.
41 Giorgio Agamben, "We Refugees", *The European Graduate School Faculty* (1994). Available at http://www.egs.edu/faculty/agamben/agamben-we-refugees.html (Accessed February 2009).
42 Evans (2005), 544.
43 Hermann Göring, "Göring Begrundet die Gesetze", *Berliner Tageblatt*, 16 September (1935), 438.
44 Agamben (1995), 145.
45 Refer to Hannah Arendt, *The Origins of Totalitarianism* (Orlando: Harcourt Inc. 1968), 269–290.
46 Agamben (1994).
47 Giorgio Agamben, *State of Exception* (Chicago: The University of Chicago Press, 2005), 3–4.
48 Julie Browning, "States of Exclusion: Narratives from Australia's Immigration Detention Centres 1999–2003" (Ph.D. diss., University of Technology Sydney, 2006), 19.
49 Refer to Carl Schmitt, *The Concept of the Political* (Chicago: The University of Chicago Press, 2007), xiv.

140 *The camp and the resort*

50 Minca (2006), 91.
51 Refer Evans (2005), 540.
52 Agamben (1995), 170.
53 Quoted in Christopher Browning, *The Origins of the Final Solution* (London: Arrow Books, 2005), 123.
54 *Ibid.*
55 Refer to Michel Foucault, (1976), 136.
56 Foucault (2003), 260.
57 Nikolas Rose, *The Politics of Life Itself: Biomedicine, Power, and Subjectivity in the Twenty-First Century* (Princeton: Princeton University Press, 2007), 57.
58 Nikolas Rose, "The Politics of Life Itself", *Theory, Culture and Society*, Vol. 18, No. 6 (2001), 2.
59 Refer to Paul Weindling, *Health, Race and German Politics between National Unification and Nazism* (Cambridge: Cambridge University Press, 1989), 60–84. Robert Proctor, *Racial Hygiene: Medicine under the Nazis* (Cambridge: Harvard University Press, 1988), 47.
60 Rose (2001), 3.
61 Evans (2005), 517.
62 It may be worth noting that the Nazis were not the only nation who implemented compulsory sterilisation laws at this time. The USA introduced and attempted to carry out sterilisation, in addition, various forms of compulsory sterilisation were also introduced by Switzerland, Denmark, Norway, Sweden and other European countries.
63 Refer to Rose (2001), 17.
64 Refer to Elisabeth Young-Bruehl, *The Anatomy of Prejudice* (Cambridge: Harvard University Press, 1998).
65 Evans (2005), 465.
66 Shelley Baranowski, *Strength Through Joy: Consumerism and Mass Tourism in the Third Reich* (Cambridge: Cambridge University Press, 2004), 7. Note, '*Tourism*' shown in *italics* is used to replace the term 'consumption' used in Baranowski's text.
67 Refer to Anson Rabinbach, "The Aesthetics of Productionin the Third Reich", *Journal of Contemporary History*, Vol. 11, No. 4 (1976), 43–74.
68 Shelley Baranowski, "A Family for Workers: The Strength Through Joy Resort at Prora", *German History*, Vol. 25, No. 4 (2007), 539.
69 The planning for the Prora Resort was loosely based on Le Corbusier's design from the early thirties for a kilometre long resort city on the Algerian coast. Klotz's design won the grand prize at the 1937 Paris international exhibition, and was promoted by the KdF as the most modern resort in the world.
70 Werner Kahl, *Der deutsche Arbeiter reist* (Berlin: 1940), 34.
71 Refer Proctor (1988), 17.
72 Axel Stelter, *An Examination of the Sea Resort Prora* (Berkley: Grin Publishing, 2008), 3.
73 Baranowski (2007), 549.
74 *Ibid.*, 558.
75 Refer to Anthony Faiola, "Hitler's Vacation Paradise is Reinvented as Condos, Hotel, Spas", *The Washington Post*, 15 December (2014), Available at http://www.washingtonpost.com/world/europe/hitlers-vacation-paradise-is-reinvented-as-condos-hotels-spa/2014/12/15/acb73eac-79b5-11e4-8241-8cc0a3670239_story.html (Accessed April 2015).
76 Detlev Peukert, *Inside Nazi Germany* (New Haven: Yale University Press, 1982), 195–196.
77 William Cook, "Inside the Holiday Camp Hitler Built", *The Observer*, 12 August (2001).

The camp and the resort   141

78 David Rousset, *The Other Kingdom* (New York: Reynal and Hitchcock, 1947), 55.
79 Agamben (1999), 26.
80 Theodor Adorno, *Negative Dialectics* (New York: Continuum, 1973), 367.
81 Refer to Paul Virilio, *Art and Fear* (London: Continuum, 2000), 5.
82 Refer to Paul Betts, "The New Fascination with Fascism; The Case of Nazi Modernism", *Journal of Contemporary History*, Vol. 37, No. 4 (2002), 549.
83 Alvin Rosenfeld, *A Double Dying; Reflections on Holocaust Literature* (Bloomington: Indiana University Press, 1980), 35.
84 Lynn Gunzberg, "Down Among the Dead Men: Levi and Dante in Hell", *Modern Language Studies*, Vol. 16, No. 1 (1986), 10.
85 Agamben (1999), 12.
86 Refer to Gunzberg (1986), 10–11, Lawrence Langer, *Holocaust and Literary Imagination* (New Haven: Yale University Press, 1975), 6.
87 Refer to Jean Amery, essayist and Auschwitz survivor, who writes: "I do not have [clarity] today, and I hope that I never will. Clarification would amount to disposal, settlement of the case, which can then be placed in the files of history. My book is meant to prevent precisely this. For nothing is resolved, nothing is settled, no remembering has become mere memory". Jean Amery, *At the Mind's Limits: Contemplation by a Survivor on Auschwitz and its Realities* (Bloomington: Indiana University Press, 1998).
88 The architectural historian Nikolaus Pevsner (who, although ostracised by the Nazis in the early years of the regime for being of Jewish decent despite his sympathetic views towards Nazism), maintained that architecture "can influence the social structure of the age; for example, directly by creating national or party symbols, or indirectly by expressing and thereby diverting ideals". Quoted in Peter Draper, *Reassessing Nikolaus Pevsner* (Burlington: Ashgate Publishing Company, 2004), 61–62.
89 Nigel Taylor, "Ethical Arguments about the Aesthetics of Architecture", in *Ethics & the Built Environment* ed. Warwick Fox (London: Routledge, 2000), 194.
90 Sybille Steinbacher, *Auschwitz a History* (London: Penguin Books, 2004), 27.
91 Yisreal Gutman, *Anatomy Of the Auschwitz Death Camp* (Bloomington: Indiana University Press, 1998), 19.
92 *Ibid.*, 20.

6 Spatial contestation and suburban riots

Following the previous discussion, which explored the various ways in which architecture may be appropriated to represent of the values and beliefs of the national body (specifically, the manner in which built form became an integral component of National Socialism), this chapter is concerned with the manner in which the urban environment, in particular, the spatial territory of the suburbs, might be associated with the values of nation. This chapter focuses on contemporary Australia, examining three riots which took place in Sydney's vast suburban sprawl, Redfern (2004), a gentrifying inner city area; Macquarie Fields (2004), a peripheral public housing estate; and Cronulla (2005), a middle-class beachside suburb. Home to 90% of Australia's population, the suburbs are subject to specific discursive formations that serve to associate finite values and attitudes with their residents. Here, individuals claim a sense of belonging to, and ownership over a particular place through various social, economic and cultural means that serve to demarcate borders and exclude 'others'. In other words, space becomes implicated in a contest between normalising practices, and difference, to which the riots, being one extreme, testify.

This chapter does not attempt to diagnose a single root cause for these riots, as they may be multiple and varied. However, it explores the manner in which various individuals (including residents, politicians and so forth) might attempt to control space through diverse means. Cronulla reveals the propagation of ideas that attempted to reclaim the territory of a suburban beach and the battle to redefine the values of place amid the changing ethnic demographic of that area. Both the Macquarie Fields and Redfern riots also demonstrate the contestability of space and the perilously thin connection between identity and place. Macquarie Fields exposes the social exclusion of its inhabitants within the urban landscape as a result of their location on the outskirts of Sydney. Redfern too brings to light the disaffection of its Aboriginal population by means of their gradual and deliberate removal from this inner city gentrified area. These examples show how the suburbs become points of (de)attachment, making distinct certain kinds of people and their associated values and characteristics. This spatial domain

Spatial contestation and suburban riots 143

is essential to the production of the national image yet it also marginalises and excludes certain others. The point at which these two poles intersect is more often than not a site of contestation resulting in social unrest, conflict and sometimes violence.

Territory and belonging: the Cronulla riots

> My suggestion is to invite one of the biker gangs to be present in numbers at Cronulla railway station when these Lebanese thugs arrive, it would be worth the price of admission to watch these cowards scurry back onto the train for the return trip to their lairs ... Australians old and new shouldn't have to put up with this scum. (Alan Jones, 2GB Radio, 7 December 2005)

In December 2005 thousands of people assembled on the beaches of Cronulla in Sydney as a 'show of strength' to voice their opposition to an alleged assault perpetrated against three off-duty surf lifesavers. Media reports in the lead up to the assembly had implicated youths of "Middle Eastern" decent as responsible for the assaults, while the high rating breakfast radio 'shock jock' and former national coach of the Australian rugby team, Alan Jones, fuelled the anger of his audience by calling for a "demonstration at the beach". He goaded listeners: "A rally, a street march, call it what you will. A community show of force".[1] Jones went so far as to broadcast a text message, which had previously only been circulated amongst a small number of radicals. It read: "Come to Cronulla this weekend to take revenge. This Sunday every Aussie in the Shire get down to North Cronulla to support the Leb and wog bashing day".[2] Many radio listeners called in to voice their thoughts and express approval for the plan to take action against those who had, so it was reported, failed to respect Australia's values and its heroes of the beach. Callers offered vitriolic ramble that only served to ignite prejudice and legitimise their hatred toward minorities in the community. In particular, one caller said: "Alan, it's not just a few Middle Eastern bastards at the weekend, it's thousands. Cronulla is a very long beach and it's been taken over by this scum. It's not a few causing trouble. It's all of them".[3] Another proudly commented: "My grandfather was an old digger and he used to say to me when we were growing up: 'Listen! shoot one, the rest will run'".[4]

On the designated Sunday an estimated five thousand people gathered at Cronulla Beach. Many were draped in Australian flags and carrying placards with racially divisive slogans such as "Aussie Pride" and "Ethnic Cleansing Unit". With their intentions clearly revealed by these messages, they only needed a catalyst to vent and justify their rage. This soon appeared in the form of a man of Middle Eastern appearance who apparently shouted: "I'm going to blow youse [sic] all up".[5] The mob attacked. Local shops were

144 *Spatial contestation and suburban riots*

looted, property vandalised and a high number of stabbings and other injuries resulting from bashings were incurred. After the riot police had subdued the attackers with force: spot fires continued throughout the night in the outlying areas. In particular, Muslim mosques and even Jewish synagogues were targeted for vandalism and associated violence.

In the aftermath of the riots, various news services and government authorities reported the events as an "aberration", the "acting out of frustrations" and the "un-Australian" conduct of criminals and thugs,[6] while carefully avoiding the moral dilemma poised by racist and segregationist attitudes towards immigrants of colour. In contrast, Professor Joseph Lo Bianco, who is best known as the author of the 1987 national policy on language and literacy, explained on ABC news radio following the riots: "In the last five, six years, there's been a deep polarisation coming into the way we talk about the national community in Australia so that there's clearly 'us and them' dichotomies being used all the time, there are clearly people who are welcome and people who are not, there are clearly people who belong and people who do not".[7] Lo Bianco suggests that people identify with their place in society, sociologically and spatially, according to how it is talked about. As such, he directly laid the blame for the polarisation leading to the riots on prominent individuals in Australia who have attempted to delimit the language of 'Australianness' and national identity. This is evidenced, for example, during John Howard's term of government with his coalition's hardline stance against 'illegal' boat arrivals and its proffering of immigration policies which deliberately steered away from 'multiculturalism' in preference of 'integration' and 'assimilation'.[8] During this time ideas of nationalism and thought on what it means to be Australian became increasingly defined by more extreme and narrow parameters, invoking images of the 'bush', the ANZACs, cricket, footy and mateship.[9] In effect, this focus on reinforcing a particular and generally easily caricatured view of Australian national identity sought to create a sense of belonging for the included majority and social antagonism towards those who threatened its imagined homogeneity, arguably culminating in the events at Cronulla.

It is the construction of such dichotomies as between 'us and them' and the manner in which the urban environment becomes associated with the values of the nation that is the subject of this chapter. Over the course of the next three chapters the themes of national identity, space and exclusion and inclusion are applied to the Australian context, highlighting specific events which have dominated Australia's news media over the past couple of decades, in particular the Sydney riots (addressed in this chapter) and 'illegal' immigration and detention (discussed in the next two chapters). With this in mind, the territory of the nation, its cities and in particular its suburbs are essential to this discussion; in effect, they become a contested ground to which certain individuals come to feel a sense of belonging and others not. The Cronulla riots were clearly about the demarcation of territory as belonging to a certain type of individual, being a place synonymous with the Australian beach lifestyle, in particular the Australian cultural icon of the surf lifesaver (the alleged victims of the instigating attack). Moreover, it is located only kilometres from Botany Bay (the landing place of Captain James Cook which preceded the White settlement of Australia), and is therefore widely considered to be a significant site in Australian history. The Cronulla riots were propagated by the idea of "reclaiming the beach" for 'Australians' from those who supposedly held no entitlement to it. According to Johanson and Glow: "One interesting feature of the riot was the identification of place with cultural values . . . Cronulla is a suburban beach that is perceived and used quite differently to Sydney's more famous beaches, such as Bondi. While the latter is often visited by backpackers and other tourists, Cronulla is more commonly patronised by locals from the suburb and other Sydney-siders".[10] For these reasons, Cronulla is perhaps more likely to be perceived by locals as a territory to be possessed, materially and sentimentally, to which the appearance of 'others' threatened to destroy their sense of belonging. With this in mind the 2005 Cronulla riots can be seen as a battle to redefine the values of place by overtly excluding others from the socio-spatial domain that represents these values.

Indeed, the Cronulla riots can be seen in the context of an emerging diversity in the ethnic background of Australian suburbanites and a growing mistrust of immigrants, in particular, Muslims since September 11, 2001. But, as David Burchell reveals, it would be a mistake to view the Cronulla riots as simply a clash between "the core culture and the cultures on the margins". He continues: "Such a conceptualisation perpetuates the idea that 'ethnic minorities' are still guests in our midst. Rather, the riots need to be seen as local communities in conflict over shared space where ethnicity is the fuel for the conflict rather than the all purpose explanation".[11] By this Burchell suggests that communities do not simply resort to violence because of ethnic diversity, but rather, come into conflict when a group of individuals associate certain values with territory and in so doing claim a 'rightful' entitlement to that space through the exclusion of others.

This view, in combination with Lo Bianco's, implies that one's sense of entitlement to space is constructed through discursive forms that work to align individuals, their feelings for themselves and the community with a view of national identity. But in reality, identities are never fully homogenised within the geographical confines of a particular territory. Yet those values and attitudes which gain ascendancy do so, as Stuart Hall indicates, "within the play of specific modalities of power" by which individuals govern themselves. He states: "They are more the product of the making of difference and exclusion, than they are the sign of an identical, naturally-constituted unity . . . Identities can function as points of attachment only because of their capacity to exclude, to leave out, to render 'outside', abjected".[12] That is to say, the notion of national identity, which implies a 'unity' of some kind, is in fact constructed on the back of exclusion. This is made possible through discursive practices that define the national image

146 *Spatial contestation and suburban riots*

and its core values. For example, notions of 'mateship', 'a fair go' and so forth attempt to define individuals who belong to a particular space as sharing specific attitudes and in some cases physical characteristics. Indeed, the Cronulla riots attempted to protect, as voiced by the many listeners of Alan Jones' radio talkback show, whether participants in the riot or not, a desire to protect certain values from 'others' who threaten the 'Australian way of life'.

In response to the Cronulla riots the then Prime Minister John Howard denied that it was an example of underlying racist attitudes within Australia and instead rationalised their cause as the combination of "incitement and alcohol, as well as people wanting to take matters into their own hands".[13] But as one editorial in *The Economist* suggests, Howard's interpretation of the events was likely shaped by his own political interests. The writer explains: "Cronulla lies at the centre of the suburban belt where he [Howard] has built a formidable political base that has kept him in power for almost ten years".[14] Indeed, the Howard administration's fixation with defining the national character, in combination with its hardline anti-immigration policies, arguably was formulated by, and no doubt helped shape, a general fear of the 'other'. Take for example, the then Parliamentary Secretary for Immigration, Andrew Robb, who reiterated the Coalition Government's concerns with relation to 'multiculturalism'. He outlined in an address to the Australian National University in 2006 that Australians wanted to redefine what it means to be a nation that accommodates people from other ethnic backgrounds rather than accepting prevailing rhetoric about the merits of multiculturalism. He argued: "Some Australians worry that progressively the term multiculturalism has been transformed by some interest group into a philosophy, a philosophy which puts allegiances to original culture ahead of national loyalty, a philosophy which fosters separate development, a federation of ethnic cultures, not one community".[15] Robb goes so far as to say that simply "co-habiting a space" was not the basis for building a strong society, rather, "those who come should unite behind a set of core values and shared identity".[16] Inevitably, this call for shared values and identity seeks to identify certain individuals as belonging to a particular place, while excluding others who do not effectively integrate with such attitudes as a result of their appearance, language, dress or other cultural traditions.

Robb's views, and others like them, serve to contextualise the events at Cronulla within a discursive framework that attempts to link the values and attitudes of certain individuals with those of a particular territory or space. To this effect, this chapter is concerned with the manner in which space becomes a means for defining national values. As Hirst points out, space seemingly becomes "constructed by forms of political power, armed conflict and social control".[17] How space, in particular the suburbs, might affect the conditions by which power may be exercised is also of key concern here. The chapter asks: how can a narrow definition of Australian values and identity play a role in sustaining a government's authority? In addition, this chapter is concerned with how individuals construct identities as a result of their location in space through the construction of borders and the reclamation of territory, like Cronulla Beach, from immigrant 'others'. As the social anthropologists Akhil Gupta and James Ferguson aptly explain: "To be part of a community is to be positioned as a particular kind of subject, similar to others within the community in some crucial respects and different from those who are excluded from it . . . these identities are not 'freely' chosen but overdetermined by structural location and . . . their durability and stability are not to be taken for granted but open to contestation and reformulation".[18] In other words, one's sense of self is governed by one's location in space, and those values that attempt to connect the individual with that place. These values work to determine, or equally undermine, one's identity in order to equate the self with the supposed values of the nation.

The analysis of the Cronulla riots leads me to two other riots which also took place in the Sydney suburbs only a year earlier, in Macquarie Fields and Redfern. These events are of interest not because they involved conflict, but rather because they demonstrate the contestability of terrain and the perilously thin connection between identity and space by which the borders of the community are defined. The riots at Redfern and Macquarie Fields reveal also the overt display of abjection, dispossession and exclusion, as these are not necessarily the result of a fear of others, although they no doubt also played a role, but rather the result of social and economic disadvantage. The Macquarie Fields riots tell the story of spatial contestation by disaffected individuals within the urban landscape of Australia's largest city. They parallel the riots of Redfern in that both events exemplify people's resentment towards their spatial isolation and inability to access the opportunities so promoted by the national imaginary of hopeful futures, prosperity and a 'fair go'. These three Sydney riots demonstrate one's attempt to redefine territory as a result of one's social, political and physical position within it.

Australian ugliness and the myth of the bush

The production of the self, and by extension the population, is manifestly twofold: on the one hand, it produces a cultural space of consolidated allegiances and a defined and distinguishable collective. Yet on the other hand, the binary division of space that follows renders visible the excluded 'other', or the deposed as a distinct identity. The operation of this duality of power, one that builds and destroys, includes and excludes, is no more evident than in the suburbanisation of the population. The suburbs are the morphological representation of the body in space, and are the loci that regulate and produce individuals as subjects in urbanised nations like Australia. In Australia, the suburbs are home to the majority of the population. In fact, 90% of Australia's 23 million citizens live in the vast expanses of suburbia. As such, it is through these spaces in which the majority of the nation's citizens reside

148 *Spatial contestation and suburban riots*

that they identify themselves as Australians. Correspondingly, Trevor Hogan states: "Australian suburban habitus, system and myth are tied directly to the nation-state project and the cultural self-understanding of the Australian people".[19] Yet the Australian image, the one which is more likely to be promoted as representative of the Australian lifestyle, does not necessarily match the suburban reality. It is somewhat paradoxical that Australia, one of the most urbanised nations in the world, tends to portray itself otherwise, for deep-rooted in the Australian imagination is the myth of the bush. Recognising this, Donald Horne points out: "It's highly inconvenient to national myth-making that Australia is probably the most urbanised nation in the world".[20] The bush holds an iconic status in Australia and features heavily in home-grown cultural enterprises such as literature, poetry, film, music and painting. The bush evokes themes of struggle and survival epitomised by familiar characters such as the bushranger, drover and stockman. The uniqueness of the Australian landscape has become a symbol of national pride, yet even before the days of Federation such depictions have not been the reality for the majority of Australians who live in the great suburban sprawl that surrounds Australia's coastal cities.

In the essay *Inventing Australia*, Richard White argues that the 'bush', towards the end of the nineteenth century, became a prominent symbol of national pride as a response to Australia's considerable urbanisation. Contrary to most historians, who have sought to explain the 'bush' in the context of the historical and topographical specificity of Australia's diverse hinterlands, White claims that the romanticisation of the bush was brought about because of a sense of urban claustrophobia in which the stories and images communicated by various writers and painters, such as Banjo Patterson, Henry Lawson and Frederick McCubbin, brought the city to the bush. White states: "Although Australia forged a national legend based on the bush, the acceptance of this legend must be related to the ideological needs of a highly urbanised population. The bush legend became the creation of urban Australia in an effort to meet the emotional demands of city life. These distinct characteristics allowed urban society to not only escape from the confines of day to day life but also adopt the bush legend as their national identity, which many Australians living in cities felt they apparently lacked".[21] The legend told about the Australian bush merely transposed the urbanised values of its writers on to the bush: their male chauvinism, their sense of freedom from the restraints of social convention and their seeming alienation from the urban environment, where all projected and represented as the 'real' Australia. Essentially, the 'real Australia' came to exist only in the city dweller's imagination of the bush, "an image of sunlit landscapes, faded blue hills, cloudless skies and the noble bushman heavy in toil".[22] However, this imagined 'bush' was not a pristine untouched wilderness, but rather an outcome of 'white' man's dominion over the land in the process of 'settling'. As Hogan further remarks: "This romanticisation was not of an arcadian idyll but of stoic pragmatic pioneers and their valiant or melancholic efforts

Spatial contestation and suburban riots 149

to subdue nature – their own making out of a new life in a seemingly hostile land of natural forces that, if not unknowable, was at least perceived as agnostic to human needs, hopes and material enrichment".[23]

In his essay *Urbanising in Australian History*, Sean Glynn argues that the imagination of the 'bush' came about at a time when Australians sought to distance themselves from British colonialism. He states: "The idea of a truly distinct and unique national character and culture, was created suddenly, at a critical time, on a somewhat flimsy and unrepresentative basis. Nineteenth century Australia, burdened with convict beginnings, had little White history to base national pride upon. It was largely due to this lack of history that the 'noble frontiersman' became the basis of Australia's national sentiment".[24] The production of the 'bush' as an Australian icon served not only to define the character and values of the national imagination, but to aestheticise the 'outback'. There followed an image of Australia portrayed as a 'white man's world', made from descendants of British stock, but also an indigenous terrain that was autonomous and resilient. Others, who did not belong to this constructed landscape, were either entirely excluded or misrepresented. Aborigines, for example, were portrayed as amiable simpletons and Chinese immigrants as dim-witted and conniving. In fact, the Federation of the Australian colonies in 1901 specifically aimed to preserve these constructed notions of national identity and values. The constitution was based around what has become informally known as the 'White Australia Policy' because it denied indigenous inhabitants citizenship, and immigration was restricted to 'white' Europeans only.

Although this type of largely idealised 'bush' is clearly constructed, its image has continued to be associated with the Australian lifestyle, and by extension, continues to reinforce the image of Australian identity. Dennis Wood, whose research interests are concerned with the imagination of space, in particular the suburbs, contends that the predominance of open parks, trees, shrubs, nature strips and water features, evident in so many Australian suburbs, is symptomatic of this view.[25] The manner in which new suburban developments market themselves as rural villages isolated from the busy city seems to be derived from this image. For Wood, these simulacra of the 'bush' conjure an image of a harmonious communal lifestyle in which residents share a fondness for 'wholesomeness' and 'virtue', including all those values commonly associated with the Australian character such as mateship, egalitarianism, stoicism, hard work and honesty. In so doing, these values become transposed from the 'bush' onto the suburban dweller. Such ideals are therefore not only confined to the 'bush' folk, but are also extended to include the suburbanite.

Consider, for example, the suburb of Ellenbrook, located on the periphery of the Perth Metropolitan area. Developed a little more than a decade ago on a former pine plantation on the outskirts of the city this suburb is marketed as a community in harmony with Australia's idealisation of rural living. An advertisement in the weekend *West Australian* newspaper

150   *Spatial contestation and suburban riots*

reads: "It's hard to tell where the community ends and the natural environment begins . . . Flanked by the rustic beauty of the Swan Valley and Gnangara and Whiteman Park, Ellenbrook sits in peaceful harmony with nature, just thirty minutes from Perth's bustling Central Business District".[26] According to Woods, this particular advertisement suggests that notions of "peace" in and "harmony" with nature are disassociated from the centre of the city, whereby Ellenbrook is located at a sufficient distance from the city not to attract unwanted elements such as crime and disorderly conduct, but just far enough so as not to be completely remote. The advertising for the Ellenbrook estate attempts to draw upon a common unity between the residents and their environment, as though producing certain desirable qualities as a result of its location beyond the 'bustle' of the city centre. But this 'nature' is not 'natural'; the indigenous landscape was destroyed years before by the establishment of the pine forest. It is a simulated nature, or as Woods describes it: "A conjured nature for a conjured community". He continues: "Thus, just as the enclave estate owners/entrepreneurs seek to remove the heterogeneous, 'vagrant' aspects of difference and otherness from the community and offer in its stead a homogeneity linked to shared interests and affiliations they also seek to remove the 'nightmare' of the uncontrollable otherness, rawness and wildness of nature".[27] This is a fake manufactured reality that attempts to construct images of a nostalgic 'bush' myth where rural communities of hardworking honest people formed genial secure neighbourhoods for their families. Such depictions, however, rely on the reality of the outside world, whereby dangers associated with that world, like socio-economic and ethnic difference and otherness, are supposedly maintained well beyond the borders of the suburban enclave.

The promotion of a suburb like Ellenbrook as a rural community correlates with what Edward Soja describes as the "third-space". In his description, the combination of the "perceptual", that which surrounds us; and the "conceptual", the way it is talked about, produces the "third-space" (because it is in between the perceptual and the conceptual).[28] According to Soja, this "third-space" brings the idealisation of identity and community into being. It is a relationship based on the imagination of space, for in the case of Ellenbrook, it acts as an anchor to which the community is invariably linked to the values of nature and the idealisation of the Australian bush. Woods further explains: "In essence the engagement and tension of the conjuring of the perceived and conceived spaces, within the walls of the estate seeks to remove the paradoxical spaces outside and install the interior as a 'paragonical' place of sameness – the illusionary third-space of the community".[29] This sameness, as described by Soja's formulation of the 'third-space', has come to characterise the suburbs. Ellenbrook even mandates sameness through its restrictive covenants, which encourage the construction of cottage-like dwellings and the use of specific building materials such as timber fences, face brick walls and pitched corrugated metal roofs. In fact, the development's design guidelines state that housing designs must be "sensitive to local topography" and incorporate "bush remnants" (like timber) in order to deliver a "new development in sync with its surroundings".[30] But beyond aesthetic sameness, the space that conjures the community must also evidence sameness in other ways, such as racial, ethnic, cultural, political and economical equivalence as well. In effect, this kind of socio-economic and ethnic sameness can be maintained in multiple ways, like targeting land prices and block sizes to young middle-class families and retirees. Sameness presents and confirms the constructed imaginary of a cohesive community, but it is not independent of difference, for difference is what is excluded by the confines of the suburban neighbourhood, beyond the enclave of the 'rural' community.

Similarly, it is within this context that the appearance of 'others', of different ethnic backgrounds, languages and cultures, threatened to destroy the imagined ideals of the Cronulla suburban enclave. Indeed, sameness attempts to promote unity, reinforcing a connection with place and providing a sense of belonging for those who fit within its parameters. Yet such connections are entirely constructed as though a veneer smoothing over the real diversity underneath. With this in mind, the architect critic Robin Boyd was also concerned with the production of suburban Australia. In his book, *The Australian Ugliness*, Boyd gives a very blunt account of suburban life in the 1950s. He writes: "Australian ugliness begins with a fear of reality . . . This is a country of many colourful, patterned, plastic veneer villas, and the White Australia policy".[31] For Boyd, the planning of Australian suburbs was linked to the constructedness of the Australian identity by the way it has been imagined as tied to a 'white' European nation. Boyd, being an architect, wanted to see a greater awareness applied to residential design that reflected the realities of the Australian environment rather than the falsification of nature that corresponded with an imagined landscape and identity.

Boyd argued that the sprawling suburbs, which had come to represent the vastness of Australia's landscape, had reduced the 'bush' to a "desert of terracotta tiles relieved only by electrical wires and wooden poles". He writes of new suburban development: "About this time the subdividers arrive, and behind them the main wave of suburbia. Then all the remaining native trees come crashing down before bulldozers, and soon rows of cottages and raw paling fences create a new landscape. The time required for this metamorphosis varies from place to place, but once any man sets his eyes on any pretty place in Australia the inexorable process of uglification begins".[32] Here, Boyd is referring to the irony of destroying the natural landscape in order to advertise it as connected to 'nature'. This is a point not lost on Wood, who echoes Boyd's observations that: "The irony here is that this destruction of the 'natural' goes against one of the major factors which *developers* utilise to sell their 'estates': that of the close connection of the estate with 'nature'".[33] Although Boyd's use of "ugliness" is perhaps largely driven by his own taste and aesthetic judgement (which tend towards

152 *Spatial contestation and suburban riots*

modernism), he is also speaking of a refusal, which he claims is part of the Australian psyche, to accept the reality of, not only the landscape, but its place in the world. According to Boyd, this inability to accept the 'wildness' of nature and the difference of 'others' is reflected in the bareness, conformity and sameness of the suburbs, which he calls 'ugly'.

With reference to the 'White Australia Policy', which was still operating in the 1950s, Boyd claims that Australians had failed to come to terms with the reality of their place in the world as part of the Asian region, and instead saw themselves as more akin to the English or Americans. He writes: "The historical, cultural, and economic justification for both these attitudes are overlaid by a slightly neurotic condition brought about by loneliness. The physical isolation from the West is only partially alleviated by radio and jet travel. Australia still feels cut off from what she thinks of as her own kind of people, and the obvious cure of her loneliness, fraternisation with her neighbours in Asia, is not acceptable. The immigration policy remains rigidly opposed to Asians and even its madly offensive, if unofficial, name of 'White Australia Policy' is sacrosanct".[34] Boyd argues that as a result of this struggle to readily identify and characterise the values of the nation, Australians have created, on the surface, the "features" that accord with this false sense of reality. But it becomes apparent that Boyd has collapsed the differences between a psychological interpretation of identity and a sociological one; it does not stand that because, as Boyd claims, Australia is alone that the suburbs are lonely places too. Boyd concludes: "This is how one turns to Featurism. Not prepared to recognise where, when, or what he is living, the Australian consciously and sub-consciously directs his artificial environment to be uncommitted, tentative, temporary, a nondescript economic-functionalist background on which he can hang the features which for the moment appeal to his wandering, restless eye".[35] Boyd's argument attempts to tie an apparent fear of difference with the constructed images of Australia, like those of the 'bush' and the sameness of the suburbs. Yet Boyd fails to recognise, in his attempt to aestheticise the issues of exclusion, that such 'features' do not spontaneously arise out of a collective desire to belong. Rather, the individuals that inhabit the suburbs of Australia are made subject to the discursive constructs that assign one's place and identity according to a number of factors such as one's socio-economic status and location in space. Those features, like parks, gardens and nostalgic rustic housing styles, have become synonymous with the suburbs because they belong to certain kinds of 'rhetoric' and media representations, amongst other modes, that bring about specific expectations and engender a kind of 'norm'. Thus, in one's desire to belong one adopts similar values, rather than, as Boyd believes, such values being inherent in the Australian consciousness as a result of its isolation.

Space is constructed through various power relations that continually intersect and render space a contest. Inevitably, place is perceived to be threatened by the appearance of others, which has the effect of identifying

Spatial contestation and suburban riots   153

those who belong as opposed to the excluded other. The 'other' threatens to destabilise the harmony of sameness and renders heterogeneity explicit, revealing the vulnerability of the body in space. Mounting concern with relation to the changing face of suburbs most often results in attempts to narrow the parameters of inclusion and thus exclude a greater number of people because they look and sound different. Take for example the pronunciations of Australian politicians like Tony Abbott (former Australian Prime Minister), who claimed that in the suburbs it is "becoming increasing harder to hear an Australian accent",[36] or Pauline Hanson, former leader of One Nation, who identified Bankstown and Cabramatta in Sydney as suburbs that threatened the "social fabric of the nation" because people there dressed differently. By contrast, Suvendrini Perera highlights: "Dress and speech are registered as acts of aggression not only against the 'values', but also against the security, of the nation . . . Women wearing hijab or burqa are subjected to a spectrum of violence from physical assault to the suspicion of concealing bombs under their burqas and accusations of 'confronting' the sensibilities of Anglo-Australia by their mere presence in public spaces".[37] The appearance of the 'other' creates a contested ground, and the need, in the mind of the included, to protect and preserve certain values that the 'other' threatens to destroy. The myth of the 'bush' attempts to 'resist' these inevitable changes by making the association between identity and place unambiguous. In this way, the disaffected other is confined to another space, outside, and excluded from the privileges of nationhood, either through the direct reclamation of suburban territory, as the Cronulla riots demonstrate, or the attempted realignment of borders as the riots at Macquarie Fields and Redfern will reveal.

Social exclusion: Macquarie Fields

Late one Friday afternoon in February 2005 three teenage males stole a Holden Commodore with the intention of taking a joyride. The police, alert to their activities, pursued the vehicle through the streets of south west Sydney. During the high speed pursuit the teenage driver lost control of his stolen vehicle at a bend on Eucalyptus Drive in Macquarie Fields, rolling the car several times and finally stopping against a tree. The two passengers died on impact, but the driver, who survived, fled the scene. Immediately after the accident, stories circulated throughout the neighbourhood claiming that the police had deliberately rammed the vehicle causing it to crash. The following night hundreds of youths gathered on the streets of Macquarie Fields in an area known as Glenquarie Estate. Agitated by the loss of two of their own they began to launch projectiles, fireworks and Molotov cocktails at the local police station. The NSW police responded by mobilising hundreds of riot police armed with batons, helmets and shields to subdue the crowd. The violence that followed lasted four nights, resulting in widespread looting, car bombings, fires and several injuries.

154 *Spatial contestation and suburban riots*

Macquarie Fields, in the heartland of western Sydney's suburban sprawl, is well known for its concentrated levels of low employment and increased levels of welfare dependence and crime, and for "unruly, uncontrollable and delinquent youths".[38] Not surprisingly, the hostilities sparked a media frenzy, TV images were broadcast all over the country and Sydney's talk-back radio ran hot with concerned listeners calling for tougher law enforcement and the better protection of Sydney's suburban streets. Politicians and media personalities alike perpetuated the 'law and order' debate by calling for tougher penalties and 'zero tolerance' policing. David Burchell, columnist for *The Australian* and author of several books on Australian politics, in his analysis of the media reporting on the riots points out the disparate approach of Sydney's two daily newspapers. He indicates that the city's conservative-leaning tabloid, the *Daily Telegraph*, headlined with "Enough is Enough", which promoted tougher law enforcement and longer jail sentences. By contrast, the city's more liberal-minded paper, the *Sydney Morning Herald*, offered a different type of analysis and proposed that the underlying causes for the Macquarie Fields riots were more the result of poverty than lawlessness. Burchell explains: "Yet none of these responses ever seemed really to cut to the heart of the matter. Since, on the one hand, communities whose members routinely plunder and deface public property are rarely healthy places in which to grow up, the first set of responses (zero tolerance, tough love, where are the parents?) always seems inadequate and even perverse. Yet the reflexive incantation of the theme of socio-economic disadvantage often seems hardly more helpful".[39] Yet these rationalities, which attempt to find a root cause for such behaviour (lack of discipline verses poverty), inevitably served to further isolate the residents of Macquarie Fields. By this means, one's location within the suburbs becomes overlaid by certain perceptions that are inevitably tied to one's moral character and social worth which position one in relation to another. In this way, the riots cannot be explained solely through economic disadvantage, but rather, that this form of disadvantage compounds one's sense of exclusion from the constructed imagination of the nation. Invariably, this has less to do with wealth and tougher law enforcement than with one's position in the context of power relations and social structures that govern the operation of society.

According to urban theorist Ali Madanipour, exclusion is a "socio-spatial phenomenon", in that those finding themselves without adequate political representation and access to employment, and marginalised from the mainstream tend to be spatially incarcerated within localised areas of the city. He claims: "The spatiality of social exclusion is constructed through the physical organisation of space as well as through the social control of space".[40] In this way, the "physical organisation" and "social control" of space is constituted by spatial divisions, whereby the socio-spatial structure of the suburbs is determined by market forces and planning policies that locate certain individuals in specific areas of the city. In the case of Macquarie Fields, this location is constituted by the periphery. At the periphery, the hinterland between the

Spatial contestation and suburban riots 155

'bush' and city, land prices are at their lowest, but they also lack adequate public infrastructure, such as transport, schools and health facilities. In addition, the periphery is notorious for its lack of employment opportunities and other commodities such as retail and government representation. Indeed, this kind of spatial sub-division, whether the result of economic or social factors, highlights the imbalance between groups of people and their ability to access the same opportunities as others.

In fact, a study conducted by Monash University in 2006 indicates that people located in the 'outer suburbs' of Australia's major cities are directly affected by factors such as inadequate transport networks, lower standards of health and limited access to public amenities. The study claims that low income households are increasingly concentrated in areas with minimal employment opportunities, thus they are required to travel long distances to find employment or other services.[41] Because travel is a barrier it also adversely affects these households' wellbeing through factors such as nutrition, as there is limited availability to fresh groceries; health services, with less access to doctors and hospitals; and of course, education, with the majority of schools and universities located in well established areas. As a consequence, these individuals are caught in a cycle of minimum opportunity. This is not because they are any less intelligent or motivated than others, as some stereotypes might suggest, but rather, their spatial situation assigns them this role. In this way, social exclusion is largely owing to limited access to resources which might benefit the livelihood and integration of certain confined individuals. Gupta and Ferguson describe this situated-ness as the "borderland", stating: "The term does not indicate a fixed topographical site between two other fixed locales (nations, societies, cultures), but an interstitial zone of displacement and deterritorialization that shapes the identity of the hybridised subject".[42] The space confined to the spatially incarcerated is, in effect, a normative space, one that assigns a particular role to individuals according to their inability to access the same resources available to the rest of the nation's citizens.

The problems of the periphery can be traced back to Australia's post-war vision of a social utopia, namely the 'great Australian dream', which corresponded to a considerable demand for home ownership and government policies supporting it. Inevitably, this required the rapid selling off of undeveloped land grouped in suburbs across all major cities in Australia. To meet the demands of all income earners, the state governments established Public Housing Commissions for the purpose of providing affordable housing to low income and disadvantaged families. In NSW alone, the Housing Commission during the 1940s built more than 12,000 homes for such families on the outskirts of Sydney, with a further 10,000 in development.[43] By the 1960s, planners had expanded the suburbs of all Australia's capital cities beyond the reach of necessary infrastructure, such as schools, shops, hospitals and public transport networks. Yet in order to appeal to the Australian sense of identity, many of these

156 *Spatial contestation and suburban riots*

suburbs were given pastoral-sounding names like Green Valley or Ambarvale in Sydney, Broadmeadows in Melbourne, and Forrestfield or Ferndale in Perth. Each of these localities, on the outskirts of the then metropolitan area, were imagined to be like little country villages set beyond the bustle of the city centre. (Ellenbrook is also typical of this phenomenon.) By the 1960s these suburbs had began to dominate the urban landscape. The Sydney suburb of Green Valley was for a short while the largest new suburb, accommodating more than 25,000 people in 6,000 new properties of public housing. Shortly after, Green Valley was surpassed by Mount Druitt as the largest public housing suburb ever built with a population of 32,000 people housed in 8,000 new homes.[44]

In realising the need to combat the ever expanding suburban sprawl and the inevitable problems of the periphery, the NSW Public Housing Commission began to construct estates of mixed cottages and town houses in order to increase living densities. In the 1970s, suburbs like Macquarie Fields, although born from virgin bush, were constructed with the supposed social needs of its residents and the ecology of the area in mind. The master planning of Macquarie Fields purported to foster social harmony and a communal lifestyle by creating a self sustaining economic environment complete with the urban infrastructure of inner city established areas. In this regard, Burchell states: "Out of this frontier wilderness, the Department of Housing planners carved neat rows of brick-veneer bungalows and angular semidetached 'villas' for a brand new suburb. But Macquarie Fields was to be more than an ordinary township. It was to be a public estate within a suburb: a little island of social experiment locked within the grand suburban sea".[45] The public housing estate (Glenquarie Estate) within the suburb of Macquarie Fields was designed in accordance with the 'Radburn' model, a town founded in 1929 in New Jersey, which attempted to create an egalitarian social utopia for middle-class America. Having its origins in Ebenezer Howard's 'Garden City', the town's planners Clarence Stein and Henry Wright aimed to adapt the communal Garden Cities of Letchworth and Welwyn in Hertfordshire England to the modern age of the car. The Radburn model is notable for the orientation of its houses which face the open space of its many parks with a secondary entrance and garage behind the house facing the street.[46] Radburn comprises a mixture of single detached homes and townhouses at a higher density than most typical suburbs, which are surrounded by common areas and an extensive interior park network connected by arcing streets, cul-de-sacs and loops. In Macquarie Fields, these laneways were named after trees such as Eucalyptus, Rosewood, Cottonwood, Tea Tree and Maple, to name a few, so as to enhance the isolationist appeal of the peripheral suburb. In addition, the invocation of a rural township, so the planners believed, was further enhanced by the meandering streets and wandering tracks and laneways through the sculptured parks and bushlands of the area.

Yet, not long after its completion and occupation, it became clear that Macquarie Fields would fail to achieve its social objectives, as Burchell reveals: "Within a couple of decades of the first concrete pours, the quaint laneways have become unsafe to walk at night, the paired semi-circular drives have turned neatly into amateur racing-tracks, and the paths through the parks make handy escape routes from the police. The neighbourhood has become a kind of monument to good planning intentions gone wrong".[47] Despite the best intentions, Macquarie Fields has become synonymous with social disaffection, and the riots only served to highlight the problems of this peripheral suburb.

Since the riots, urban theorists have hypothesised whether town planning was responsible for the social delinquency of the Macquarie Fields residents. In an attempt to address the social problems of the area plans were already in place, prior to the riots, to reorientate the houses to face the street in an effort to make them more visible from the street. In addition, various designs have been proposed to do away with the numerous laneways and cul-de-sacs to improve the traffic flow and accessibility of the suburb's streets. These two planning features in particular, it is argued, are responsible for many of the problems of the area, in that they "provide insufficient scrutiny of the public areas from the residents and that the many laneways give access and escape routes for thieves".[48] Nonetheless, the orientation of the homes and the cul-de-sac streets, even when combined with socio-economic disadvantage, do not necessarily result in civil uprisings, violence and riots, although they might be conducive to such events. Despite any conclusive evidence for the complete spatial determination of delinquent behaviour, authorities have now proposed to raze the entire 'Radburn precinct' which includes not only Macquarie Fields, but also the neighbouring suburbs of Green Valley, Minto, Claymore and Bonnyrigg. So far, more than 400 houses have been demolished with many more to come down. The residents have been moved away, in some cases against their will, to other suburbs, while the new land made available from the demolished estates will be sold to private development.[49]

Like most suburbs in Sydney's south west, Macquarie Fields epitomises the social isolation of a peripheral suburb. Yet there is no one single explanation for the events at Macquarie Fields. Poor urban planning and inadequate housing do not cause riots, although they may have acted as a catalyst for such disaffection. The riots were perhaps ignited by people's frustrations resultant from their inability to access the same privileges as the majority of citizens. As Burchell further notes: "In our era, we've managed to fill our little would-be utopias with a new class of public beneficiaries distinguished by their almost complete dearth of political, financial and televisual leverage of any kind . . . No serving politician or planner, ever went to live in Green Valley or Macquarie Fields. The locals there can't strike or stop work, or lobby local dignitaries. Instead, like the urban 'mob' of pre-franchise English cities, they have to throw bricks and break things to make themselves heard".[50] The riots, in a way, put Macquarie Fields back on the map. There is an ironic logic in wanton destruction of public and private

158 *Spatial contestation and suburban riots*

property, even if what they have seems so little, for in response resources seem to automatically pour into the place through a renewed focus in government infrastructure and resources. Those residents now relocated, as a result of the NSW's housing authorities' policy to distribute public housing throughout all areas of the city, will also obviously benefit from their relocation into areas where opportunities are greater.

The problem with places like Glenquarie Estate in Macquarie Fields is not that the urban planning did not produce the social utopia as intended, but rather, that it contributed to the spatial isolation of its residents as a result of the inadequate provision of public amenities. In a way, it served to deny residents access to public infrastructure such as transport, employment and education, effectively detaching them from mainstream society.[51] The conglomeration of so many welfare dependants and unemployed in one area only serves to strengthen stereotypes about the individuals that inhabit these areas. Effectively, their circumstances become greatly diminished as a result of their 'situated-ness' in space and the discursive formation of welfare dependency and social identity.

Disaffected locals: Redfern

In February 2004, a seventeen-year-old Aboriginal boy was recognised by a passing police vehicle investigating a bag snatching, while riding his bicycle from his mother's house in the inner Sydney suburb of Redfern. What happened next is sketchy, even after three independent enquires: however, it seems that there was some sort of pursuit during which the boy, 'TJ', lost control of his bicycle while turning a corner and impaled himself on a metal railing causing fatal injuries to his chest and neck. The next evening, his grieving friends and relatives gathered in an area of Redfern commonly known as 'The Block'. The gathering also attracted discontented Aboriginal youths from all over Sydney who blamed the police for the teenager's death. In an effort to prevent further numbers from joining the gathering the police closed down the local train station and began to barricade the area. As anger mounted a clash erupted between Aboriginal youths and the police in which the violence escalated into a full-scale riot which continued throughout the night. The train station was set alight, cars were fire bombed, and 40 police officers were injured.

In the aftermath, the Director of Redfern's Aboriginal Crossroads Ministries, Ray Minnecon, wrote an impassioned letter to a Sydney newspaper describing the Aboriginals' struggle for identity in a place like Redfern. He wrote: "For almost 200 years we were locked away from the new Australia that was built on our land . . . We are not happy with many of the results of that nation-building process . . . We are not happy at our forced exclusion in the building process . . . And we are still picking through the rubble of that terrible history, not made by our own hands, to rediscover ourselves, our identity and our place in the new nation . . . I live with the hope that my people will find our place and our space in the most alien and inhospitable place of all to the Aboriginal culture and people – the City of Sydney".[52] In his letter, Minnecon speaks of the Aboriginals' forced exclusion from the nation-building process. Here, he is not necessarily referring to their physical exclusion (although this has certainly occurred through their high rate of incarceration and the 'stolen generation'), but rather, their exclusion from the story of the nation. This process has not only resulted in their disaffection from the nation-state, but also their confinement to marginalised spaces of government housing, remote communities, illegal camps and homelessness. To this regard, the Aboriginal politician, Aden Ridgeway, later commented: "What happened on Sunday night [in Redfern] was an extreme expression of the mistrust between Aboriginal youth and the Police Services set against a backdrop of poverty, a lack of jobs and limited education . . . 'The Block' has its share of drugs, alcohol and dysfunction problems, just like any other community where poverty is rife. What is exceptional here is that we have a community of Aboriginal people living in Australia's largest and wealthiest city. They have life's entire infrastructure at their fingertips – and yet the opportunities of life in the big city are not within their reach".[53] This domain of Aboriginality is constituted by certain perceptions, like observations of endemic crime and poverty that sustains their position on the margins of society. Aboriginal households and communities are amongst the poorest in Australia. In effect, this cycle of poverty and alienation is self-reinforcing, perpetuating notions of dispossession and alienation, thereby excluding many indigenous Australians from the privileges that come about from being part of the nation.

The Redfern area has long been associated with violence and criminal behaviour. This lawlessness and lack of civility has been used to justify plans to demolish 'The Block', as the then NSW opposition leader John Brogden commented following the riots: "Put aside all the social problems that are well-known about down here in Redfern, and none of what happened last night is acceptable. The fact that 40 or 50 police were injured whilst they stood there and copped it from young Aboriginal thugs and others is an unacceptable position going forward. I'd bring the bulldozers in because I think allowing this to happen every couple of years, which is what's going to happen, will never fix the problem".[54] Brodgen's comments reveal a widely-held desire to remove The Block, its inhabitants and their social problems from the sub-urban landscape entirely. Redfern is undergoing a process of gentrification. As an inner city suburb close to Sydney's central business district, it has become home to high-rise apartments inhabited by wealthy young professionals. Wendy Shaw also highlights this in her interrogation of the Redfern riots: "The promise is for an urbanism that is free of fear, for person and property, through urban regeneration. Gentrification, the brightening and 'whitening' of inner Sydney space, is a stark contrast to conditions on The Block . . . This settlement at the heart of Australia's largest city unsettles commonly held views about entitlements to comfortable

160 *Spatial contestation and suburban riots*

living, particularly for the increasingly affluent neighbourhoods that encircle it".[55] This small parcel of Aboriginal occupied land seems to be the last hurdle for a complete rejuvenation of Redfern. The Block's association with disorder, dirt and crime was only enhanced by the 2004 riots, while the underlying causes of disaffection, under-privilege and poverty were seemingly glossed over and ignored. "The only hope for many non-Aboriginal locals, and others, is that The Block will eventually disappear, and so too will the threat of more 'race riots' in the gentrifying city".[56] The removal of the Aboriginal other serves two purposes: one, it produces racial sameness within this suburban terrain, and two, it diminishes the threat of the other. In this way, as Brogden intimates, the new residents of Redfern's gentrified areas will be able to cultivate and maintain an idyllic lifestyle, however contrived or precarious it may be, without interruption from the unwanted 'other'.

At this point, urbanism becomes overwritten by race, in that the wealthy privileged Australians believe themselves to possess a greater entitlement to the city. Apart from having been excluded from the production of nationalism, 'poor blacks' do not belong to areas of gentrification because they supposedly induce a sense of fear by their very presence. Sherene Razack argues, with relation to Native Americans in Canada, that the relationship between white settler society and indigenous people continues to be structured by racial hierarchies. She states: "In the national mythologies of such societies, it is believed that white people came first and that it is they who principally developed the land; aboriginal people are presumed to be mostly dead or assimilated. European settlers thus become the original inhabitants and the group most entitled to the fruits of citizenship".[57] Redfern, although occupied by Aboriginal people, is not seen as Indigenous land by the general public, but a space given to them by the Aboriginal Housing Commission by a 'white' federal government. As such their connection to place is tenuous at best because they are seen to have no claim to 'ownership'.

Similarly, the relocated residents of Macquarie Fields, while experiencing better amenities, also say that they are now "more lonely than ever in their lives, because they're the only public housing residents in a street of 'privates'".[58] Here, the differences between public housing and private development seem to also play a role in practices of exclusion, whereby one's sense of belonging is predicated on one's ability to claim possession of a piece of land. While government housing authorities attempt to provide residences for the under privileged, the very fact they occupy a 'public house' serves to stigmatise and exacerbate their sense of exclusion from the 'normal' population.

Redfern, a working-class suburb, was designated for Aboriginal housing in the 1970s. At the time, this reflected a significant shift in policy by the Whitlam government from the 'paternalism' of state intervention, which saw as one of its methods the forced removal of Aboriginal children from their families, to a policy of 'self determination'. 'Self determination'

Spatial contestation and suburban riots 161

supposedly gave the Aboriginal people the ability to determine their own political, economic, social and cultural development, and the potential to overcome disadvantage. Yet The Block still exists as an excluded zone, a community of economic disadvantage, unemployment, poverty, low education, overcrowding, suicide and continued welfare dependence. As such, the Redfern riots can be seen as the result of the uneasy negotiation between the way Aboriginals have been situated within the city as having less entitlement to occupy suburban space and the resulting effect of disaffection from the production of nation. Renee Newman-Storen argues that when individuals are defined by spaces like Redfern, they exist in a contradictory tug-of-war between agency and disempowerment. She remarks: "Conflict can be understood as an engagement between physical bodies and a collision of bodies of knowledge, intersecting in a simultaneous quest for acknowledgment".[59] In this way, one's sense of belonging is both a "lived embodied experience" and a discursive exchange that produces subjects of individuals through the reiterative overlay of power and space.

Redfern is a complex, contested and controversial suburban space. It is the only suburb in Australia to have a state government minister and a department designated specifically to watch over it. The police are visible in high numbers and confrontation, harassment and intimidation are daily occurrences. Redfern could be seen as a "place of cultural pride and autonomy for the Indigenous Australia"; instead, as Zanny Begg points out: "It is an antiquated remnant of a more paternalistic state which invested in public housing".[60] Here the government agencies who maintain ownership over the residences of Aboriginal people in The Block not only physically locate particular individuals in specific places, but also reiterate discursive formations of poverty, race and welfare that define people's identity and sense of belonging.

The story of the land is basically a racial one which characterises certain kinds of people and condemns them to an anachronistic space and time. As the former Prime Minister Paul Keating stated in his 1992 Redfern address: "It might help us if we non-Aboriginal Australians imagined ourselves dispossessed of the land we have lived on for 50,000 years – and then imagine ourselves told that it had never been ours. Imagine if ours was the oldest culture in the world and we were told that it was worthless. Imagine if we had resisted this settlement, suffered and died in the defense of our land, and then were told in history books that we had given up without a fight. Imagine if non-Aboriginal Australians had served their country in peace and war and were then ignored in history books. Imagine if our feats on sporting fields had inspired admiration and patriotism and yet did nothing to diminish prejudice. Imagine if our spiritual life was denied and ridiculed . . . ".[61] Here Keating pleads for the acceptance of Aboriginal people, not only within the urban landscape, but within the imagined nation. Unfortunately, this sense of disaffection, which has served to exclude Aboriginal people from employment, education, medicine and other opportunities, only reinforces, in the

162 *Spatial contestation and suburban riots*

minds of non-Aboriginal people, their image as a threat to the solidarity of the nation-state. In effect, Aboriginal people have been disaffected from the suburban space of the nation because they do not belong to the imagination of nationalism.

The Macquarie Fields riots tell the story of spatial contestation by disaffected individuals within the urban landscape of Australia's largest city. It parallels the riots of Redfern in that both events exemplify people's resentment towards their spatial isolation and inability to access the opportunities so promoted by the national imaginary of hopeful futures, prosperity and a 'fair go'. The solution to both, as advocated by the political right, is complete redevelopment, whereby it is proposed that the complete renewal of such land will supposedly extinguish the related social problems. Yet while certain individuals are excluded from the privileges of nationhood as a result of their location, race or other distinguishing features to which a border may be defined, the terrain they occupy may very well continue to be a volatile space. This does not suggest that one's behaviour is spatially determined, but rather, one becomes subject to particular discursive forms, like poverty, race and welfare, as a result of one's location in the city. Locations like the Australian beach, the periphery and the gentrified inner city become associated with particular values through a multitude of factors that, in effect, assign individuals a role to play in 'normal' society. In this manner, the discursive associations that construct identities serve to exclude certain individuals in order to define the collective 'we'. The "riotous thugs" who supposedly instigated the Redfern and Macquarie Fields riots may be simply removed and relocated, their claims to ownership, not only to the land but also to citizenship, are made void because they do not belong to the images of nationhood. By contrast the Cronulla riots add another dimension to the interplay between territory and belonging, for the Cronulla riots were not directed at government or law enforcement, but rather at the reclamation of territory that had seemingly been taken over by 'others'. In effect, as Wendy Shaw points out, this so-described "show of force" was a dominant display from those who, in believing to possess ownership over the urban terrain, attempted "to prescribe the norms or benchmarks against which to identify difference, including ethnic or 'racial' difference".[62] All three riots reveal the battle for ownership over space. The Macquarie Fields and Redfern riots were arguably brought about as a result of people's sense of exclusion from the constructed images of the nation, while Cronulla was more about reclamation in order to preserve those same constructed values.

Making up the nation

The preceding examples of suburban conflict demonstrate the contest between bodies in space in the marking out of territory. Sydney is not nearly as dangerous as these riots suggest, particularly given how the media has commonly betrayed such events as dangerous disruptions to civil peace, and

Spatial contestation and suburban riots 163

law and order. Other cities too have not been immune from such events. Consider the many riots in the United States over the past century, most recently the Rodney King riots in Los Angeles (1992),[63] the Paris riots in 2005 or even the Athens riots in 2008, all involving the residents of 'poor' neighbourhoods clashing with police. However, it is a gross oversimplification to associate criminality and violence with race and economic disadvantage. For as the Cronulla riots demonstrate, the middle class to wealthy educated 'white' suburbs are also not impervious to such events. As described, Cronulla, a wealthy beachside suburb of Sydney, "is a place that sits easily at the heart of the geographical imagination of 'decent' old-fashioned (white) Australia".[64] Cronulla was more than a 'revenge attack', and was rather the active defence of borders that typify nation and one's entitlement to urban space. It was the product of discursive strategies of "alignment and non-alignment" that, as Shaw identifies, "serve the principle belief in a kind of Australian-ness that is exclusive and exclusionary; it is non-ethnicised/racialised (or 'white')".[65] At this point, one becomes a witness to what Ghassan Hage describes as the "surface": the imagination of a unified national body (the territory and its citizens) that looks after it and protects it. In other words, it constructs a type of governmental/geopolitical entity that assumes entitlement over a territory, above the rights of 'others', of the kind that "the nation belongs to me".[66]

The possession of national citizenship endows the self with an entitlement to all those legal, social, cultural and normative dimensions that induce a sense of belonging and hope. Hage points out that this capacity to distribute "hope" is the secret to the nation-state's enduring capacity to secure the allegiances of individuals. The description by the eighteenth-century historian of the rise of nationalism, Jules Michelet, of the *Birth of the Frenchman* still bears relevance today. He describes the moment of birth of the *Frenchman* as when he is immediately "recognised" and "accounted" for as a person. In so doing, the nation-state provides him with a claim to dignity and moral worth, while at the same time he is made to feel "in control over the national territory". Hage elaborates: "No sooner is he born than he is put . . . in possession of his native land. But more importantly, the sense of being included, being accounted for and being in control, all add up to what is the national's capacity to receive what Michelet called his share of hope".[67] In this way, one's sense of belonging creates the illusion that one's association with place is greater than some other's. In this process, the state concerns itself with the collectivisation of individuals, a kind of 'making up the nation'. Although the geographic boundaries of a state are wholly arbitrary, it is the belief in their fixity, as Browning asserts, "which provides the strength of the nation-state's construction of rights and territorial limits".[68] Those found beyond these limits and marginalised by the national image find themselves lacking the rights and privileges pertaining to the inclusive citizen.

The geopolitics of producing citizens emphasises disjunction and division in the attempt to unite an identified collective. Nonetheless, the self is

164 *Spatial contestation and suburban riots*

not the product of 'unity', rather as Hall recognises: "a point of temporary attachment to the subject position which discursive practices construct for us".[69] Identity requires only the most basic of binary oppositions in order to link the individual to place. The spatial domain with which the citizen is associated is a volatile and reactionary site. In the suburban context it is the product of exclusion and inclusion which seeks to position the self in relation to or in reliance upon local authority. As such, the spatial representation of the public domain becomes a valorised and private space, accessible to the included few and overtly secured in order to guard against the presence of the 'other'. The dislocation of marginalised people from the mainstream, the exclusion of certain groups of people, racial division, class division and political unrest are more often than not the consequence of social regulation, nation building and the narrow characterisation of citizenship. The point at which these two poles meet is more often than not a site of contestation, resulting in social unrest, conflict and sometimes violence.

With this in mind, consider the Australian detention centre as a site established not only for the exclusion of others, but also for the purpose of defining the values of the included citizen. The following chapter is concerned with the redefinition of sovereign territory for the exclusion of others and the architecture that facilitates such purposes.

Notes

1 David Marr, "Alan Jones: I'm the person that's led this charge", *The Age*, 13 December (2005).
2 *Ibid.*
3 2GB, *Alan Jones Show*, 8 December 2005. Refer to ABC *Media Watch* Avail. http://www.abc.net.au/mediawatch/transcripts/s1898662.htm (Accessed December 2009).
4 *Ibid.*
5 Paul Sheehan, "A Hot, Wet Trail – Yet Police Remain Clueless in Cronulla", *Sydney Morning Herald*, 30 January (2006).
6 Refer to Suvendrini Perera, "Aussie Luck: The Border Politics of Citizenship Post Cronulla Beach", *ACRAWSA e-journal*, Vol. 3, No. 1 (2007), 2.
7 Karen Percy, "Words Hurt: Cronulla Violence Fuelled by the Language of Division", ABC *The World Today*, 12 December (2005). Available at http://www.abc.net.au/worldtoday/content/2005/s1529175.htm (Accessed January 2010).
8 Refer to Hsu-Ming Teo, "These Days it's Harder to be Different", *The Sydney Morning Herald*, 7 December (2006), Louis Foster and David Stockley, *Australian Multiculturalism: A Documentary History and Critique* (Clevedon: Multilingual Matters Ltd, 1988), 65.
9 Refer to Clemence Due, *The Terror of Racism: Constructing the Good White Nation Through Discourses of Values and Belonging* (Everyday Multiculturalism Conference Proceedings, Macquarie University, 2006).
10 Katya Johanson and Hilary Glow, "Re-Thinking Multiculturalism; Performing the Cronulla Beach Riot", *The International Journal of the Humanities*, Vol. 5, No. 3 (2007), 37.
11 David Burchell, "Both Sides of the Political Divide Stoop to Playing the Race Card", *The Australian*, 27 January (2006).

Spatial contestation and suburban riots 165

12 Stuart Hall, "Who Needs Identity", in *Questions of Cultural Identity* ed. Stuart Hall and Paul du Gay (London: Sage Publications, 1996), 4–5.
13 AAP, "PM Refuses to Use Racist Tag", *Sydney Morning Herald*, 15 December (2005).
14 Editorial, "On the beach", *The Economist*, 17 December (2005), 41.
15 Quoted in Lachlan Heywood, "National Identity in Spotlight", *The Courier Mail*, 27 November (2006).
16 *Ibid.*
17 Paul Hirst, *Space & Power: Politics, War and Architecture* (Cambridge: Polity Press, 2005), 3.
18 Akhil Gupta and James Ferguson, *Culture, Power and Place: Explorations in Critical Anthropology* (Durham: Duke University Press, 2001), 18.
19 Trevor Hogan, "Nature Strip: Australian Suburbia and the Enculturation of Nature", *Thesis Eleven*, Vol. 74 No. 54 (2003), 60.
20 Donald Horne, *The Lucky Country* (Camberwell: Penguin Books, 1964), 16.
21 Richard White, *Inventing Australia; Images and Identity* (Sydney: George Allen and Unwin, 1981), 101–106. Refer Graeme Davison "Sydney and the Bush; An Urban Context for the Australian Legend", *Intruders in the Bush: The Australian Quest for Identity,* ed. John Carroll, (Melbourne: Oxford University Press, 1982), 109–130.
22 Bradley Webb, "The Urban Context of the Bush Legend", *History Essays*. Available at http://www.ncs.net.au/history/essay_06.html (Accessed December 2009).
23 Hogan (2003), 60.
24 Sean Glynn, "Urbanisation in Australian History", *Images of Australia* ed. G. Whitlock and D. Carter (Brisbane: University of Queensland Press, 1992).
25 Dennis Wood, "Selling the Suburbs; Nature, Landscape, Adverts, Community", *Transformations*, No. 5 (December 2002).
26 *The West Australian*, real estate section, 9 May (1998).
27 *Ibid.*, 9.
28 Refer to Edward Soja, *Thirdspace: Journeys to Los Angeles and Other Real and Imagined Places* (Cambridge: Blackwell, 1996).
29 Wood (2002), 2.
30 Refer to Sally Paulin, *Sense of Place and Community Ownership*, 11 July (2008), 11. Available at http://yourdevelopment.org/factsheet/view/id/48#bg (Accessed December 2009).
31 Robin Boyd, *The Australian Ugliness* (Ringwood: Penguin Books, 1963), 9.
32 *Ibid.*, 35–36.
33 Wood (2002), 1.
34 Boyd (1963), 71–72.
35 *Ibid.*, 90.
36 Tony Abbott, "The Real Issue is the Changing Face of our Society", *The Australian*, 31 May (1990). Quoted in Adam Jamrozik, "From Lucky Country to Penal Colony: How a Politics of Fear Have Changed Australia". Keynote Address to the *Refugees and the Lucky Country Forum.*
37 Perera (2007), 3.
38 Mai Le, et al. *Youth and the Criminal Justice System*, 7 Nov. (2006). Avail. http://cts.hss.uts.edu.au/students06/Group2/overview_x.html (Accessed March, 2009)
39 David Burchell, "Dysfunctional Dumping Grounds", *The Australian*, 10 Feb. 2007.
40 Ali Madanipour et. al, "Social Exclusion and Space", in *The City Reader* ed. Richard LeGates and Frederic Stout, (London: Routledge, 2007), 182.
41 Kate Colvin, *Transport and Disadvantage* (Monash University, 2006). Available at http://209.85.173.132/search?q=cache:-TGHG9W5ACEJ:www.monash.edu.au/cemo/Transport2006/kateColvin%2520%2520Transport%2520and%2520

166 Spatial contestation and suburban riots

disadvantage%2520conference.doc+Kate+Colvin,+Transport+and+Disadvantag e&hl=en&ct=clnk&cd=1&gl=au (Accessed July 2009).

42 Gupta and Ferguson (2001), 18.
43 Refer to http://www.housing.nsw.gov.au/About+Us/History+of+Public+Housing+ in+NSW/The+1940s.htm (Accessed May 2009).
44 Refer to http://www.housing.nsw.gov.au/About+Us/History+of+Public+Housing +in+NSW/The+1960s.htm (Accessed May 2009).
45 David Burchell, "Trying to Find the Sunny Side of Life", *Griffith Review Edition 15: Divided Nation* (Sydney: Griffith University, 2007b), 4.
46 Refer to Peter Hall, *Cities of Tomorrow* (Malden: Blackwell Publishing, 2002), 128–138.
47 Burchell (2007b), 4.
48 Quoted in "Bulldozing the Past", *Sydney Morning Herald*, 2 August (2008).
49 *Ibid.*
50 Burchell (2007b), 16.
51 Refer to David Burchell, "Introducing . . . Social Exclusion", guest speaker at the State Library of Queensland, 18 April 2007.
52 Ray Minnecon, "Despair the Reality for a Race Lost in the Alien Space of Redfern", *Sydney Morning Herald*, 17 February (2004).
53 Aden Ridgeway, "The Underlaying Causes of the Redfern Riots Run Throughout Australia", *The Australian*, 18 February (2004).
54 Quoted in AAP, "Brogden's Riot Response: Bulldoze the Block", *The Sydney Morning Herald*, 16 February (2004).
55 Wendy Shaw, "Riotous Sydney; Redfern, Macquarie Fields, and (my) Cronulla", *Environment and Planning D: Society and Space*, Vol. 27 (2009), 431.
56 *Ibid.*, 432.
57 Sherene Razack, *Race, Space, and the Law: Unmapping a White Settler Society* (Toronto: Between the Lines, 2002), 2.
58 Quoted in "Bulldozing the Past", *Sydney Morning Herald*, 2 August (2008).
59 Renee Newman-Storen, "The Redfern Riots; Performing the Politics of Space", *Proceedings of the Conference of the Australasian Association for Drama, Theatre and Performance Studies* (2006), 2.
60 Zanny Begg and Keg De Souza, *There Goes the Neighbourhood: Redfern and the Politics of Urban Space* (Sydney: Published in tandem with the Performance Space exhibition, 2009), 6.
61 Paul Keating, speech at Redfern Park, 10 December 1992.
62 Shaw (2009), 428.
63 Refer Janet Abu-Lughood, *Race, Space and Riots* (Oxford: Oxford University Press, 2007), 227–268, and Mike Davis, *City of Quartz* (New York: Vintage Books 1990). This latter book is notable for its cultural dissection of Los Angeles, predicting, as some have described it, the tensions that led to the 1992 LA riots.
64 Shaw (2009), 439.
65 *Ibid.*
66 Ghassan Hage, *Against Paranoid Nationalism* (Annandale NSW: Pluto Press Australia, 2003), 33.
67 *Ibid.*, 14.
68 Julie Browning, "States of Exclusion: Narratives from Australia's Immigration Detention Centres 1999–2003" (Ph.D. diss., University of Technology Sydney, 2006), 132.
69 Hall (1996), 6.

7 The architecture of indefinite and mandatory detention

This chapter is a direct response to the Australian government's ongoing commitment to mandatory and indefinite detention. While this study focuses on the Howard era (1996–2007) it also decries the inability or unwillingness of subsequent governments to end detention. To this end, this chapter is concerned with the attitudes and politics that situate a certain type of architecture, like makeshift military barracks, transportable dongas, shipping containers and tents, in remote and inhospitable regions of Australia. It is here argued that detention is far more than just an administrative process to determine one's legitimate claim to asylum, and even more than a deterrent to prevent further dangerous ocean crossings. Rather, the practice of mandatory detention is derivative of discursive forms that criminalise the refugee and so justify their incarceration as a form of punishment for arriving in Australia uninvited. Indeed, the detention centre constitutes an architectural space that demonstrates how certain discursive practices with relation to national identity and citizenship provoke a political intervention that professes to act in the interests of the nation. The detention centre is an architecture of exclusion, one that exploits the vulnerability of one group of people in order to influence the behaviour of another. To this end, those incarcerated within Australian detention facilities become the 'exception', whereby their trauma is ostensibly transmitted to the public as 'spectacle' in order to depict the 'other' as potentially dangerous to the Australian way of life. Mandatory and indefinite detention is an extremely cruel practice. Moreover, it is perpetuated by a government that finds it politically convenient to deny certain individuals their human rights in order to present itself as tough on border security.

This chapter examines the status of the refugee as an individual without rights, made subject to the Australian government's policy of indefinite and mandatory detention. Here the location and composition of the immigration detention centre plays a role in the portrayal of asylum seekers as criminals, whereby their exclusion is effectively justified through discursive forms that seek to delimit the values and identity of the citizen.

The grey zone

> The exercise yard surrounded by a high and dangerous perimeter fence is the only sovereignty for the detainees. The touch of sunlight and breath of fresh air rejuvenates the life of the mentally drained detainees. 'The heaven' is what has been referred to by all detainees as the only place where they indulge in personal activities. But 'the heaven' is constantly guarded by the 'devils' that perform the evil task of invading privacy . . . The officers in charge of guarding the heaven take joy in proving their freedom, thus demoralising the detainee to its lowest. Like a pack of dogs the detainees are let out to the yard for a small period of time, on the hour till the wee hours of the morning. The shortage of various recreational and entertainment activities has a profound effect on the detainees' emotional, mental and physical status. (Wasim, immigration detainee)[1]

In early February 2000 media reports began to emerge about the Curtin Air Base near Derby in Western Australia's Kimberley region (then transformed into an immigration detention centre) that approximately 300 of the 1,147 detainees had entered their seventh day of a hunger strike. More dramatically, it was reported that certain Afghani detainees had resorted to "bizarre" acts of self harm, even to the extent of sewing their lips together.[2] More than a decade later, this form of protest has become all too familiar in Australia's detention centres, yet at the time, as Peter Mares recalls: "The incident at Curtin was unprecedented".[3] The protesters at the Curtin Immigration Detention Centre (IDC) were reportedly aggrieved about the length of time it took to process their claims for asylum. Moreover, they remonstrated about the conditions in the camp, which were described by a doctor attending the facility as "sub-human".[4] The Curtin IDC was opened in 1999 following multiple boat arrivals from Indonesia, making use of a disused RAAF base; temporary demountables, shipping containers and tents, surrounded by razor wire, were hastily assembled to accommodate the refugees.[5] In the camp, detainees complained about unhygienic conditions and inadequate toilet facilities, and about having to queue for hours for meals (as the mess hall could only seat 250 people at a time). They objected to the lack of air-conditioning in the accommodation and described the sweltering desert heat as unbearable. In fact, the detainees claimed that the shipping containers, which were used for accommodation, would get so hot that one would receive burns from leaning against their steel panels.[6] But above all, the detainees complained about being cut off and isolated from the rest of Australia as there were no telephones, no access to any form of news media and no ability to send and receive mail. Understanding this, Ian Rintoul from the Refugee Action Committee warned: "The very remoteness, the weather, the lack of facilities, the fact that people know that when they go there that they are going to be there

The architecture of indefinite and mandatory detention   169

for at least six months, or potentially longer . . . does mean that there is the possibility of more protests and self harm".[7] With this in mind, this chapter examines the process by which the asylum seeker is able to be detained, in often deplorable and harsh conditions, beyond the reach of adequate legal representation and basic human rights. This chapter is concerned with the attitudes and politics that situates a certain type of architecture like transportable dongas, shipping containers and tents in remote inhospitable regions of Australia, for the exclusion of certain individuals.[8] Implicated in this process is the architect, who in bringing about the means for the procurement, and in many cases the conversion of existing military barracks into detention centres, is complicit in such dehumanising practices. However, a more in-depth discussion on the ethical implication of the architect's participation in the design of detention centres, in particular the Christmas Island IDC, will be addressed in the next chapter.

Australia's practice of detaining 'unauthorised' arrivals is one of the most stringent in the world. Since 1992 Australian governments have enforced a policy of mandatory and indefinite detention. However, this chapter focuses on the Howard era (1996–2007). Although there is some crossover into more recent debates, Howard's legacy still has a profound effect on the development of current day immigration policy. Accordingly, all 'unauthorised arrivals' entering Australia's sovereign territory or intercepted in the nation's 'migration zones' are detained until their status can be determined. Moreover, the Howard government deliberately exploited this process in an effort to protect Australian borders and preserve a narrow and idealised view of Australia's cultural identity. It was (and is) a policy that dehumanises asylum seekers, representing them as inherently undesirable and unfit to make Australia their home. To this end, the activist Julian Burnside QC argues: "Refugees are the most powerless people on the face of the earth. For them, human rights have virtually no meaning. It is the fate of many minorities to be marginalised and disempowered; but rare in a modern, developed, democratic country to see one group singled out for such harsh treatment as asylum seekers in Australia. Specifically, it is disturbing to see a group so vilified, so demonised by the forces of government that their humanity disappears from the moral equation".[9] This notion of vilification, as described by Burnside, is most evident by the conditions of the detention camp. Indeed, by early 2002, not only Curtin but all Australia's immigration detention centres had become sites of protest, riots, acts of self harm and suicide attempts. As Annie Sparrow worker at the Woomera detention centre recounted: "I saw people stitching their lips who felt forgotten, people who had been there upwards of eight months or even a year, people who had done their utmost to comply with detention centre rules and immigration department requirements during that time, and had never before been part of the hunger strikes or the riots . . . People were driven to such an extreme measure because the only form of control they had left was what went in and out of their mouths. By lip-stitching they are saying 'we

170 *The architecture of indefinite and mandatory detention*

are absolutely helpless.' It is the deepest expression of despair".[10] Despite criticism by many respected individuals and agencies within Australia and abroad, such as the UNHCR and Amnesty International, the Howard government refused to accept other alternatives to its detention policy. In fact, it attempted to increase its political popularity through the harsh treatment of vulnerable people, who were assumed guilty of 'queue jumping' until they could prove themselves otherwise. Indeed, in November 2001, Australians voted to return the Howard government on a promise, following the Tampa Crisis, to be even tougher on border protection. With this in mind, this chapter questions how we might begin to understand the political space articulated by the construction of detention facilities, as neither prisons nor places of protection, and neither inside nor outside the rule of law.[11] The detention facility is a space of "intricate ambivalence".[12] On the one hand, it seeks to exclude, while on the other, it is also entreated to protect.

The intermittent arrival of asylum seekers, usually by boat from Indonesia, now routinely sparks heated and vigorous debates regarding the vulnerability of the nation's borders and the need for government to better protect Australian citizens from external threats. These arguments have become the building blocks for actionable government policy which takes form, in part, as architectural projects such as detention facilities. These buildings, of the type represented by those at Curtin (1999–2003, reopened 2010–2014), Woomera (1999–2003), Baxter (2002–2007), Port Hedland (1991–2003), Christmas Island (2008–current), Nauru (2001–2008) and others institute a space governed by the indistinction between law and lawlessness, regulating the body of the detained and confining them to a space that is inherently violent. This is a space in which life, to borrow from Agamben, is reduced to the "bare" minimum. In effect, it is a form of 'sovereign' power enacted over not only the lives of inmates, but also those beyond its perimeter – making for the Australian community. The detention facility exists within a 'grey zone', between inclusion and exclusion. Isolated and hidden from the public gaze, the IDC's presence is intended to provide a sense of security and reassurance in that it 'holds' potentially dangerous individuals at arm's length from the citizen.

In Australia, the politics of division have successfully exploited susceptible groups of people for the purpose of influencing the behaviour of citizens in the broader community. These policies are implemented in such a way that many people believe that the institutionalisation of asylum seekers is a necessary modus operandi for maintaining the status quo. Despite the fact that 85% of asylum seekers are eventually recognised as genuine refugees, all are viewed with mistrust, and therefore detained until such a time that their status can be determined, no matter the length of time it takes to do so. As the refugee activist James Jupp explains: "Just because a small minority of applicants practice fraud, whole categories are subject to excessive scrutiny and restrictions".[13] The asylum seeker becomes a 'life expendable', not because they are a threat to citizens, but because the spectacle of

The architecture of indefinite and mandatory detention 171

their trauma and literal exclusion behind razor wire reinforces the idea that Australia is a safer and more secure nation as a result.

Indeed, images of their suffering, protests and self harm are used against the refugees as a means of enhancing perceptions that these people are potentially dangerous and inimical to the Australian way of life. In this way, the trauma of refugees incarcerated in Australia's immigration detention centres becomes transmuted as a spectacle. Here Pugliese argues: "The razor wire fences of these prisons generate a double movement of both enclosure and exposure. The potential for exposure is what enables refugee trauma to be telegenically transmitted as spectacle".[14] For Pugliese, the spectacle of refugees surrounded by razor wire and living in subhuman conditions dispenses object lessons on deterrence whilst simultaneously representing the refugee as a threat to the Australian way of life. In addition, the detainee, who in possessing nothing of value (with the exception of their bodies) is reduced to performing spectacular acts of violence and self harm like cutting themselves with razor wire, setting fire to themselves and burying themselves. In effect, these actions serve to confirm, in the mind of a majority of citizens, that such individuals are unfit for inclusion into Australian society. In this way, the detention camp becomes a component of discourse on Australian identity and the privileges of citizenship, whereby the trauma of the refugee becomes tolerated and even justified. To this end, the former Premier of Western Australia, Richard Court, declared following the protests at the Curtin IDC that the detainees "had a nerve to be complaining", instead he continued, they should show "a little bit of gratitude . . . ".[15]

The rhetoric generated from government combined with a relatively benign media has sought to depict asylum seekers as intrinsically dangerous, as a people capable of throwing their babies overboard, criminals and possibly 'terrorists'. The use of such terms serves to justify their exclusion and contributes to their criminalisation, to the point that they are seen as deserving of their incarceration. Indeed, the detention centre is a 'heterotopian' space, an architectural assembly for the reprimand and exclusion of certain kinds of people from the mainstream socio-political domain. Foucault describes these spaces as the representation of disciplinary power, in that they explain how certain discursive practices aimed at delimiting the national character and the identity of the citizen become associated with forms of political intervention. Such intervention manifests itself through a variety of technologies, such as new laws, educational practices and even architectural forms.[16] These forms, like the built (and sometimes temporary) structures of the detention centre, are used not only to confine, but also to invest the public with particular rights and privileges through their participation in Australian society. The detention facility represents the physical and wilful exclusion of those who do not belong. It is constitutive of the regulation of not only the state, but also those who are deemed acceptable members of the community.

172 *The architecture of indefinite and mandatory detention*

The stateless individual

> I feel like I am located between the devil and the deep blue sea. If I stay in the camp I am wasting my life and yet I cannot go back. I've never committed any crime against humanity. I've just acted and practised according to my rights as a human back in Afghanistan. (Anonymous, immigration detainee)[17]

Prior to analysing the architecture of indefinite and mandatory detention, it is worthwhile examining the status of the refugee, if only to contextualise their treatment in Australian managed immigration detention centres. The refugee is literally outside the country of his/her nationality, lacking the rights and protections naturally afforded by citizenship. Nonetheless, the refugee is not an individual completely devoid of rights. According to the UNHCR *Convention and Protocol Relating to the Status of Refugees* a refugee is defined as: "One who . . . owing to a well-founded fear of being persecuted for reasons of race, religion, nationality, membership of a particular social group or political opinion, is outside the country of his nationality and is unable or, owing to such fear, is unwilling to avail himself of the protection of that country . . . ".[18] A refugee is therefore entitled, under the laws of the convention, to make a claim for asylum outside their country of nationality. However, as Julie Browning points out in her research on Australian immigration policy, the refugee's claim is counterbalanced by the discretion of the receiving state to accept or deny entry.[19] As Bulent Diken explains: "Our society seems unable to decide whether the asylum seeker is the true subject of human rights, which it invites everybody to accept as the most sacred of the sacred, or simply a criminal, a thief, who threatens 'us' with abusing 'our' welfare system".[20] Here Diken recognises the contradiction, on the one hand, between the state's enforcement and protection of human rights as it applies to its citizens, while on the other, its capacity to make arbitrary decisions about whom the same rights should apply to because they do not belong. In this way, it is interesting to note the change in terminology since WWII with relation to asylum seekers. Once classified as 'stateless', the current and more frequently used 'displaced person' seemingly legitimises the state's inability to recognise the legal status of refugees.[21]

Expanding upon this notion, Judith Butler recognises that the refugee's status is one of transition and movement between existence and the autonomous sovereign state. She explains: "When and where a 'refugee' is expelled from one state . . . there is often no place to go, even as one arrives someplace, if only in transit. It might be within the borders of a given state but precisely not as a citizen; so one is received, as it where, on the condition that one does not belong . . . ".[22] Those individuals who exist outside the bonds of citizenship are found to be, in Butler's view, "wanting" and subject to "discursively constituted fields of power" that will determine their admission or continued deprivation.[23] As such, the refugee is accepted or

The architecture of indefinite and mandatory detention   173

alternatively denied entry into the national body subject to discursively constructed criteria, including but not limited to such conditions as: ethnicity, religion, affiliation, appearance, speech, education, skill and so forth.

Hannah Arendt in her writings on the refugee in *The Origins of Totalitarianism* links the "rights of man" with that of the nation-state in order to demonstrate how the asylum seeker is excluded from law by their inclusion in detention. She claims that the 'natural' or inalienable rights purportedly belonging to all mankind (as incorporated into the US Bill of Rights) break down at the moment they can no longer be applied to every individual within the state.[24] She adds: "The conception of human rights, based upon the assumed existence of a human being as such, broke down at the very moment when those who professed to believe in it were for the first time confronted with people who had indeed lost all other qualities and specific relationships – except that they were still human. The world found nothing sacred in the abstract nakedness of the human being".[25] In this manner, the rights of humankind become separated from the individual when they are found outside the confines of the nation-state.[26] As Costas Douzinas declared, "one is a human being to a greater or lesser degree because one is a citizen".[27]

The separation of the rights of human beings from the rights of the citizen is most evident in the detention centre. These form a zone for the exclusion of others, a space of exception whereby the rights of one group are withdrawn in order to supposedly 'protect' the rights of another. In this way, Arendt's analysis of stateless people following the Second World War is still pertinent today, providing an interesting parallel with the Australian Government's treatment of current-day asylum seekers. Arendt asserts: "The first great damage done to the nation-states as a result of the arrival of hundreds of thousands of stateless people was the right of asylum, the only right that had ever figured as a symbol of the rights of man in the sphere of international relationships was being abolished".[28] In this manner, Arendt recognised that only when an individual is a citizen do they enjoy the full protection of the law, suggesting that humans are not all 'born equal', but become equal dependant on their ability to gain membership in a group that can guarantee the mutual recognition of human rights. Once one finds themselves outside the confines of that social order, they are no longer guaranteed those same rights. Here Arendt recognises: "A man who is nothing but a man has lost the very qualities which make it possible for other people to treat him as a fellow man".[29]

The significance of statelessness, according to Arendt "consists in the absence of a distinct place in the world; the loss of home, occupation, language, family and rights induced by the deprivation of legal and political status".[30] Indeed, statelessness is not an aberrant phenomenon, but rather a normalised condition predicated by a sovereign power to exclude. Elaborating this point Hayden explains: "In ceasing to belong to any rights-guaranteeing community whatsoever, the stateless person stands in stark

174 *The architecture of indefinite and mandatory detention*

contrast to the citizen located in the public sphere. Whereas the latter become fully human in a common world shared by others, the former are alienated from this world and lose their relevance to others".[31] Furthermore, Butler adds, speaking in relation to Guantanamo Bay, "Since the stateless are not stripped of status but accorded a status and prepared for their dispossession and displacement; they become stateless precisely through complying with certain normative categories. As such, they are produced as the stateless at the same time that they are jettisoned from judicial modes of belonging. This is one way of understanding how one can be stateless within the state, as seems clear for those who are incarcerated, enslaved, or residing and labouring illegally. In different ways, they are, significantly, contained within the polis as its interiorised outside".[32] Here the architectural spaces of internment camps and detention centres alike become a tool in the process of entitlement and disenfranchisement, whereby the disenfranchised are detained by the law but denied access to the law. In essence, the stateless person is consigned to a space of lawlessness and withheld rights precisely because they are not guaranteed the protection of the state. Sites designed specifically to accommodate refugees, as evidenced by the Australian detention centre and others akin to it (including the internment camps described by Arendt), encompass those individuals who are suspended from the law by the law that enables their incarceration, thus becoming, as Matthew Holt reveals, "a place, zone or area which is neither in the common juridical and political order nor completely outside it".[33]

From the outset, Australian detention centres have been geographically located on the margins, away from major population centres in remote desert regions of Australia. However, as a way of further emphasising Australia's commitment to border protection, the Howard government also opened detention facilities beyond the Australian mainland like Christmas Island (discussed in the next chapter) or on Pacific islands like Nauru (2001–2008) and the Manus Islands (2001–2004). Offshore detention served to further emphasise the refugee's displacement not only beyond the Australian mainland (which is their desired destination), but also, as Arendt recognised following the Second World War, out of reach of the law and the rights of citizenship. Browning adds: "In sending people to Manus Islands and Nauru and in denying legal appeals, the government rendered meaningless the treaty-ensconced right to seek asylum. In this sense offshore detention intensified the conditions of exclusion".[34] Interestingly, offshore detention was judged to be illegal by the High Court of Australia in 2010 following a proposal to open a detention facility in East Timor. The court ruled that the Australian government's failure to provide statutory law to asylum seekers detained in offshore detention centres was a breach of natural justice.[35] Consider the remarks by human rights lawyer Darren O'Donovan in relation to the High Court's decision: "Few court cases have made more visible the remorseless technical intricacies of modern government, functional division of labour, the layering and division of

The architecture of indefinite and mandatory detention 175

decisions, which diffuses responsibility for the total process. It returns us to the writings of Hannah Arendt who argued that the ideal of the 'rights of man' exists in a continual confrontation with the position of the stateless people, who lack the right to have rights which secure membership of a nation-state".[36] Despite the court's ruling, mandatory detention has continued unabated on Christmas Island and at other remote locations in Australia. To this end, the following section will examine how notions of 'sovereignty' enable governing authorities to make 'exceptions' to the rule of law for the better management of the population.

Sovereign power and 'the state of exception'

> Sunsets and sunrises help you ponder what life has in store for you. The present overtakes the past and sadness overtakes the future. Patience would be a virtue, but the truth lies in the period of torture. Torture from the constant itch of freedom makes the hours tick slower and slower. Isolation from society for a long period, cramped centres and the uncertainty of the detention period result in detainees attempting suicide or acts of self mutilation. The constant fear of being supervised and mustered makes anyone feel demeaned. (Wasim, immigration detainee)[37]

In detention human rights and laws are effectively suspended under the jurisdiction of the state for the 'benefit' of the state – or, as it might be better justified – "for the security of the nation".[38] Judith Butler argues that with this suspension of the law the state attempts to legitimise its power while at the same time diminishing the built-in structures of accountability by inducing a state of emergency. Along with this suspension of the law comes a new exercise of state sovereignty in which to attempt the better management of the population. To explain this she refers to Foucault's notion of 'governmentality', which is understood as the means by which political power regulates a population.[39] Here Butler argues that 'governmentality' has emerged as a form of power distinct from 'sovereignty'. She explains: "Governmentality operates through state and non-state institutions and discourses that are legitimated neither by direct elections nor through established authority . . . it gains meaning from no single source – rather it operates diffusely, to dispose and order populations, and practices and beliefs".[40] Butler adds that 'sovereignty' has emerged as the mode by which the state is able to assert its authority over a population when linked to a particular territory. In this way, both 'sovereignty' and 'governmentality' work together to enable the state to either suspend or contort law to its own benefit or in some cases fail or never fully realise their aims.

With the exercise of sovereign power the state is no longer subject to the rule of law. As Butler points outs: "Law can be suspended or deployed tactically and partially to suit the requirements of a state that seeks more

176 *The architecture of indefinite and mandatory detention*

and more to allocate sovereign power to its executive and administrative powers. The law is suspended in the name of 'sovereignty' of the nation, where 'sovereignty' denotes the task of any state to preserve and protect its own territoriality".[41] Thus, with relation to indefinite detention, the state allocates itself the power to exclude certain individuals who are deemed a danger or threat to the security of the nation by withholding access to basic human and legal rights. Accordingly, Agamben contends that 'sovereignty' asserts itself at the moment the state constitutes a state of exception to the rule of law. He explains: "The paradox of sovereignty consists in the fact the sovereign is, at the same time, outside and inside the juridical order. If the sovereign is truly the one to whom the juridical order grants the power of proclaiming a state of exception and, therefore, of suspending the order's own validity, then the sovereign stands outside the judicial order and, nevertheless, belongs to it, since it is up to him to decide if the constitution is to be suspended *in toto*".[42] In this way, the sovereign can both institute laws and suspend certain people from the law. This 'suspension' does not relate to their immunity from law, although this is possible, but rather their deprivation from the protection of the law, for the purpose of better managing the state and the population.

The exercise of sovereign power and the suspension of the law are exemplified, in the Australian context, by the exceptional placement of detention facilities in isolated desert regions of Australia, or more recently, under the 'Pacific Solution' legislation, on small remote islands. Howard's solution to the problem of detaining asylum seekers outside the law but inside Australian territory was to formulate a legislative 'state of exception', called the Pacific Solution. The Pacific Solution enabled the transportation of asylum seekers to detention camps located on small island nations in the Pacific, such as Nauru and the Manus Islands, rather than allowing them to stay on the Australian mainland. In addition, the Howard government in 2001 amended the *Migration Act* to excise external territories from the 'migration zone' – these territories included Christmas Island, Ashmore Reef, Cocos Island and hundreds of other territorial islands. This meant that any non-citizen arriving in these zones was not entitled to make a claim for refugee status, thus becoming unrecognisable by the law and excluded from due legal process. As Davidson comments: "The excision of the migration zone creates a physical buffer oriented toward the 'outside' so as to preserve the privileges and extend the rights of the core, where the thus protected and fully empowered citizenry resided".[43] In this way, the Australian Government has preferred to re-consider the extent of its sovereign territory in order to deny foreigners a claim to asylum and rights provided under international law because 'technically' they have not arrived in Australia. The excision of territory from Australia has little impact on citizens, in that no documentation is required to travel between territories. Its desired effect is on the non-citizen refugee who has no claim to legal rights and is thus mandatorily detained and isolated from the national population indefinitely.

The architecture of indefinite and mandatory detention   177

This redefinition of space is evident in other spaces of detention around the globe, including the Guantanamo Bay detention facility in Cuba. This fortified United States naval base which jailed refugees prior to the capture of alleged Al-Qaeda terrorists, strategically does not afford the same constitutional rights to detainees on the American mainland. Although under American jurisdiction and control, Guantanamo Bay is situated outside American sovereign territory, thus denying those individuals incarcerated there access to the law. As McLoughlin and Warin point out: "This state of exception is peculiar to the cartography of Guantanamo Bay and its placement within legal geographies, for the prison is simultaneously outside the United States, and within the United States in order to permit 'coercive interrogation'".[44] This situation was justified by the Bush administration as working in the best interests of the security of the American nation. In Europe, several countries such as Germany, Switzerland, Spain and France have also excised territory in order to control the flow of refugees and 'illegal' immigrants from entering into their sovereign territory. However, in contrast to Australia, these excised territories do not exclude offshore and remote regions of national territory, but rather, the internal territory of airports. For example, the creation of so-called 'international transit zones' in French airports denies refugees the right to asylum because they are not considered to have entered French national territory, and as a consequence French authorities are under no obligation to examine their request. In these spaces, the state has no obligation to provide asylum seekers or any alien with the same rights afforded to its citizens, whereby the state reserves the right to excise territory in order to deprive certain individuals of the rule of law.[45] In effect, the external territories become the exception to the law by the law inside the state.

The distinction between 'governmentality' and 'sovereignty' is important because it helps describe how power works. Thus, in relation to indefinite detention, sovereignty produces the suspension of law, "a rival form of political legitimacy", as Butler explains, "one with no structures of accountability built in".[46] 'Governmentality' seeks to produce the subject in compliance with the law, yet 'sovereignty', while concerned with the management of populations, does so through exclusion. One means by which this is achieved is through the inhumane treatment of refugees – in contrast to the citizen who is encompassed by the mechanisms of national identity and belonging. Thus, it is equally important to recognise that the 'state of exception' instituted by state sovereignty not only excludes but also constitutes the national community. Here Diken recognises that the production of the population is not constructed on the back of a simple exclusion, but rather it is produced by including the excluded. He declares: "What is excluded by the law or abandoned at the margins of politics, of the polis, maintains its relation to the law as its suspension . . . The refugee is abandoned only to be included in the domain of power".[47] According to the mechanisms of sovereignty, power emerges not as the expression of social

178 *The architecture of indefinite and mandatory detention*

unity, as 'governmentality' might explain, but rather as the expression of dis-unity that offsets the citizen in contrast to the 'other'.

The 'state of exception' not only excludes the 'other' from the law, but also seeks to define and characterise the values of individuals for their inclusion, subjectification and production in the national body. Diken further elaborates: "The social bond itself has the form of exception, or un-bonding, in which an exclusionary inclusion politicises the subject, in our case the refugee. Thus, every time the refugee is 'excluded' we should be looking for the inclusive gesture that follows it, which is part and parcel of the social bond between 'us' and 'them'".[48] One might point to Howard's attempts to add terms like 'mateship' to the constitution as one of many inclusive gestures made during his time in office. Yet the attempt to polarise the population sets one against another for the purpose of gaining the allegiances of the included and at the same time enact upon the excluded a legally constituted, enforceable and justifiable ban or suspension of the law.

Sovereign power is distinct from governmentality because the former has the ability to constitute the exception, whereby the 'state of exception' removes the distinction between life and law, and outside and inside.[49] Sovereign power is realised in the detention facility, because it is not an institution designed to safeguard certain laws, but rather to put in force the legal violence against the 'other'. In this way, the built structures of the detention facilities become the embodiment of the Howard government's "determination to permanently jettison the excluded".[50] Australian-run detention facilities have become a space for the enactment of the exception, both inside and outside Australia's juridical order. The individual placed within the confines of detention, having no claim to any legal status, is abandoned outside the rule of law and made subject to 'bare life'. The individual located outside the detention facility, while entitled to the rule of law, becomes enclosed and defined by the nation-state. Indeed, sovereign power is capable of totally subsuming the majority of the population by excluding others in the interests of the nation. This is not to say that mandatory detention is not without its opposition, yet those who protest risk being seen as working against the interests of the state. The detention facility is a reminder of the extent to which sovereign power can succeed in substantiating the mistreatment of certain individuals for the purpose of sustaining the authority of the governing body.

Although Howard's successors, the Labour governments under Kevin Rudd, ended the 'Pacific' Solution', they did not change their stance on the practical effectiveness of mandatory detention. Furthermore, the return of the Coalition under Tony Abbott on a platform of strengthening Australia's borders through the implementation of 'Operation Sovereign Borders', whereby naval vessels intercept and turn around rickety fishing boats, and the reopening of the offshore detention centres in Nauru and Manus Island in 2012, is testament to Australia's commitment to exclusionary politics. For as long as it remains Australian policy to locate detention facilities outside

The architecture of indefinite and mandatory detention 179

the rule of law it stands to reason that mandatory and indefinite detention will have profound and troubling implications for the welfare of some of the world's most marginalised people. If it is necessary to legitimately assess every claim for asylum, surely this can be achieved in a humane manner devoid of the necessity to transmit the process as a means of sustaining the authority of the governing body and delimiting the citizen. Mandatory detention is an ineffective and extremely costly way to process such claims, yet its value to the government, in particular the Howard government, is enormous. But sadly, as Burnside observes: "In twenty years time our children or grandchildren will ask, 'What did you do to try and change this?' Those without an answer will show themselves to be complicit in a terrible moral wrong".[51] The process of isolation and incarceration in some of Australia's most remote locations employs space and architecture in ways that enable the subjectification of the population. In this case, the buildings that constitute the immigration detention centre become convenient not only for the practicality of being able to provide basic amenity and accommodation, or because of their geographically remote locations, but rather to further the interest of the sovereign and thus enable the better management of Australia's population. For those detained inside the confines of the detention camp, their voice is reduced to acts of protest and self harm. Unfortunately, such acts are still an all-too familiar fixture in the Australian news media. With this in mind, the following section will examine the effect of "externalisation",[52] geographical containment and lawlessness on the operation of the detention camp, its composition and its impact on the health and welfare of the detainee.

Managing Australia's borders: inside Woomera

> When we came first to Woomera, we didn't believe we were in Australia . . . Because the things that happened – they wouldn't happen in Australia. It must be another country.[53]

In the years that followed the Curtin hunger strike, Australian immigration detention centres were plagued by numerous major riots and incidents of self harm. But as Browning recognised, detainees have also attacked the "material space of detention and the architectonics of their incarceration".[54] Detainees have set fire to buildings, pushed down barriers and cut through razor wire fencing. In response, the Department of Immigration has employed, in many cases, aggressive means to suppress the protests and restrict the damage to property. In December 2002, not long before its closure, Woomera experienced a mass break-out and days of rioting in which 13 accommodation units were burnt down. In fact, over Woomera's three years of operation, 12 major incidents were reported by the Department of Immigration in which tear gas and water cannons were deployed as a tactical response to quell the violence.[55]

180 *The architecture of indefinite and mandatory detention*

Described as the "worst" of all Australian detention facilities,[56] the Woomera detention centre incarcerated more than 1,500 men, women and children at any one time. Located approximately 500km north of Adelaide in the South Australian Simpson Desert, the Woomera detention camp was established at the site of an abandoned military barracks at a former missile testing ground. During the 1950s Woomera boasted a population of over 7,000 people, but when the US military pulled out in the 1980s the town's population plummeted, leaving a population of just 325 in 1999. When the detention centre was opened, the town consisted of rows of abandoned houses, an abundance of underutilised services and a vacated military ground. Peter Mares explains: "When there was a sharp increase in arrivals of boat people on Australia's northern coast, Woomera appeared to offer a nice fit with the town's underutilised facilities and its isolation".[57] But when asked in an interview why the detention facility needed to be located in such a remote and inhospitable region of Australia, Phillip Ruddock, the then Minister for Immigration, denied both the punitive and deterrent aspects of the facility and simply answered by saying that it was a convenient location because "there was an airport nearby".[58]

As the camp's population rapidly increased, the original 1950s brick barracks became augmented by transportable dongas and rows of tents enclosed

Figure 7.1 November Compound, Woomera Detention Centre, 2002. Taken as part of a fact-finding mission for the Human Rights and Equal Opportunity Commission's National Inquiry into Children in Immigration Detention.

http://www.humanrights.gov.au/

by a razor wire fence. Within the confines of the Woomera IDC, detainees were subject to a complete lack of basic amenity and grossly inadequate conditions. For example, there were limited toilets and wash rooms which required detainees to line up for hours in order to use them. As one South Australian lawyer noted: "Two working toilets for 700 people, both leaking, sand on the floors to 'mop up' the effluent, four working showers, hot water only available after midnight . . . no air conditioning, no flyscreens, there are millions of flies . . . ".[59] In time, a playground was erected for the children, but as a parliamentary enquiry into the standard of accommodation pointed out, there were no children using it because the temperature, which often exceeded 40°C, was not "conducive to outdoor activity".[60] One year after Woomera's opening the detention centre received somewhat of an upgrade. A new high security building was constructed for the isolation of "high risk detainees" – otherwise known as solitary confinement. In addition, the detention centre was divided into five separate compounds through internal barricades and checkpoints, for the "better management of detainees". And the 4 metre-high perimeter fence was replaced by a more solid barrier made from closely spaced steel palisades to prevent further escapes. But despite these so called 'improvements', the camp continued to be plagued by riots, breakouts, hunger strikes and suicide attempts. In April 2003, owing in part to substantial political pressure, the Woomera site became untenable and the site was closed. Thus, the detainees were transferred to the nearby purpose-built Baxter detention centre located 200km further south. More recently, the Woomera site has been proposed for nuclear waste disposal, leading Zygmunt Bauman to suggest that like toxic waste, "the refugees become human waste, and sealed off in tightly closed containers".[61]

Isolated within the confines of the Woomera detention centre, the refugee is cut off from the outside world in a visceral display of exclusion. Anyone attempting to enter the camp from the outside, such as nurses and welfare officers, is subject to stringent security checks and restrictions designed to regulate the experience of the visitor and ultimately discourage them from entering. Life inside the detention facility is routine, based upon sleep, meals and 'muster', when every few hours detainees are called to gather for a head count. As Browning observes, detainees are "caught in a space of isolation and obfuscation, theirs is a cycle of boredom, hope, anxiety and frustration".[62] Everyday choices have been withdrawn from the detainee. These include freedom of movement, the ability to access health, recreational and legal services, to choose appropriate clothing, or to eat and sleep according to one's preference. Every movement within the facility is subject to regulation and surveillance, and every aspect of life is regimented in accordance with the procedures dictated by detention management. It is not uncommon for detainees to be subject to threats and in some cases physical violence, handcuffing, solitary confinement and deprivation for failing to obey procedures or to curb resistances.

182 *The architecture of indefinite and mandatory detention*

Indeed, the effect of temporal-spatial detention is further compounded by the way asylum seekers are treated. A visiting psychiatric nurse, Dr Glenda Koutroulis, at the Woomera IDC was critical of the "military way" detainees were dealt with, often with contempt and by means of reducing them to a number. She writes: "Woomera is a totally traumatising, alienating experience because they are not treated with any humanity. I have never held so many crying, sobbing men in my life who asked me, 'Why are you doing this to us? I am not an animal' they say, 'I am not criminal'. All I could do was apologise for shame of Australia doing that to them".[63] A detainee's time in detention, compounded with the traumatising effect of past experiences, has prolonged and serious consequences for their health. Psychologists describe the literal "breaking down" and the "fundamental loss of will" suffered by long term detainees who are: "reduced to catatonia – a non speaking human shell".[64] Here, one is reminded of Primo Levi's 'Muselmann', whereby the detainee is stripped of rights and the normality of the outside world rendering life worthless. In Levi's account the 'Muselmann' is the walking dead of the concentration camp, the limit of the human condition, a life exposed to death. Obviously, detention centres, though deplorable, are not concentration camps comparable to those built by the Nazi regime. Nonetheless, there are parallels between the two structures in the manner that life is reduced to a bare minimum, and in comparisons not only of scope and numbers, but also of morality.

Interestingly, the task of managing the facility was awarded to ACM (Australian Correctional Management, a subsidiary of Wackenhut Corporations, operator of the American private prison system). Arguably, the treatment of detainees and the day-to-day operation of the facility bore a greater resemblance to a maximum security prison than that of a refugee processing and reception centre. Recognising this, Simon Philpott's analysis is telling. He states: "ACM's ability to make refugee detention profitable partly arises from its capacity to operate detention centres at a lower per-head cost than the government . . . Financial effectiveness, rather than the welfare of asylum seekers, has featured prominently in government discourse in favour of privatised centres".[65] Indeed, outsourcing custodial services not only relates to the Australian government's desire to save money, but also locates allegations of human rights abuses, brutality and assault outside the public domain and beyond the sphere of government oversight and responsibility. To this end, Philpott concludes: "There seems little doubt that despite government claims of taxpayer value for money in the detention and care of asylum seekers, the market has not been kind to asylum seekers themselves . . . Perhaps of greatest concern is the fact that by placing the market between itself and the asylum seekers, the Australian government, and the people it represents, can be shielded from the moral questions that might be raised by the policy of mandatory detention primarily in the context of commercial confidentiality".[66] Effectively, the refugee not only finds themselves self stateless and trapped within an uncertain legal domain, but

The architecture of indefinite and mandatory detention   183

also in the hands of a company whose primary concern is to profit from their incarceration.

By minimising its responsibility for the operation of detention facilities, the government can masquerade its reasons for isolating detainees, typically in disused remote military barracks, as a fillip to economic activity in the local town. More recently the Western Australian town of Northam, also with disused army barracks, has been transformed into a site for the detention of asylum seekers. Despite vigorous objections from the local population, local government authorities have supported the plan on the basis that a detention centre will provide the town with additional economic activity. The Wheatbelt Development Commission website states: "The Australian Government announced the establishment of an immigration detention centre at the Department of Defence Northam Training Camp in October 2010. It will be important for Wheatbelt communities to capture the positive financial and social benefits, including an economic boost, increased employment opportunities, contracting and tender opportunities, and departmental and detention service provider staff joining local sporting and cultural groups".[67] Much like the hundreds of prisons which have sprung up in small rural towns all over the US, the prison-town concept has brought with it unintended consequences.[68] For example, during the operation of the Woomera detention centre, local employment remained effectively unchanged because specialised detention staff needed to be flown in from the major cities. In fact, Woomera's reputation as a place to live has diminished considerably owing to negative attitudes about the detention centre, which has resulted in the further depletion of the town's economic viability and reduced population numbers.[69] To this end, architects, project managers, construction companies and the like who participate in the procurement of such facilities for the purpose of detention cannot limit their moral obligations by pretending to act in the best interests of small town communities. For despite the possibility of commercial gain the long-term effects on both the detainees and community are, as experienced in the US and Woomera, extremely harmful.

In reality, any government willing to incarcerate certain individuals because they do not belong does so because their obligations to uphold basic human rights are outweighed by their desire to normalise certain entitlements and further extend the powers of the governing body. "Getting tough"[70] will not stem the movement of displaced people seeking a better life. Indeed, placing asylum seekers in detention not only punishes 'others' but serves to delimit the population through the ever narrowing parameters of border politics. Consider briefly the US-Mexico migrant barrier and the Israel-Palestine security wall, both of which derive from a similar discourse relating to exclusion. Here Michael Sorkin suggests: "Each of these barriers has been touted as providing security for one side or the other, but each clearly marks a failed politics and aggressive intransigence".[71] All such barriers, both physical and sometimes virtual, not only protectively enclose

184 *The architecture of indefinite and mandatory detention*

the citizen, but attempt to define the other. They enable space to be clearly demarcated by the border, as a 'statement' of territorial sovereignty. On the inside, one is encompassed by the nation-state, on the outside one loses entitlement even to the basic claim of human rights and dignity.

In the case of Australian immigration detention centres, the withdrawal of basic human rights simply to deter other people from a dangerous border ocean crossing simple does not stack up. At this point one might agree with Hage, who states: "We cannot defend our border in a totally racist and totalitarian way and then claim – or pretend to – live within that border as a non-racist, democratic society".[72] The detention centre occupies the space in-between inside and outside, it is a space that is materialised when exception becomes the rule. There is no doubt, as Tazreiter concludes, that detention is a "policy decision and a strategic and administrative practice which is unambiguously about containment, separation and punishment".[73] Although she may have being referring to the detainee, detention is not without its effects on the population as a whole.

Notes

1 Quoted in *From Nothing to Zero* ed. Julian Burnside (Melbourne: Lonely Planet Publications, 2003), 36.
2 Refer to Chris Masters, "A Well Founded Fear of Persecution", *ABC Four Corners*, 13 March 2000. Available at http://www.abc.net.au/4corners/stories/s110015.htm (Accessed October 2010). For an analysis of the media reporting with relation to detention centres refer to Natascha Klocker and Kevin M. Dunn, "Who's Driving the Asylum Seeker Debate? Newspaper and Government Representations of Asylum Seekers", *Media International Australia incorporating Culture and Policy*, No. 109, November (2003), 71.
3 Peter Mares, *Borderline* (Sydney: UNSW Press, 2002), 9.
4 Refer to Mares (2002), 13. Mark Colvin, "Mixed Reaction to Reopening of Curtin Detention Centre", *ABC PM* (19 April 2010). Available at http://www.abc.net.au/pm/content/2010/s2876919.htm (Accessed September 2010). Jessica Baird "Playing the Waiting Game in 42 Degree Heat", *Amnesty International*, 1 November (2010). Available at http://www.amnesty.org.au/refugees/comments/24022/ (Accessed January 2011).
5 The Curtin detention centre was decommissioned following riots in 2002 by the Howard government, but was subsequently reopened by the Rudd-Gillard government in 2010 following an increase in asylum seeker arrivals. Refer to Simon Santow, "Asylum Seekers Sent to Curtin 'Hell Hole'" *ABC News*, 19 April (2010). Available at http://www.abc.net.au/news/stories/2010/04/19/2876159.htm (Accessed January 2011).
6 Refer to Julie Browning, "The Only Thing They Have to Bargain With in Their Own Self: Masculinity and Protesting Immigration detention", *Transforming Cultures eJournal*, Vol. 2 No. 1, November (2007), 10.
7 Santow (2010).
8 The inhospitable temporary accommodation measures at the Woomera detention centre stand in stark contrast to the fashion for the 'transient' in high-brow architectural circles, in particular, theory that fetishizes shipping containers and the condition of portability. It has been recently proposed that the vacant shipping containers at Woomera could be sent to Christmas Island as a solution to

The architecture of indefinite and mandatory detention   185

overcrowding. However, one architectural critic in proposing his objection to such a decision suggested that these containers would be better served as remote indigenous housing. Iain Hall writes:

> The problem for so many bureaucrats, activists and latte sippers is that they are just not capable of thinking outside the square to finding housing solutions that solve the problems at a reasonable cost. Housing made from shipping containers does not have to look second rate or makeshift. It can be stylish, practical and affordable but importantly you can create dwellings that are extremely durable that can be built up in modules to suit the needs of any size family or community. Of course you can bet that what stops the use of surplus shipping containers as a starting point for the creation of some innovative housing solutions, is not their fitness for the purpose but a fear that this will be seen as a second rate housing option for our first Australians. The people who think like this are actually troglodytes who clearly know squat about architecture, design or building. The problem is not how can we afford to build McMansions in the remote parts of the country but how do we house people who need housing. A real solution needs those in power to think outside the brick veneer paradigm go to a clean sheet of paper and consider lateral thinking options like this. (Available at http://iainhall. wordpress.com/2009/10/16/thinking-inside-the-big-boxes-for-indigenious-housing/ [Accessed January 2011]).

9 Quoted in Burnside (2003), VI.
10 *Ibid.*, 32–33.
11 Refer to Fiona Jenkins, "Bare Life: Asylum Seekers, Australian Politics and Agamben's Critique of Violence", *Australian Journal of Human Rights*, Vol. 18 (2004).
12 Julie Browning, "States of Exclusion: Narratives from Australia's Immigration Detention Centres 1999–2003" (Ph.D. diss., University of Technology Sydney, 2006), i.
13 James Jupp, *From White Australia to Woomera* (Cambridge: The Cambridge University Press, 2002), 67.
14 Joseph Pugliese, "The Tutelary Architecture of Immigration Detention Prisons and the Spectacle of 'Necessary Suffering'", *Architectural Theory Review*, Vol. 13, Issue 2, August (2008), 206.
15 Quoted in Mares (2002), 11.
16 Michel Foucault, "Of Other Spaces: Utopias and Heterotopias", *Lotus*, Vol. 48, No. 9 (1985/6), 9–17.
17 Quoted in Burnside (2003), 9.
18 UNHCR, *Convention and Protocol Relating to the Status of Refugees* (Geneva: UNHCR Media Relations and Public Information Service, 2007), 16.
19 Browning (2006), 7.
20 Bulent Diken, "From Refugee Camps to Gated Communities: Biopolitics and the End of the City", *Citizenship Studies*, Vol. 8, No. 1, March (2004), 83–84.
21 Refer Hannah Arendt, *The Origins of Totalitarianism* (Orlando: Harcourt Inc. 1968), 279.
22 Judith Butler and Gayatri Chakrovorty Spivak, *Who Sings the Nation-State?* (Oxford: Seagull Books, 2007), 6.
23 *Ibid.*
24 Refer Giorgio Agamben, *Homo Sacer: Sovereign Power and Bare Life* (Stanford: Stanford University Press, 1995), 126.
25 Arendt (1968), 299.

186 The architecture of indefinite and mandatory detention

26 Included in the confines of the nation-state is international travel with a valid visa.

27 Costas Douzinas, "Postmodern Just Wars: Kosovo, Afghanistan and the New World", in *Law After Ground Zero* ed. John Strawson: (London: Glass House Press, 2002), 31–32. Refer to Costas Douzinas, *The End of Human Rights* (Portland: Hart Publishing, 2000), 85–108.

28 Arendt (1968), 280.

29 *Ibid.*, 300.

30 Patrick Hayden, *Political Evil in the Global Age: Hannah Arendt and International Theory* (New York: Routledge, 2009), 55.

31 *Ibid.*, 56

32 Butler and Spivak (2007), 16.

33 Matthew Holt, "Biopolitics and the 'Problem' of the Refugee", in *Critical Perspectives on Refugee Policy in Australia* ed. Michael Leach and Fethi Mansouri, (Burwood: Deakin University, 2003), 99.

34 Browning (2006), 190.

35 In November 2010, the full bench of the High Court unanimously ruled that two Sri Lankan asylum seekers were denied "procedural fairness" under the Migration Act. The bench found that the government had made an "error of law" by not allowing the pair, who were detained offshore, the legal right to appeal to Australian courts. The decision means that asylum seekers who are intercepted in excised territory, like Christmas Island, Ashmore Island and Cocos Island, cannot be treated differently than those who arrive on the mainland. The lawyer for the two Sri Lankans explained that the Migration Act has resulted in a two-tier system, whereby asylum seekers who land offshore have different avenues of legal recourse to those who land onshore. "Now, any decision made by an immigration official in East Timor or Nauru could also be subject to review. At the very least, asylum seekers in offshore detention centres like Christmas Island will now have access to the courts". Refer to Alexandra Kirk, "Immigration Facing 'Chaos' After High Court Decision", *ABC Kimberley*, 10 November (2010). Available at http://www.abc.net.au/news/stories/2010/11/11/3063298.htm?site=kimberley (Accessed October 2011).

36 Darren O'Donovan, *Echoes of a Distances Humanity; Australia's High Court and Offshore Asylum Seeker Detention*, 16 November (2010). Available at http://www.humanrights.ie/index.php/2010/11/16/echoes-of-a-distanced-humanity-australia%E2%80%99s-high-court-and-offshore-asylum-seeker-detention/ (Accessed January 2011).

37 Quoted in Burnside (2003), 35.

38 Refer to Judith Butler, *Precarious Life* (London: Verso, 2004).

39 Refer to Michel Foucault, *The Foucault Effect: Studies in Governmentality* ed. Graham Burchell, Colin Gordon and Peter Miller (Chicago: University of Chicago Press, 1991), 87.

40 Butler (2004), 52.

41 *Ibid.*, 55.

42 Agamben (1995), 15.

43 Robert Davidson, "Spaces of Immigration 'Prevention': Interdiction and the Nonplace", *Diacritics*, Vol. 33, Nos. 3/4, Fall (2004), 2–18.

44 Pauline McLoughlin and Megan Warin, "Corrosive Places, Inhuman Spaces: Mental Health in Australian Immigration Detention", *Health and Place*, Vol. 14 (2008), 256.

45 Refer to Attila Ataner "Refugee Interdiction and the Outer Limits of Sovereignty", *Journal of Law & Equality*, Vol. 3, No. 1, Spring (2004), 7–29.

46 Butler (2004), 66.

The architecture of indefinite and mandatory detention 187

47 Dikens (2004), 85.
48 *Ibid.*
49 Refer to Agamben (1995), 18.
50 Refer to Browning (2006), 38.
51 Burnside (2003), VII.
52 Jennifer Hyndam and Alison Mountz, "Another Brick in the Wall? Neo-Refoulement and the Externalisation of Asylum by Australia and Europe", *Government and Opposition*, Vol. 43, No. 2 (2008), 250.
53 Quoted in D. Campbell, "In Woomera", *The Guardian Weekly*, 25 May (2002), 25–31.
54 Browning (2007), 2.
55 Refer to "A Last Resort", *Human Rights and Equal Opportunities Commission*, 13 May (2004). Available at http://www.hreoc.gov.au/Human_RightS/children_deten tion_report/summaryguide/7_safety.htm (Accessed October 2010).
56 Refer to Jupp (2002), 194.
57 Mares (2002), 36.
58 Refer to ABC *Lateline* transcript, "Labour Rethinks Detention Stance", 28 January (2002).
59 Quoted in Fiona Redding et al., *We've Boundless Plains to Share*, Peoples Inquiry into Detention, November (2006), 30.
60 Refer to http://www.aph.gov.au/House/committee/mig/report/hilton/5chapter.pdf (Accessed June 2008).
61 Zygmunt Bauman, *Wasted Lives; Modernity and its Outcasts* (Cambridge: Polity Press, 2004), 85.
62 Browning (2006), 73.
63 Quoted in Penelope Debelle, "Blowing the Whistle on Hidden Suffering in Woomera", *The Age*, 24 April (2002).
64 Browning (2006), 13.
65 Refer to Simon Philpott, "Protecting the Borderline and Minding the Bottom Line: Asylum Seekers and the Politics in Contemporary Australia", *Refuge*, Vol. 20, No. 4 (2003), 69.
66 *Ibid.*, 70
67 http://www.wheatbelt.wa.gov.au/northam/ (Accessed December 2010).
68 The location of prisons in small rural towns is intended to boost population numbers, as the US Census counts prisoners in the population data of the place in which they are incarcerated. Both federal and state agencies distribute programmes and services, and allocate the number of local representatives according to this census data. Thus, a high number of prisoners can sometimes double or triple the town's population and result in a greater share of tax dollars and political representation.
69 Woomera's current population is approximately 200.
70 Philip Ruddock, "Get Tough or Prepare for the Flood" *The Australian*, 24 October (2009).
71 Michael Sorkin, *Against the Wall* (New York: The New Press, 2005), vi. Refer to Wendy Brown, *Walled States, Waning Sovereignty* (New York: Zone Books, 2010).
72 Ghassan Hage, *Against Paranoid Nationalism* (Annandale NSW: Pluto Press Australia, 2003), 45–46.
73 Claudia Tazreiter, "Security Against the Few: Asylum Seekers as Pariahs in Australian State", *Research Conference on Poverty, International Migration & Asylum*, Helsinki (2002), 12.

8 Architecture and ethics
Competition for the Christmas Island detention centre

In continuation of the theme of detention, this chapter queries the ethical responsibility of architects who participate in the design and procurement of the Australian detention centres. It focuses on the architectural competition for the Christmas Island detention centre, which attempted to shift public perceptions of mandatory detention by calling for an innovative and humane design solution to the political and ethical problem of mandatory detention. To this end, the government sought the assistance of architects to redefine the image of immigration detention. Indeed, the Department of Immigration and Citizenship had hoped that the principles of 'good design' in architecture would alleviate the negative effects that recent media images of riots and hunger strikes had had on the government. But beyond the PR, the Christmas Island detention centre is a key component in the government's apparatus to deter further 'boat arrivals' from entering Australia's sovereign borders by sea. It is a policy of containment through the exclusion of 'others', and derivative of a discursive construct that seeks to delimit the Australian character and present certain individuals as dangerous and undeserving of basic human rights. Architects who lend their services for the fulfilment of such practices, regardless of their personal views, contribute towards the acceptance of such policies in the community. Architects have an ethical obligation to consider the social impact of their work. This is a point on which the design for the Christmas Island detention centre falls well short of what should be the acceptable standard both within and outside the profession.

Creating 'limbo land'

> The right to seek and enjoy asylum is recognised as a basic human right . . . Confinement within a narrowly bounded or restricted location, including prisons, closed camps, detention facilities or airport transit zones, where freedom of movement is substantially curtailed, and where the only opportunity to leave this limited area is to leave the territory . . . is inherently undesirable. (Universal Declaration of Human Rights)[1]

In early 2002, Australia's conservative government, upon winning the federal election and another term in office, announced the construction of a new purpose-built detention facility on Christmas Island. The island, located in the Indian Ocean 360km south of Java Indonesia, and 1,400km north-west of Australia, had recently been excised from Australia's migration zone by well-crafted legislation (along with Ashmore reef, the Cocos Islands and hundreds of other peripheral territories to the north of Australia). Seemingly justified by the terrorist attacks in New York on September 11, 2001, the Federal Parliament immediately passed legislation to amend the Migration Act. The amendments, dubbed the 'Pacific Solution', were comprised of three central strategies for the control of 'illegal' immigrants. Firstly, unauthorised arrivals landing in the excised migration zones had no right to apply for a visa. Secondly, the Australian Defence Force commenced operations to routinely intercept and turn around boats containing asylum seekers. And thirdly, asylum seekers who arrived on Australian shores were to be deported offshore to locations such as Nauru and the Manus Islands for the processing of their refugee claims. The proposed Christmas Island detention facility was to become the prototype for offshore detention, where the asylum seeker is strategically positioned off the Australian mainland, out of sight of the Australian population, and beyond the reach of legal processes and basic human rights.

A press release announcing the shortlist of architects participating in the design competition for a permanent 'Immigration Reception and Processing Centre' (IRPC) on Christmas Island was issued by the Minister for Immigration at the time, Phillip Ruddock. The release attempted to shift public perceptions of mandatory detention from being a place where asylum seekers were effectively punished to a place that could more efficiently process claims for asylum. Ruddock stated: "I wish to emphasise that immigration detention is administrative in nature and is not, in any way, designed for purposes of punishment. Immigration detention facilities are not corrective facilities and it is essential that the final design for the facilities reflects and are [sic] sympathetic with this central concern of the Government".[2] For this purpose, the Government sought the assistance of architects to redefine the image of immigration detention and claimed this was a "great opportunity" for architectural offices to "showcase their talents and potentially earn international recognition in an environment where the illegal movement of people around the world is a growing international problem".[3] He continued: "The Government is looking for innovative and environmentally friendly designs that demonstrate a clear regard for the personal needs and dignity of the residents . . . I expect that a range of innovative designs will result from this process and that they will meet the Government's need to provide detention infrastructure that is humane, non-punitive and sensitive to the needs of people held under this process of administrative detention".[4] The Minister's choice of words,

190 *Architecture and ethics*

with their emphasis on innovation, dignity and the need to create a positive environment for the administration of refugees, was an appeal to the design profession to provide an architectural solution to the political and ethical problem of mandatory detention. As Stephen Cairns points out: "For this politician [Ruddock], the principles of 'good design', 'style' and 'advancing quality', would, in a quite pragmatic way, alleviate the negative effects that media images of detention centres had had on his government".[5] Thus, by framing the problem of immigration detention as a 'design opportunity' the government hoped to sidestep a number of fundamental ethical and political concerns with regards to the deleterious effects of mandatory detention and the treatment of asylum seekers.

Christmas Island is a small multiracial community with a population of approximately 1,200 people. At least 65% of the island's 135km² is designated as National Park consisting of untouched pristine rainforest inhabited by numerous species of unique flora and fauna. For over a century since European settlement, the island's main economic activity has been phosphate mining. However, since the 1990s the Australian government has been closing down these mine sites and in April 2007 it announced that no more new mines would be opened due to the threat they posed to the unique environmental fabric of the island. But the termination of the Island's main economic resource brought about much consternation within the Christmas Island community. As Don Newton, an island resident commented at the time: "Without the mine, the island is nothing . . . If they're going to take away the mining, they need to replace it with something else, otherwise there'll be a huge vacuum".[6] To counteract the declining economy and the potential exodus of its residents, the Christmas Island community sought to capitalise on the island's unique ecology and promote tourist-based economic growth. Knowing this, the Howard Government considered that the construction of the new detention facility would provide a "significant boost to the local economy". As Wilson Tuckey, former Minister for Infrastructure declared of the new detention centre, "Overall, the development of this facility, the first purpose designed and built facility in Australia represents a major opportunity for Christmas Island. This decision heralds an era of increased local employment opportunities and major economic development for one of our most remote regions".[7]

Despite such comments, it was never entirely clear how the detention facility would provide a fillip to economic activity. The former Labor minister and long time critic of Howard's immigration policies Carmen Lawrence responded by echoing local sentiments in stating: "It [the detention centre] is not providing any economic activity for the people on Christmas Island at the moment and is not likely to for most of the time. For the small number of people needing assessment, it is a very expensive way to do it. The people would prefer to have a tourist facility rather than a detention centre".[8] Christmas Island's Shire President, Gordon Thompson, was also vocal in his opposition to the detention centre and made it clear that residents were worried about the effects a detention centre might have on the island's tourism industry. He remarked: "We'll have an invasion of people who'll turn the Christmas Island economy from a mining and tourism economy into a prison type economy".[9] He continued: "Regardless of the plans for the detention centre, it was not welcome by most islanders. We don't want a prison on Christmas Island at all. We don't want a prison for refugees anywhere".[10]

Despite these concerns, the federal government proceeded headlong with its plans to build a new purpose-built detention centre on Christmas Island. In so doing, the Department of Immigration attended to the urgent preparation of the island's infrastructure in order to accommodate the construction and ongoing operation of the facility. These new works included a second port facility on the east coast of the island to ensure building supplies could be delivered in all weather conditions, and a new transport corridor from the new loading facility to the building site. In addition, the government built a 160-room hotel for security guards in the seaside area of the island and living quarters for workers at the detention centre who were to be flown in. In the vicinity, new tennis courts, a swimming pool and a recreation centre were also constructed. But despite this unprecedented upgrade to the island's infrastructure, many locals remained concerned about the likely impact a full detention facility might have on the day-to-day operation of the island, and in particular, on perceptions of the island from abroad.

The Australian Government spent more than AU\$500 million transforming Christmas Island into the ultimate "limbo land".[11] But no matter how it is justified by the Federal Government, the key objective for the Christmas Island detention centre is to play a strategic role in sending out a warning to 'illegal' immigrants. By selecting Christmas Island as the location for the detention centre the Federal Government has deliberately targeted the Australian territory closest to Indonesia and therefore the place most refugees will attempt to access in order to gain a foothold into the Australian mainland. "The detention centre is needed to deter potential unauthorised refugees trying to reach Australian shores", claimed the former Minister for Human Services Joe Hockey. "We want to send a strong message to all potential people smugglers that if you try to illegally land people in Australia those people will be sent to Christmas Island, they will not be able to stay on the mainland".[12] In fact, the policy of offshore detention is analogous with what Machiavelli described as the "paradox of deterrence". That is to say, if deterrence involves some sort of threat, the success of that threat is dependent on its communication and the willingness to use it. As Michael McCanles explains: "The 'paradox of deterrence', then, is that we have a discourse that has meaning only insofar as it refers to arms, while arms in turn only have meaning insofar as they are articulated through discourse".[13] Similarly, the Christmas Island detention centre is an essential component in the government's armoury against 'illegal' immigration. Its meaning is derived through discourses that relates to the necessity to deter 'illegal' immigration

192   *Architecture and ethics*

and to keep potentially dangerous people outside of Australia. Indeed, the Christmas Island IDC not only promotes ideas relating to Australian identity and 'culture', but it also serves to reassure the public that the dangerous 'other' is maintained well beyond the Australian mainland.

While Christmas Island offers a strategic base for intercepting and detaining asylum seekers trying to reach Australia, the island also provides the added benefit for government policy makers of being literally distant and isolated from the Australian mainland. As a result, the Australian government has succeeded in literally distancing the asylum seeker from the Australian population. Consequently, the refugee is denied proper legal representation and human dignity as discussed in the previous chapter. This chapter, however, is concerned with the ethical implications of such an architecture, in which the architect is invited to participate in a competitive tender for the design and construction of a detention centre. Detention centres are an exclusionary apparatus designed to delimit ones sense of belonging in relation to the nation-state. The perceived need for such facilities raises not only political questions but moral ones too. Understanding this, it is asked whether architects should lend their services to a government for the purposes of mandatory detention. The existence of detention centres perpetuates a discourse that represents asylum seekers as potentially dangerous, whereby the government, acting in the interest of the nation, must be increasingly tougher on border protection. Indeed, is this an activity to which architects should competitively bid for its facilitation?

Island detention

Following the announcement of the four shortlisted architects,[14] the Department of Immigration announced in mid-2002 that the Walter Construction Group had been awarded the contract for the design and construction "of what will be the first purpose designed and built IRPC in Australia". The statement from the office of Phillip Ruddock read: "The design will be based on a concept developed by Phillips Smith Conwell Architects. The design concept was assessed by DIMIA (Department of Immigration, Multiculturalism and Indigenous Affairs) as being an excellent response to the design brief issued in April to four architectural firms which were selected last year following an open tender process".[15] The original design concept, on which the agreement was made, was for a 1,200-person facility to be built in 39 weeks for a cost of approximately AU$250 million. However, as work progressed toward the final design resolution delays in the project timeline and increases in the budget began to emerge. As the Auditor General outlined: "By September 2002, the project estimate had increased to AU$427 million with a delivery period in the order of 120 weeks".[16] Despite this setback, the government reconfirmed its commitment to the proposed Christmas Island detention centre. However, amid rising costs and a reduction in the number of boat arrivals in 2003, the Australian Government

Architecture and ethics 193

Figure 8.1 Christmas Island detention centre site.
DIAC Images – Wikimedia Commons.

announced that the proposed 1,200 person facility was to be scaled back to 800 places for a revised total cost of AU$276 million with a 14-month construction period. As a result of these changes, the 're-specified' detention facility's delivery method was also amended to reflect a more traditional model rather than a fast track approach and the contract with the Walter Construction Group was terminated.[17]

Following almost two years of industry consultation, design changes and budget revisions, the project was retendered in late 2004 and a new construction contract was signed with the Australian construction corporation Baulderstone Hornibrook in early 2005. Based on Phillips Smith Conwell Architects' 're-specified' design and after three years of construction, the Christmas Island detention centre was handed over to the Department of Immigration for operation in April 2008, but remained empty, despite being fully staffed, for a number of months. Described as a "gigantic scar" on the pristine environment of Christmas Island, the detention centre comprises more than 50 buildings on a site located at the remote north-west end of the island. Sited on an old phosphate mine, known as Mining Lease 138, the buildings that make up the detention compound are, at a glance, ordinary structures and hardly notable works of 'architecture'. As Pamela Curr, campaign coordinator for the Asylum Seeker Resource Centre, reported following her tour of the completed detention facility: "The design seems

194   *Architecture and ethics*

to concentrate more on clear CCTV viewing paths than anything else". She further adds: "As you drive through the first set of heavy electric gates into the vehicle airlock, you know that you are in a high security prison with every permutation of steel grilles and wire mesh . . . Everything is caged, lights, gym, cameras, everything".[18]

"With characteristics both in common with and uncommon for a prison",[19] the buildings that constitute the detention facility consist of five separate and individually secured compounds with associated administrative, educational and recreational facilities. Four of the five compounds are identical in planning, form and appearance, each consisting of a central facilities building flanked by two mirrored rows of four separate structures for accommodation. The four accommodation compounds, named white, blue, green and gold, are designed to house both families and individuals. The family accommodation units each contain six single rooms with provision for a double bed or bunk and a bathroom in an area no larger than 48m². Each cell opens onto a communal area that contains a covered outdoor kitchen and dining facility enclosed by roller shutters. The general accommodation units are similar in layout to the other units, but instead house 12 single rooms, each with a double bed or bunk. These rooms are built on two floors, with the upper level overlooking the communal covered outdoor area. The fourth unit is a contingency dorm (in the case of a sudden increase of detainees) with 24 bunk beds divided into two groups for male and female internees. The central facilities building accommodates general recreation and activities rooms, mess hall, medical facilities, interview rooms and a central surveillance room for monitoring the flanking accommodation units. In addition, the compounds include facilities for the detention of children, including childcare facilities, playgrounds, preschool classrooms and a nursery for babies, despite promises that no mother and child would be held in detention.[20]

Described as "Australia's Guantanamo" by refugee advocates, the level of security and surveillance is far higher than any other detention centre in Australia and would appear to be more suited to a maximum security prison than a facility for processing refugees' claims to asylum. Each accommodation cell is fitted with electrically operated lockable doors that are remotely activated from a central point. There is a card override lock accessible from the outside and a 'request to exit' button and intercom on the inside of each room. The covered outdoor kitchen and dining area are complete with wall mounted speakers, locator beacons to identify every individual in the unit (all detainees carry electronic identity tags), motion PTZ (pan tilt zoom) cameras linked to a remote control room in Canberra, reed switches to protect the perimeter of the unit and security alarms. The open courtyard between the accommodation units and the central facilities building are subject to multiple detection devices such as bistatic microwave probes (for detecting movement), microphonic listening cables, field lighting and PTZ cameras mounted on the roof, under the eaves and around

Architecture and ethics 195

Figure 8.2 Christmas Island detention centre 'break out' cages to allow detainees fresh air during lockdown.

Project SafeCom, http://www.safecom.org.au.

the perimeter. Each compound is surrounded by a series of parallel fences, microwave probes, checkpoints for guards on patrol, field security cubicles fitted with duress alarms for the guards and a plethora of surveillance cameras. Furthermore, the perimeter of the entire facility is controlled by an entirely different level of security with lighting, field cubicles, microwave probes and a 10m-wide 'no go zone' situated immediately in front of the electrically energised fences and guard towers.

In addition to the state-of-the-art surveillance and security technologies, the Christmas Island detention centre also incorporates cells for solitary confinement called 'management' units.[21] Highlighting the punitive nature of detention, the fifth accommodation compound, 'red' block, is a 'high security' prison "designed for the most violent, instable and dangerous detainees".[22] Refugee advocate David Manne, who was granted access to the unit before it opened, described the accommodation as "cruel, inhumane and degrading". In his account he described "small metal cells in which the beds were moulded out of the same piece of metal flooring",[23] with no natural light except for a small breakout cage for exercise. Solitary confinement is known to cause significant physiological distress to those

196 *Architecture and ethics*

restrained in such a manner. In fact, a psychiatrist visiting the Baxter facility described detention management strategies as "primarily punitive" and inconsistent with mental health management. She further stated that in some cases management techniques included physical harm, ridicule, hand-cuffing and confinement for months.[24] As the Royal Australian and New Zealand College of Psychiatrists stated with relation to the treatment of asylum seekers: "The use of inappropriate behavioural management techniques is of great concern . . . These techniques are not considered to be standard treatment of behavioural disturbance resulting from mental illness, and are not acceptable to international psychiatric bodies".[25] The inclusion of isolation cells in the Christmas Island detention facility demonstrates that the Australian government is willing to use techniques of incarceration (even allowing torture, by some measures) normally reserved for maximum security prisons and 'hard-core' prison populations to solve a political problem. Isolation cells further reinforce the punitive character of mandatory detention and further isolate the asylum seeker from the mainstream population.

Architecture and ethics

The political debate as to whether architects should participate in the development of detention centres or similar projects is one that cannot be divorced from ethics. Ruddock's competition for the detention centre was an attempt to find an 'architectural' solution to the political challenges of mandatory detention. Indeed, one can question whether this has been achieved in the design of the Christmas Island detention centre. Doubtlessly, the design better facilitates the 'management' of detainees, for it is a practical and functional response to the brief. Yet the ethical implications regarding the procurement of such structures must go beyond concerns for practicality, budget, aesthetics and the environment, as typically conceived, and rather analyse the appropriateness for architects to lend their services to aid particular political outcomes.

Therefore, it is necessary to ask whether an architect who accepts a commission to consult and contribute towards the design of a detention centre is participating in the endorsement of this practice. Considering this, the Architect's *Code of Professional Conduct* states that the architect is obliged to "thoughtfully consider the social and environmental impact of their professional activities".[26] Yet the absence of such debates in the public domain, and in particular from within the profession, is surprising. "In recent years", as Anderson and Ferng point out: "there has been little interest among architectural scholars in analysing the offshore processing of asylum seekers".[27] To highlight this point, upon the announcement of the design competition for the Christmas Island detention centre the Royal Australian Institute of Architects (RAIA) issued a media release entitled *Doomed Detention Centres*. However, the release warned architects not to participate in the design competition because of the potential loss of copyright for submitted designs. No mention of the morality of mandatory detention was made. The statement reads: "The Department of Immigration and Multicultural Affairs is conducting an architectural services competition which requires all competitors to give up the copyright in the designs they submit, as well as waive their moral rights in their designs . . . The Department clearly wants to create centres that are well designed, innovative and leading edge . . . It is very unfortunate that the process it has put in place is unlikely to produce the best results".[28] Indeed, the process is unlikely to produce any good "results". But, notwithstanding the architect's rights to copyright, the greater moral concern should be focused on the "social impact" of such works of architecture. In fact, this should have been the main reason to dissuade architects from competing in the design competition for the Christmas Island detention centre.

Furthermore, one wonders what personal views the architects responsible for the Christmas Island detention centre hold with regards to mandatory and indefinite detention? However, such questions ultimately seem superfluous as their expertise in procuring such a facility could not be a greater indication of their tacit support for such policies. Indeed, Phillips Smith Conwell Architects have a history of providing design services for correctional facilities, including the Villawood immigration detention centre redevelopment and the Townsville Women's Correctional Centre. In 2003, at the Hansard Committee on Public Works, convened to investigate the viability of the re-specified Christmas Island IDC, a query was raised about the level of experience and competence of the architects commissioned to perform the task. In response, Mr Carseldine, director of Phillips Smith Conwell Architects, replied: "There have not been any purpose-built detention centres in Australia previously. Our past experience is in correctional centres and fairly major institutional projects. The correctional centre experience goes back 24 years. That includes work in Victoria, Tasmania, predominantly Queensland and also New Zealand. Those are our qualifications for working on this project".[29] Supplementary to this response, the committee pressed the Mr Carseldine further; the transcript reads as follows:

> Mr Brendon O'Connor (Deputy Chair): "You mentioned that you are involved in correctional centres, prisons. In your view, does a detention centre for unauthorised arrivals that may include families require a different design than a facility for people that are convicted and detained? Does the design reflect the different needs you have had to accommodate?"

> Mr Carseldine: "It is significantly different but, at the same time, there are some common characteristics . . . The issue of security and safety is just as important in prisons as it is in a detention centre . . . However, what we look at in detention centres, as well as that, is giving people

198 *Architecture and ethics*

a much higher level of freedom of movement within the centre . . . If I put up a design for an 800 person prison, you would definitely see some similarities, but I could point out to you some quite different features, particularly in the design of the accommodations areas".[30]

In a later committee seating, Mr Carseldine described the 'different features' relating to the design of the accommodation areas as "non punitive" where "security is discreet". He elaborates: "The innovative planning divides the centre into two zones. A 'green heart' links living spaces, gardens, recreation, areas and community facilities. This series of boulevards, gardens and sports fields create a self-contained human scale 'village' accommodating the day-to-day activities of the residents".[31] In his analysis of the ways and means by which the Christmas Island IDC has been translated into a solution to a political problem, Peter Chambers describes these words and the work they relate to, as the "working parts of an interactive, normative process that is explicable, justifiable, and rational on the grounds given in the [government's] brief". According to Chambers, the architect's commitment to transparency delivers the green heart, simultaneously demonstrating the effectiveness of the collaboration with the government's process to ensure its passage through the senate. Chambers elaborates: "The IRPC is not fortified, but it is a thoroughly defensible structure, legally explicable as humane, efficient and secure . . . As the 'villagers' mingle freely in the green heart, they can easily forget they are being detained and surveilled . . . The green heart retains a high degree of indeterminacy . . . It is an empty open space that the free play of people, and only the free play of people, can activate and thus transform . . . Fundamentally, the 'green heart' suggests that it is the responsibility of the detainees to take possession of and deploy their negative liberty through their social interactions . . . The role of the architect here is simply to exercise due diligence in constructing the enabling conditions of an indeterminate number of utopias, private individual utopias that can and must be transformed into 'community' through interaction in the 'village'".[32] As Chambers identifies, the architect's experience is most apposite at being able to translate, seemingly through words alone, the government's brief for the detention facility into an architectural proposal that ignores the deleterious effects of detention by providing a justifiable design outcome, one less likely to experience opposition in both the bureaucratic and public domain because of its appeal to normality. Yet, due to their level of experience, the architects, rather than justify the need for such a facility and its various requirements, might have raised and sort to address, at various times throughout the briefing and design process, numerous issues concerning the potential harmful effects detention is known to inflict upon its detainees. In fact, the decision to remain silent on these matters, for whatever reason, further enables the realisation of such governmental policies and the perpetuation of discourses that seek to exclude 'others'.

In their analysis of the architectural consequences of detention facilities, Anderson and Ferng claim that "such buildings housing detainees embody political borders connecting methods of detention with national anxieties around refugees, as a means of controlling the edges of Australian territory". Furthermore they argue: "Spatial designs of detention centres demand thorough investigation of their potential to subvert ethical attempts to create humane and habitable spaces. An architecture program and its related functions must reconcile the flagrant disparities that exist between design and security apparatuses used to detain asylum seekers".[33] In this sense, architecture embodies the physical apparatus of Australia's complicity in exacerbating the refugee crisis, whereby architects become agents for furthering the cycle of the imprisonment of asylum seekers and its general acceptance in the broader community.

Architectural practices might suggest that it is not their responsibility to question the motivations of a client. Likewise, should every member of the public be required to scrutinise the motivations of everyone they provide a service to? With this in mind, Harvard professor Serge Chermayeff criticised the reduction of architecture from a profession into "nothing more than a business, and one that thoughtlessly conformed to a politics of individual free enterprise".[34] He further remarks: "The architect should be a leader, not a mercenary who thoughtlessly sells design services to any client able to pay".[35] Especially, I might add, a client engaged in the detention of asylum seekers. Notwithstanding, it is important to recognise that architects are equally capable of being informed by and also of informing social values through the practices and beliefs that demand the construction of certain buildings. For example, an architect might agree with the policy of mandatory detention and therefore consider their participation as perfectly appropriate. To this end, Elizabeth Farrelly enquires of the announcement of the shortlisted architects: "Should such an architect, invited (hypothetically) to participate in such a competition, opt in, in the hope of improving an egregious situation, or out, keeping his conscience dry? Should the everyday architect feel obliged to scrutinise and approve his client's business dealings before accepting a commission?"[36] Indeed, such questions are not easily answered. Nevertheless, when an architectural brief demands the incorporation of particular inhumane activities, such as solitary confinement and the detention of children, it becomes incumbent upon anyone to query the necessity for such systems? If the architect accepting the commission to design a detention centre fails to speak out and address any adverse situation with regards to its function it is likely that the lack of opposition towards its procurement will contribute towards its possible acceptance in the broader community. Architects have an ethical and professional obligation to not only ensure that buildings comply with relevant building codes and standards, but also to fully comprehend the social impact of their work on the public at large and on those who are expected to occupy the facility. Architects play a role in the fabrication of a particular reality. Their very involvement promotes the inevitable requisite

200 *Architecture and ethics*

that mandatory and indefinite detention is the best solution to the perceived and constructed problem of 'illegal' immigration. In fact, innovative design solutions relating to the problem of immigration detention may not require any new architecture at all, but perhaps greater awareness of the deleterious effects of mandatory detention and the plight of asylum seekers.

From 'white elephant' to 'breaking point'

At the time of the Labor government's election in 2007, the total number of asylum seekers detained in Australia was in decline. According to the Department of Immigration and Citizenship's Annual Report for 2007–2008, there were 402 people in immigration detention on 30 June 2008, a 9% decrease from the previous year.[37] Though the former coalition government attributed this to its tough policies of deterrence, in reality, the number of asylum seekers worldwide had decreased.[38] In fact, when construction on the $500 million detention facility on Christmas Island was completed in 2008 it lay dormant for seven months while authorities debated about what to do with Howard's 'white elephant'. Christmas Island locals questioned why so much money had been wasted on the construction of the facility when it could have been redirected to upgrade numerous other infrastructure projects sorely needed on the island. Indeed, the Shire President Gordon Thompson, along with others, proposed that the structure could be put to better use by converting it to an educational facility, holiday resort, or even a scientific research facility for monitoring climate change.[39] Thompson stated that "the detention centre was a political project for the Howard Government and a colossal waste of money", and urged the newly formed Rudd government to find another use for the facility.[40]

On this matter, Labor remained circumspect arguing that the Christmas Island IDC had been designed for a specific purpose and to change the building would have severe cost implications. Warren Snowdon, whose electorate includes Christmas Island, responded by saying: "Since this was established we've questioned the motives of the (Howard) government, they've spent a hell of a lot of money to appease their own political interests . . . But the problem we've got now is that we've got the Australian tax payer being landed with this establishment and its ongoing upkeep".[41] Although Snowdon's explanation seems to justify the retention of the Christmas Island facility, ultimately the need to reassure Australia's public of the government's ongoing commitment to border security still outweighed any other concern related to the mandatory detention of asylum seekers.

Indeed, the Christmas Island facility remained fully staffed and in operation even while it remained vacant, for it acted as insurance against the possibility, as it was perceived by the government, of large numbers of refugees arriving in Australian waters. Thus, when 37 'boat people' were intercepted 200km off the coast of Darwin in December 2008, Kevin Rudd announced that they would be the first asylum seekers to be incarcerated in the Christmas Island facility. By claiming to have no choice but to open its doors, the federal government, despite pressure not to use the facility, validated the former Howard Government's decision to build it in the first place.[42] In response the Human Rights Commissioner, Graeme Innes, expressed his disappointment, telling journalists: "The previous government built a high-tech security prison and this Government has sadly decided to use it . . . Christmas Island is not the place to hold asylum seekers".[43]

Although the newly elected Rudd government had declared an end to the Pacific Solution, it did not end mandatory and indefinite detention. In fact, the Senator for Immigration, Chris Evans, told reporters that although the Rudd government was committed to maintaining strong border protection it should do so by treating people with dignity. He said: "Labor rejects the notion that dehumanising and punishing unauthorised arrivals with long-term detention is an effective or civilised response. Desperate people are not deterred by the threat of harsh detention – they are often fleeing much worse circumstances".[44] Evans also acknowledged that the policy of mandatory detention had damaged Australia's reputation amongst the international community. He continued: "The implementation of this [new] approach would go a long way toward meeting our international commitments, including people who have travelled to Australia to escape fear, persecution and injustice in their own countries. It would assist in repairing the shameful reputation Australia has developed for the way it has treated such people over the last decade or so".[45] Despite this, Senator Evans reaffirmed the government's commitment to the Christmas Island IDC for the purpose of "conducting health, identity and security checks of adult men".[46] Indeed, Christmas Island has become central to the government's plans for incarcerating asylum seekers. After its opening all other remote mainland detention centres were closed down and their detainees transported to Christmas Island.

In the years that followed the opening of the Christmas Island detention centre refugee movements around the globe have surged, due primarily to the ongoing conflicts in Sri Lanka and Afghanistan. Consequently, the Christmas Island IDC has reached its breaking point. At the beginning of 2010 the Immigration Department reported that the Christmas Island detention centre had more than doubled its capacity with 1,674 people in detention, 200 of whom were being held in tents due to overcrowding.[47] In addition, the makeshift Phosphate Hill camp and the former construction workers' camp had become home to hundreds of women and children as a form of "community housing".[48] As a result, the government announced a $40 million upgrade to the facility in which 81 demountable buildings were set up on the island to help relieve accommodation pressures.[49] But, as more boat loads of people continued to arrive, the Christmas Island detention

202 Architecture and ethics

population rapidly swelled, reaching a peak of 2,971 people in November 2010.[50] A report in the *Australian* stated: "Last night, detainees were sleeping in rooms designed for teaching English or for conducting interviews with immigration officers, as officials sought to make room for the island's growing detainee population. A spokesman for the Department of Immigration and Citizenship said the island could adequately accommodate all those who had arrived".[51] In reality, not only are amenities severely compromised by the increasing population at the Christmas Island detention centre, but so is the island's infrastructure, with local flesh water supplies running low and the sewage system under strain.

With current numbers beyond capacity the facility is struggling to cope and conditions are in major decline. Recreation space has become taken over with beds, there are large queues for toilets and basic food supplies have been withdrawn from the communal spaces. During periods of overcrowding tensions between detainees have increased: in 2010 a man climbed a light pole and threatened to throw himself to the ground, and 150 Sri Lankan and Afghani men attacked each other with broom handles and tree branches resulting in 37 injuries, three of them critical.[52] In 2011, 250 detainees protesting about conditions in the centre threw rocks at detention staff and set fire to the accommodation blocks causing millions of dollars worth of damage.[53] In early 2014, nearly 400 detainees took part in a hunger strike with many sewing their lips and attempting suicide.[54] Refugee advocates are calling the island a "penal colony", with the huge numbers detained there likely to have a significant impact on the island's perception the world over. In fact, the then Prime Minister, Julia Gillard, conceded that detention numbers have placed a great burden on the island, and as a consequence would reopen older detention facilities like Baxter and Port Augusta and construct more new detention centres shortly.[55]

The recent increase in asylum seekers has placed considerable pressure on the government to further toughen immigration legislation to prevent further 'illegal' boat arrivals from entering Australian waters.[56] It is clear that placing people in detention has not deterred or prevented more boat arrivals. Yet the operation of detention centres, in particular the Christmas Island IDC, continues unabated because it represents the government's 'tough' stance on border protection. Indeed, it is politically convenient for the incumbent government to isolate certain individuals outside of the population despite the inhumane conditions to which they are exposed. Thus with relation to the ethical responsibility of architects, one must ask whether it is appropriate to willingly compete for services that adversely and deliberately affect people's lives. Architects should query the necessity for such buildings and political infrastructure, rather than promoting and proliferating the need for such practices by their involvement. The architects responsible for the design and procurement of the Christmas Island detention centre, and other buildings like it, cannot remain ambivalent in the face of political policies that deliberately deprive certain individuals of their dignity and human rights. Indeed, architects who contribute towards the discursive construct of immigration detention through the design of detention centres make an ethical choice to serve a particular public and, more significantly, to disregard the implications of their work.

Notes

1 UNHCR, *The Universal Declaration of Human Rights: Adopted and proclaimed by General Assembly resolution* 217 A (III), 10 December 1948.
2 Phillip Ruddock, Minister for Immigration and Citizenship, Media Release, *Architects Shortlisted for New Permanent Detention Facilities Design Competition,* 3 April 2002. Available at http://www.minister.immi.gov.au/media/media-release/2002/r02023.htm (Accessed August 2007).
3 *Ibid.*
4 *Ibid.*
5 Stephen Cairns, *Drifting; Architecture and Migrancy* (London: Routledge, 2004), 26.
6 Quoted in Nick Squires, "Tougher Times for Christmas Island?" *CSM,* 1 August (2007), 1.
7 Wilson Tuckey, Minister for Regional Services, Territories and Local Government, Media Release, *New Detention Facility for Christmas Island,* 12 March 2002. Available at http://www.ministers.infrastructure.gov.au/wt/realeases/2002/march/wt08_2002htm (Accessed June 2008).
8 Quoted in Ross Peake, "They Had Fled their War-Torn Countries but Found Australia Would not Abide By . . . " *The Canberra Times,* 15 December (2007), 2.
9 Quoted in "Christmas Island Detention Centre Comes Under Fire", *ABC Lateline,* 13 May (2002).
10 Quoted in K. Elliot "Australia's Guantanamo on remote Xmas Island", *Perth Indymedia,* 26 November (2006).
11 Refer to Paige Taylor, "Christmas Island Centre in Limbo", *The Australian,* 6 March (2007).
12 Quoted in "Island Centre 'Could Be Like Guantanamo'", *Mercury,* 17 November (2006).
13 Michael McCanles, "Machiavelli and the Paradox of Deterrence", *Diacritics,* Vol. 14, No. 2, Summer (1984), 13.
14 The list comprised Crone and Associates, Phillips Smith Conwell Architects, Codd Stenders and a consortium consisting of Guymer Bailey Architects, Sinclair Knight Merz and Peter Hunt Architects. Refer to Phillip Ruddock, Minister for Immigration and Citizenship, Media Release, *Architects Shortlisted for New Permanent Detention Facilities Design Competition,* 3 April 2002.
15 Department of Immigration and Citizenship Newsroom, *Contract Signed for the Christmas Island Detention Facility,* 17 June 2002. Available at http://www.newsroom.immi.gov.au/media_releases/429 (Accessed August 2007).
16 Refer to Australian National Audit Office, *Construction of the Christmas Island Immigration Detention Centre* (2009), 9. Available at http://www.anao.gov.au/uploads/documents/2008-09_Audit_Report_43.pdf (Accessed March 2010).
17 Refer to Australian Government Department of Finance and Administration, *Proposed Christmas Island Immigration Reception and Processing Centre: Statement of Evidence to the Parliamentary Standing Committee on Public Works,* September 2003.
18 Quoted in Sophie Black, "Inside the Christmas Detention Centre", *Crickey,* 19 August (2008).
19 Peter Chambers, "Society Has Been Defended: Following the Shifting Shape of State Through Australia's Christmas Island", *International Political Sociology,* Vol. 5 (2011), 30.

204 *Architecture and ethics*

20 In May 2005, Federal Liberal backbencher Petro Georgiou, supported by colleagues including Judi Moylan, Bruce Baird and Russell Broadbent, crossed the floor to vote against Howard's immigration policies, and threatened to introduce a Private Member's Bill to soften the government's mandatory detention policy. Three days later, The Prime Minister John Howard announced that as a compromise changes would be made to the detention policy. These included releasing families with children into community housing and, in addition, those detained for more than two years would be subject to investigation.

21 In March 2005, an advisor to the then Minister for immigration Amanda Vanstone admitted that solitary confinement is used as punishment within detention facilities (Refer Burnside, 2005). When the practice was brought to the public's attention via the Cornelia Rau affair, the then Federal Government intimated that the policy of solitary confinement would be abandoned. The RANZCP have since reported that immigration detention centres do not have "adequate mental health staff, appropriately trained supervisory staff, or adequate capacity to review and monitor 'biological' treatments". Refer to *Submission to the Senate Legal and Constitutional References Committees into the Administration and Operation of the Migration Act 1958*, 29 July (2005), 3. In addition, the advice from trained psychiatrists who visit detention centres is most often ignored in preference for more punitive measures such as solitary confinement. As the Cornelia Rau affair demonstrates, along with other Australians who have been wrongfully detained in immigration detention facilities due to mental illness such as Vivian Alvarez, solitary confinement cells form part of the frequent management of people in distress.

22 Paige Taylor, "Six Sri Lankan Detainees Held in Christmas Island 'Red Block', *The Australian*, 9 November (2009).

23 *Ibid.*

24 Refer to Lynda Crowley-Cyr, "Mental Illness and Indefinite Detention at the Minister's Pleasure", *University of Western Sydney Law Review*, Vol. 9 (2005), 53.

25 *Ibid.*

26 RAIA, *Code of Professional Conduct* (2006).

27 Sean Anderson and Jennifer Ferng, "No Boat: Christmas Island and the Architecture of Detention", *Architectural Theory Review*, Vol. 18, No. 2 (2013), 214.

28 Architects Institute of Australia, *Doomed Detention Centres*, 19 June (2001). Available at http://www.architecture.com.au/i-cms?page=513 (Accessed December 2010).

29 Commonwealth of Australia, *Official Committee Hansard: Joint Committee on Public Works*, 31 October (2003), 10.

30 *Ibid.*

31 Australian Government Department of Finance and Administration, *Proposed Christmas Island Immigration Reception and Processing Centre: Statement of Evidence to the Parliamentary Standing Committee on Public Work*, September 2003, 10.

32 Peter Chambers, "The Passage of Authority", *The International Journal into Island Cultures*, Vol. 6, No. 2 (2012), 129–130.

33 Anderson and Ferng (2013), 214.

34 Quoted in David Monteyne, "Shelter from the Elements: Architecture and Civil Defence in the Early Cold War", *The Philosophical Forum*, Vol. 35, No. 2, Summer (2004), 196.

35 *Ibid.*

36 Elizabeth Farrelly, "The Moral of the Storey", *Sydney Morning Herald*, 15 June (2002).

Architecture and ethics 205

37 Refer to Department for Immigration and Citizenship Annual Report 2007–08: Output 1.5 Immigration Detention. Available at http://www.immi.gov.au/about/reports/annual/2007-08/html/outcome1/output1-5.htm (Accessed October 2011).

38 Kazimierz Bem et al., *A Price Too High; The Cost of Australia's Approach to Asylum Seekers* (Calton: Oxfam Australia, 2007), 13.

39 Refer to David Weber, "No Detainees in Christmas Island Detention Centre", *ABC Online: AM*, 24 May (2008), and "Call to Turn Detention Centre into Research Facility", *ABC News*, 23 May (2008).

40 "Please made to ALP Over Christmas Island Detention Centre", *ABC News*, 27 November (2007).

41 "Christmas Island Centre Too Expensive to Abandon: Snowdon", *ABC News*, 27 November (2007).

42 Refer to Jewel Topsfield, "Boat Influx Opens Howard's White Elephant" *The Age*, 19 December (2008).

43 Quoted in Alison Caldwell, "Opening of New Christmas Island Detention Centre", *ABC Online: AM*, 19 December (2008).

44 Quoted in Emma Rodgers, "Sweeping Changes to Mandatory Detention Announced", *ABC News*, 29 August (2008).

45 Quoted in Melissa Jenkins, "Rudd Govt Softens Asylum Seeker Laws" *Sydney Morning Herald*, 29 July (2008).

46 Refer to Senator Chris Evans, *Rudd Government Committed to Christmas Island Detention*, 18 August (2009). Available at http://www.minister.immi.gov.au/media/media-releases/2009/ce09074.htm (Accessed December 2010).

47 Paul Maley and Paige Taylor, "Christmas Island at Breaking Point", *The Australian*, 27 January (2010).

48 Michelle Dimasi, "The Christmas Island Challenge", *Inside Story*, 5 November (2008).

49 AAP, "Christmas Island Detention Centre to Expand", *The Australian*, 31 October (2009).

50 Flip Prior, "Christmas Island Hunger Strike Over", *The West Australian*, 27 November (2010).

51 Maley and Taylor (2010).

52 Refer to Nicolas Perpitch and Paige Taylor, "Island Detention Centre Inmates Run Riot", *The Australian*, 23 November (2009).

53 Andrew Martin, "Christmas Island Escape Highlights Bad Conditions", *Direct Action*, Issue 31, April (2011).

54 Katrin Long, "Asylum Seekers' 'Mouths Sewn Shut' During Christmas Island Protests", *ABC News*, 1 June (2014).

55 James Massola, "Two New Detention Centres to be Opened", *The Australian*, 18 October (2010).

56 Refer to Philip Ruddock, "Get Tough or Prepare for the Flood" *The Australian*, 24 October (2009).

9   Apparatus

Conclusion

In 2009, Giorgio Agamben published a short essay entitled 'What is an Apparatus?' in which he investigated Michel Foucault's use of the word *dispositif*, or 'apparatus' in English. Agamben points out that Foucault began to use the word around the mid-1970s when he became concerned with the subject of 'governmentality'. For Foucault, 'governmentality' is an activity or practice capable of shaping the knowledge and guiding the conduct of some person or persons.[1] But Foucault was not simply referring to the politics and government of a particular state, but rather to the productive influence of power to 'govern' and make subjects of individuals within a particular state. Indeed, 'apparatus' is connected to 'governmentality' because it represents and facilitates the operation of power. This is exemplified in Foucault's book *Discipline and Punish*, which studies the application of disciplinary techniques that resulted in the invention of the modern penitentiary system. Here Foucault argues that whole aspects of modern societies could be understood by reconstructing certain 'techniques of power' "designed to observe, monitor, shape and control the behaviour of individuals situated within a range of social and economic institutions such as schools, the factory and the prison".[2] To this extent, architecture has a role to play as an element of an 'apparatus' because it is brought about and facilitates the operation of power. As previous chapters illustrate, examples of an 'architectural apparatus' include the Australian immigration detention centre, because it facilitates not only the detention of refugees, but also the formation of a national identity. Indeed, the detention centre is an exclusionary device whereby individuals on the outside are made subject to forms of knowledge that inform particular values and attitudes about what it means to be an Australian citizen.

In an interview, Foucault gives the following explanation for his use of the term 'apparatus': "What I'm trying to single out with this term is, first and foremost, a thoroughly heterogeneous set consisting of discourses, institutions, architectural forms, regulatory decisions, laws, administrative measures, scientific statements, philosophical, moral and philanthropic propositions – in short, the said as much as the unsaid. Such are the elements of the apparatus . . . ".[3] An apparatus is a set of practices and mechanism that aims to normalise particular forms of knowledge and ways of thinking amongst those individuals within a certain conceptual and physical space. As Agamben reaffirms, this entails: "A set of practices, bodies of knowledge, measures, and institutions that aim to manage, govern, control and orient – in a way that purports to be useful – the behaviours, gestures and thoughts of human beings".[4] Undeniably, some architecture, in particular buildings sponsored by political regimes, aspire to such ambitions. Take for example the architecture of Albert Speer, discussed in chapter 4. Under the instruction of Adolf Hitler, the architecture was intended to represent the strength and authority of Nazi Germany. But the question raised by buildings like those constructed in the Königsplatz in Munich was whether they alone were capable of transforming the attitudes and values of a group of people. Architecture, when viewed as part of an apparatus, suggests that the power to make such transformations does not derive from the top down, or by the imposition of a particular authority, but rather, it operates on all levels of social interaction whereby individuals come to regulate their conduct and form beliefs and opinions about particular things. This process of subjectification results from and gives order to a 'discursive formation'. Both not only produce knowledge through language, but also shape and influence what we do.[5] As such, architecture belongs to this process, whereby discourse produces the meanings we associate with certain forms and regulates our conduct within a space.

Foucault's conception of the 'apparatus' foregrounds the relationship between discourse, and knowledge and power that concern this book. He states: "The apparatus is thus always inscribed in a play of power, but it is also always linked to certain limits of knowledge . . . This is what the apparatus consists of: strategies of relations of forces supporting and supported by types of knowledge".[6] Considering this, this project has attempted to extend Foucault's analysis of prisons, insane asylums, schools, hospitals and factories (whose connection with power is perhaps self evident), to show how other forms of architecture and space (including heritage buildings and the suburbs), are also derived from interplays of power. Analogous consideration can be made concerning the apparatus of detention, whereby Australian detention facilities, both in remote and overseas locations, serve to protect an imagined ideal of what it means to be Australian. In this way, the architecture of detention not only incarcerates certain 'others' inhumanely, as shown, but also elicits and promotes certain national interests in order to sustain the authority of the government. Indeed, community concern sparked by the ongoing arrival of refugees by boat has caused Australia's political parties of all forms to act, and act urgently and harshly, in order to appear to be protecting Australia's borders and therefore its values. The detention centre as actually built, whether a temporary makeshift camp of shipping containers and tents or the maximum security facility on

208 *Apparatus*

Christmas Island, equally belong to this apparatus by deliberately excluding the 'other' from the perceived benefits of Australian citizenship.

An apparatus is rooted in the very process of rendering those values which we prescribe as 'human'. To this end, architecture plays a significant role by informing one's sense of place and identity along with those values that become associated with the constructed landscape. Of interest in previous chapters have been the laws and means that convcy meanings about our identity and our place in the built environment to a majority of individuals within a culture. These meanings include one's sense of inclusion, or alternatively displacement, as a result of their location within the urban territory of the city. This was further analysed in Chapter Six, which examined the Cronulla riots, whereby the individuals who believed themselves to belong to this particular space sort to 'protect' certain core values and characteristics even through violent means. These examples demonstrate how the formation of one's identity relates to the making of difference and to exclusionary forces that are constructed through discursive means making for the subjectification of individuals. As Agamben remarks: "Foucault has demonstrated how in a disciplinary society, apparatuses aim to create – through a series of practices, discourses and bodies of knowledge – docile, yet free, bodies that assume their identity and their 'freedom' as subjects in the very process of their subjectification. Apparatus, then, is first of all a machine that produces subjectification, and only as such is it also a machine for governance".[7] The governance of the subject is therefore managed by the apparatus, for it participates in the production of knowledge producing docile yet malleable bodies. An extreme case of this apparatus at work is evident in the Nazi-organised death camps, like Auschwitz, discussed in chapter 5. Auschwitz not only brought about the death of millions of Jews, but also diminished resistance to the crimes of National Socialism, if only through the people's ambivalence rather than their active participation in such atrocities. In other words, the tangible representations, like the camp and the resort (discussed in that chapter), were brought about as a consequence of the German people's desire to identify themselves as part of the nation's included at the expense of the 'other'.

Architecture belongs to discourse. It is a 'statement' which delimits knowledge in a particular field. In so doing, architecture gives tangible form and solid representation to those values which are thought to be inherently associated with its location or occupiers, as exemplified by Hugo's writing on the Notre Dame cathedral and the dictates of the Athens Charters, discussed in chapters 2 and 3. Yet architecture conceived in this way derives meaning only discursively. Building form in itself cannot set the limits of knowledge relating to its location and occupants. To assert a similar point, Arendt draws an analogy with the ancient Greeks in which she claims that the architecture of Athens provided a tangible representation of the law – it being "the product of making". She claims that the ancient Greeks did not institute knowledge, nor impose particular forms of conduct, but rather provided a tangible representation of such values through the construction of the political centre of the city, like the Agora. Arendt asserts: "In their opinion, the lawmaker was like a builder of the city wall, someone who had to do and finish his work before political activity could begin. To them, the laws, like the walls around the city, were not results of action but products of making. Before men began to act, a definite space had to be secured and a structure built where all subsequent actions could take place, the space being the public realm of the polis and its structure the law; legislator and architect belonged to the same category. But these tangible entities themselves were not the content of politics (not Athens, but Athenians, were the polis) . . . ".[8] Seen in this way, architecture is without any formal content, but rather meanings are attributed to it by the populace. Yet the people in question are not simply one cohesive social body and agency with the capacity to interpret and make decisions. Rather, the populace is made of multiple and diverse subjects who share a similar outlook and values because they are identified with and formed by the same discursive formation. An apparatus plays a role in the governance of individuals because it produces ways of knowing. Thus, to understand how and why specific laws, practices and of course architecture are brought about – like buildings for the detention of refugees – requires an investigation of the processes of subjectification and the rules in which power relations inform the conduct and beliefs of individuals to which they are provided concrete form.

This book has been concerned with architecture as an element of 'apparatus' and how it might arise from, guide and affect the conduct of individuals within its confines, as well as delimit knowledge within a particular field. Contrary to popular opinion, architecture is not capable of guaranteeing specific meanings or determining the conduct of others. Although it may better facilitate certain activities, it is always part of an apparatus – belonging to a larger historical, material, conceptual and behavioural ensemble – to which buildings are not only ascribed meanings but brought about according to the norms of a particular time and place. This effect becomes essential to the governance of a population, whereby space is utilised as a resource of power. Sovereign territory, urban planning and architecture all have a role to play, at various scales, in the production of identities because they facilitate, at a very basic level, the inclusion of certain people at the expense of others. Finally, this book asked the ethical question of whether the architect should lend their services to the procurement of certain types of architecture that intend to harm other human beings. While recognising that the architect too is the product of discourse, it suggests that individuals are capable of speaking out against certain practices rather than contributing to their acceptance and normalisation in the community. Here the architect, like any other individual who chooses ambivalence and silence over resistance, must recognise that they too have provided an endorsement of such activities and therefore have contributed to the perpetuation of specific norms and forms. To this end, Agamben provides a fitting reminder that such ethical concerns will

210 *Apparatus*

continue to pervade the production of knowledge "so long as those who are concerned with it are unable to intervene in their own subjectification, any more than in their own apparatus".[9] Although, as Foucault suggests, architects lack the power to transform the attitudes and values of society,[10] they may certainly contribute to the normalisation of certain activities by helping to procure certain types of buildings. This resultant architecture becomes a 'statement', or a component of discourse, which further perpetuates certain ways of thinking – described by Foucault as an apparatus for the subjectification of individuals. As such, architects bear a measure of responsibility, though they may see themselves as simply providing a design service.

Notes

1 Refer to Colin Gordon, *The Foucault Effect: Studies in Governmentality* ed. Graham Burchell, Colin Gordon and Peter Miller (Chicago: University of Chicago Press, 1991), 2.
2 *Ibid.*, 3–4.
3 Foucault, *Power/Knowledge; Selected Interviews and Other Writings, 1972–1977* ed. Colin Gordon (New York: Pantheon Books, 1980), 194.
4 Giorgio Agamben, *What is an Apparatus?* (Stanford: Stanford University Press, 2009), 12.
5 Stuart Hall, *Representation; Cultural Representation and Signifying Practices* (London: Sage Publishing, 1997), 44.
6 Foucault (1980), 196.
7 Agamben (2009), 19.
8 Hannah Arendt, *The Human Condition* (Chicago: University of Chicago Press, 1998), 194–195.
9 Agamben (2009), 24.
10 Refer to Michael Foucault, "Space, Knowledge, and Power", *The Foucault Reader* ed. Paul Rabinow (London: Penguin Books, 1984), 247.

Index

aestheticisation 15–19, 50, 114, 118; political construct 14, 135–6; self fashioning 116

Agamben, G: apparatus 206–10; the ban 116; bare life 117, 124, 170; ethics 135–6; the exception 11; exclusion 120–1, 125–8; sovereign power 118, 122–3, 130, 178

apparatus 10, 116, 206–10; culture 49; governmental 188, 192, 199

architecture as text 4, 8, 23, 26, 34–5, 40, 49

Arendt, H: Eichmann, A. 89–91, 108; denationalisation 126; human rights 173–5; law 208–9

asylum seeker: boat people 11, 123, 180, 200; detention 168–70, 183, 192, 199–202; portrayal 167, 171, 196; rights 120; treatment 19, 172–7, 182, 189–90, 196

Auschwitz 90, 115, 135–7, 208; the camp 114, 117

bare life 123, 130, 178

Barthes, R. 13–14, 35, 41

Bauhuas 108

biopolitics 114, 116–20, 129, 136–7

body politic 114, 129, 137

Ceausescu, N. 13–15

Christmas Island 190–1; competition 189; design 197–8; immigration detention centre 5, 169–70, 174–6, 188, 192–6, 200–2

CIAM 62–4, 79

Citizenship: rights 27, 122, 124, 160, 162–64, 171–4; Nuremberg Law 125–31; white Australia policy 149

constructivism 7, 50

Curtin immigration detention centre 168–71, 179

detention 10, 117, 126, 167, 169–71, 173–5; indefinite and mandatory 176–9

determinism: cultural 6; historical 56, 59, 64–6, 71

Deleuze, G. 80

dialectic 7, 16, 32

docile bodies 208

Eco, U. 41–3

Eichmann, A. 89, 91, 108

enunciative modality 4, 9, 23, 46, 49, 78–9; *see also* Foucault, M.

final solution, the 89, 126, 135

Foucault, M: biopower 117–18, 127, 129; discourse 7–9, 11, 77–9, 81; governmentality 206; heterotopias 171; knowledge 6; panopticon 4; power 2–3, 18, 119, 122, 210; statements 80

Frauenkirche Cathedral, Dresden 56, 72–3, 83

gargoyle 29–33

Giedion, S. 35–6

Goldhagen, D. 16, 90

Gothic architecture 23, 27–33, 34, 36–9, 42

governance 5, 8–9, 18, 208–9

governmentality 175, 177–8, 206

Guantanamo Bay 11, 126, 174, 177

Gutenberg 37, 49; printing press 25–6

212 *Index*

hermeneutics 67, 71, 77
Hirst, P. 3–4, 78, 102, 122, 146
holocaust 89–90, 121, 127, 135
Howard government: rhetoric 12;
  Christmas Island IDC 190, 200–1;
  immigration policy 169–70, 174,
  176, 178–9; national identity 144,
  146
Hugo, V: Notre Dame de Paris 23–6,
  32, 35, 39; language 26–7, 33–4,
  37–8, 42–4, 45, 49

identity: Australian 148–53, 171, 192;
  cultural 5, 61, 120–3, 169; national
  13, 58, 60, 76, 125, 144–7, 167, 206;
  self 12, 83, 124, 164, 208
immigration: illegal 19, 144, 177, 189,
  191, 200; policy 152, 167, 169, 172,
  190

knowledge 3–5, 44, 77–8, 207–10
Koolhaas, R. 1–2
Konigsplatz, Munich: Nazi era 88, 91,
  99–102; post war 103–7

Labrouste, H. 44–5, 49
Le Corbusier 58, 62
leisure 118, 131–5

medieval 30–3, 38, 42
modernism 9, 65, 81, 94
muselmann 115, 137, 182

nation-state 123, 125, 148, 162–3, 173
National Socialism 93–5, 96–101,
  106–9; Nazi 16, 88–92, 102–6,
  122–8, 133–5, 137–8, 207; Third
  Reich 118–21, 129–32
nationalism 58, 82, 144, 163
neo-classical architecture 12, 45–6,
  93–5, 107
Notre Dame: *de Paris* (novel) 24–5, 35,
  44; Cathedral 26–9, 31–2, 37

Pacific Solution, the 188, 190, 201, 213
physiognomy 32
place 5, 10, 145
power 2–3, 9–11, 18, 82, 93, 145–7,
  206–10; bio 122, 127, 131, 136;
  disciplinary 4, 171–2; juridico 118,

127; over life 114–15, 121, 129–30;
  power/knowledge 5, 119; sovereign
  116, 118, 124, 170, 173, 175–8;
  space 152, 161
Primo, L. 106, 115, 182
Prora resort 114, 117, 120, 131–5,
  137

Rabinow, P. 2, 17–18, 77, 79
Refugee(s) 169–74, 176–82, 192, 199
Reichstag, Berlin 12
riot: Cronulla 143–7; Macquarie Fields
  153–7; Redfern 158–63
Rohe, M. van der 94, 108

Saint Mary's Cathedral, Perth 67–72,
  77, 83
Saint Michael's Cathedral, Coventry 75
sameness 12, 150–3, 160
serious speech act 79, *see also*
  Foucault, M.
Speer, A. 92, 94–5, 97, 102, 106–9,
  132
spirit of the age 34–9, 57, 66, 70, 82
sovereign 8, 116–18, 126–7, 129–31,
  170, 173, 175–9; *see also* power;
  Agamben, G.
state of exception 116, 127–9, 175–8
statement(s) 4, 8–9, 14, 57, 65, 78–84,
  184, 210; *see also* Foucault, M.
Ste-Genevieve Library, Paris 44–6
Strength through Joy (KdF) 117–20,
  131–3, 136
subjectification 11, 17, 89, 124, 178–9,
  207–10
surface of emergence 9, 78, 80; *see also*
  Foucault, M.

Troost, P. L. 94–5, 100–2, 104

Viollet-le-Duc, E. E. 27–33, 36–7

Weimer 94, 108
Woomera immigration detention centre
  169, 179–84
Wright, F. L. 37–8

zeitgeist 32, 66
zone of indistinction 115–16, 121,
  124, 136